Studien zur Freizeit- und Tourismusforschung 3

Andreas Kagermeier und Joachim Willms (Hrsg.)
Tourism Development in Low Mountain Ranges

Studien zur Freizeit- und Tourismusforschung

Herausgegeben von Hans Hopfinger, Andreas Kagermeier und Monika Rulle

Band 3

Andreas Kagermeier und Joachim Willms (Hrsg.)

Tourism Development in Low Mountain Ranges

Mit 57 Abbildungen und 4 Tabellen

2010

Verlag Metagis-Systems, Mannheim

Umschlagfoto:
Harzer Tourismusverband

Printed in Germany
Layout und Satz: Freizeit- und Tourismusgeographie, Universität Trier

Verlag: Meta-GIS-Systems, Mannheim
ISBN: 978-3-936438-34-5
ISSN: 1869-7909

Bibliografische Information Der Deutschen Bibliothek
Die Deutsche Bibliothek verzeichnet diese Publikation in der Deutschen Nationalbibliografie;
detaillierte bibliografische Daten sind im Internet über http://dnb.ddb.de abrufbar.

Bibliographic information published by Die Deutsche Bibliothek
Die Deutsche Bibliothek lists this publication in the Deutsche Nationalbibliografie;
detailed bibliographic data are available in the Internet at http://dnb.ddb.de.

Information bibliographique de Die Deutsche Bibliothek
Die Deutsche Bibliothek a répertoiré cette publication dans la Deutsche Nationalbibliografie;
les données bibliographiques détaillées peuvent être consultées sur Internet à l´adresse http://dnb.ddb.de.

Table of contents

Searching for innovative products

Authors

Prof. Dr. Werner Gronau
Tourism & Transport Research Center
University of Nicosia
46 Makedonitissas Avenue, P.O. Box 24005
CY-1700 Nicosia
gronau.w@ttrc.info

Prof. Dr. Sven Groß
Management von Verkehrsunternehmen, Hochschule Harz
Friedrichstraße 57-59, 38855 Wernigerode
sgross@hs-harz.de

Dipl.-Geogr. Laura Herlitz
Freizeit- und Tourismusgeographie, Universität Trier
Behringstr., 54286 Trier
herlitz@uni-trier.de

Prof. Dr. Andreas Kagermeier
Freizeit- und Tourismusgeographie, Universität Trier
Behringstr., 54286 Trier
andreas@kagermeier.de

Dr. Rudi Kaufmann
School of Business, University of Nicosia
46 Makedonitissas Avenue
P.O. Box 24005, CY-1700 Nicosia
kaufmann.r@unic.ac.cy

Dipl.-Geor. Andreas Lehmberg
Harzer Tourismusverband e. V.
Marktstr. 45, 38640 Goslar
A. Lehmberg@harzinfo.de

Dipl.-Geogr. Nadine Lichter
InvesTour GmbH
Burgstraße 4, 54636 Bickendorf
nadinelichter@yahoo.de

Dipl.-Kffr. Kathleen Lumma
Kompetenzzentrum Hochschule Harz
Arbeitsbereich Tourismus, Hochschule Harz
Friedrichstraße 57-59, 38855 Wernigerode
klumma@hs-harz.de

Yianna Orphanidou, M.A.
Tourism & Transport Research Center
University of Nicosia
46 Makedonitissas Avenue, P.O. Box 24005
CY-1700 Nicosia
orphanidou.y@unic.ac.cy

Dipl.Geogr. Julia Raulf
Geographisches Institut Ruhr-Universität Bochum
julia_raulf@hotmail.com

Dr. Markus Rebstock
Fachhochschule Erfurt
Institut Verkehr und Raum
Altonaer Straße 25
99085 Erfurt
rebstock@fh-erfurt.de

Prof. Dr. Frank Schaal
International Business School Berlin
Wilmersdorfer Straße 117
10627 Berlin
InvesTour GmbH
Burgstraße 4, 54636 Bickendorf
schaal@investour.de

Prof. Dr. Joachim Willms
Tourism Futures Institute
37085 Göttingen
jw@tourism-futures.org

Tourism Development in Low Mountain Ranges – An Introduction –

Low mountain regions have been developed into tourist destinations from the beginning of commercial tourism in the 19th century. The early industrialisation of the lowlands in the river valleys and basins and the attendant rise of an industrialised urbanitiy made the nearby nature-oriented low mountains perfect destinations for recreational tourism in spas and mountain resorts. Apart from its nature low mountain regions often have cultural heritage as a potential attractor for tourism.

But since the end of the 20th century, tourism, leisure and recreation are on the move. Especially tourism, leisure and recreation in low mountain ranges faces various challenges due to important and sustainable changes forced by "glocalised" impacts like climate change, economic transformations, environmental degradation, aging societies, shifting values, new competitive markets and new ICT.

The contributions in this book seek to examine the complexity of tourism, leisure and recreation within the geographic frame of low mountains and their corresponding valleys and its changing interdependencies of nature, endogenous and exogenous culture.

Trier & Göttingen, Spring 2010

A. Kagermeier *J. Willms*

New approaches of adressing tourists

Andreas Kagermeier & Joachim Willms (eds.): Tourism Development in Low Mountain Ranges.
Mannheim 2010, p. 13 - 22 (= Studien zur Freizeit- und Tourismusforschung, Vol. 3)

Target-group-oriented bundling of tourism products as a possible key for a long-term perspective in low-mountain ranges
– A Cypriot Perspective –

Werner Gronau, Rudi Kaufmann & Yianna Orphanidou (Nicosia/Cyprus)

Abstract

The global competition of destinations on the one hand and the similarity of many low mountain ranges regions on the other hand form a very competitive environment for any kind of destination marketing and management. At the same time the demand for active, authentic and cultural orientated forms of tourism is constantly raising. New offers such as spa tourism and gastronomic tourism resulted in an enormous market segmentation and a steadily increasing number of potential target groups. At the same time the market segments for those offers are getting smaller and smaller. Already today many of these new forms of tourism are not sufficient on its own but need additional side products. Furthermore a growing overlapping of target groups and tourism products has to be considered. It is vital that this overlapping is understood as a chance of combining several tourism products in order to create a region specific tourism product, which is able to address a bigger target group and therefore can become a real alternative to established tourism products in other regions such as, for instance, “sun & beach” for coastal regions.

Following up an empirical study on the agro tourism sector, the potential of combining tourism products such as culinary, hiking and cycling tourism in the low mountain ranges of the Troodos mountains in Cyprus is presented. The compatibility of tourists’ interest in those different segments is presented, as well as possible ways to combine them in one product.

1 Introduction

1.1 Framework conditions

In recent years tourism product development became a rather complex job, not just the demand is constantly changing due to several aspects such as the individualisation process within the society, as described by *Beck* (1994) but also the supply-side is constantly upgrading and differentiating its products. Quite often product diversification in the leisure and tourism industry is understood as a logical result of the ongoing individualisation of the society. This interpretation may be true for the early periods of the diversification process, but the enormous product diversification one can see in today's leisure and tourism market can only be ex- plained by an ongoing self-supporting process mainly driven by the lack of creative ideas of the marketers. It seems as if there is not one single niche in the market which cannot be addressed as a unique and specific tourism product. By screening state of the art tourism products we find a huge amount of products belonging to one category. Sports tourism represents a good example: Of course there is not just sports tourism, but water sport tourism, which then gets differentiated once more into various products such as canoeing, kayaking or rafting tourism. By witnessing this enormous differentiation the question arises, whether all these so called tourism forms can or should be interpreted as stand alone tourism products. Considering the constantly decreasing market potential for those very differentiated products, it seems that in many cases additional side products are needed, or these so-called 'tourism products' turn out to be just side products themselves. In brief maybe a small add-on to the famous marketing slogan "Differentiate or Die!" may be allowed, when having the situation in the leisure and tourism industry in mind: "Differentiate or Die!" views "Differentiate till you Die!"

1.2 Product bundling as an option

Nevertheless all stakeholders in the tourism and leisure industry, including the consumers, have to find ways to cope with this very heterogeneous market. The answer given by the consumers - as has been elaborated in several studies - is the combination of several products, which is then anticipated by the supply side by offering product bundles. Especially when it comes to the bundling of tourism products on the supply side, the question arises which products meet the expectations of similar target groups and is there a possibility to identify typical product bundles which are likely to be successful.

Of course such bundles have to meet several general standards, they should:

- be applicable to different destinations
- guarantee a decent demand
- include various activities
- be based on existing products, though not neglecting upcoming trends
- represent a proper set of products for the specific target group.

Having all those before mentioned needs in mind the task seems to be quite hard to achieve, but the reality at the markets may give us some hints on how to solve the problem.

2 Geographical type settings of spatial contexts as base for tourism product bundling

2.1 Competitive Environment in Tourism Industry

The global competition of destinations on the one hand and the similarity of destinations on the other hand form a rather competitive market. At the same time especially the similarity of destinations can be used if it comes to tourism product bundling. To a certain extent the “famous” sun & beach tourism can be interpreted as a bundle of sun and beach related tourism products, which is implemented all over the world, based on a similar regional characteristic such as the proximity to a beach. From a geographic point of view the similarity of a certain type of spatial context existing in various destinations forms the base for a spatial context based bundle of tourism products. In other words the spatial context of a sunny coastline is the only need for the implementation of a sun & beach product. Therefore the existing geographical typesetting of spatial contexts may be a good starting point for the bundling of tourism products, especially due to the fact that those categories of spatial contexts can be identified all over the world. In relation to the product bundling for a sunny coastal context a product bundle for a low mountain context can be developed as well.

To what extent product bundling in a specific geographical context is possible and to what extent this product bundle is then transferable to similar spatial contexts in other destinations is the content of this case study from Cyprus.

2.2 Bundling Steps in the context of geographical typesetting

The process of bundling tourism offers into geographical typeset specific designated bundles and can be separated into 4 phases:

- Clarification of geographical typesetting,
- Clarification of the supply option in the given context by the identification of typical tourism products for the specific geographical typeset,
- Clarification of the demand by the identification of tourism target groups in the given geographical typeset,
- Creation of geographical typeset specific target group orientated product bundles.

The first step is the identification of the given geographical typeset, based on climate zones, geomorphologic features, natural and cultural features and the height range of a specific region a certain type of geographical typeset can be identified. For example a low mountain range in a moderate climate zone with rich cultural heritage sights at a level of 500-1000 meters.

In a second phase based on the specific geographical typeset typical tourism products are supposed to be identified. In order to create an overview on possible options and existing products it is important at this step to integrate all possible products into the given typeset while not just concentrating on the given ones. To stick to the example of the already mentioned typeset, possible products are, various forms of culinary tourism, biking, hiking and trekking tourism, spa and health tourism forms, cultural tourism due to the given heritage sites, etc.

The third phase focuses on the demand side by identifying the existing tourism target groups and their specific needs by examining their motivations, interests and satisfaction level.

In the final phase the existing supply side gets screened by the results of the demand analysis as well as the supply options the specific geographical typeset is offering.

In order to clarify the before introduced method, in the following the approach will be applied to a case study from Cyprus.

3 A case study from Cyprus

In order to provide the reader with an overview on the destination of Cyprus and the regional specifics a short introduction on Cyprus and its tourism development will be given within the next paragraphs.

3.1 Tourism Industry in Cyprus

3.1.1 The destination development of Cyprus

Since the independence of Cyprus in 1960, tourism was seen as the main source of income for the islands economy, consequently a national effort towards the development of a modern tourism destination was pressed ahead. The initial successful development was drastically interrupted by the country being at the brink of a civil war and the final Turkish intervention in 1974. The loss of the so far existing main tourism spots in Kyrenia and Famagusta led to the establishing of new tourism areas. Typical for the development in the late 1970s and the early 1980s, the classical "sun & beach"- destination was developed. The high acceptance of Cyprus' tourism offers led to a rapid development of accommodation infrastructure during the 1980s and early 1990s. The rising cost of living within Cyprus, the upcoming of new Mediterranean destinations in the mid of the 1990s and finally the lack of a diversification strategy in the national tourism industry, consequently led to a noticeable decline in the tourism industry in the end of the 1990s. Realising the decline, a new strategy plan, called Strategic Plan 2010 was elaborated. This plan, however, focuses mainly on making up for the missed out trend towards the diversification and upgrading of the tourism product. Nevertheless this new plan set new and very valuable trends for the establishment of new tourist offers aiming for new target groups. The newly established Cyprus agro tourism program can be seen as one of the successful outcomes of the new strategy.

3.1.2 The exceptional situation for "Agro-Tourism" in Cyprus

Due to the Turkish intervention in 1974 especially the rural areas faced a dramatic change. The loss of the major part of the Turkish-Cypriot community which amounts in some regions to up to 1/3 of the whole population led in some regions of southern Cyprus to abandoned or depopulated villages, especially in the low-mountain ranges. Due to the fact that the major part of the Greek Cypriot refugees coming from the northern parts moved to the urban areas this unequal allocation of the population could never be compensated. This fact of course armed dramatically the already beginning migration to the cities in the mid 70'ies. Consequently the depopulation of rural areas and low-mountain regions showed a much stronger result than in comparable countries. Considering these developments EU-funds have been used by the Cypriot government already in 1975 to strengthen the low mountain ranges. Already in these first activities in the context of for example the regional developing project in the Pitsillia the rural revitalization should also be enhanced by the implementation of tourism in this spatial context. Therefore the original roots for "agrotourism" in Cyprus can already be identified in the early 1980s. These - at that time isolated - private endeavours towards establishing some kind of "agrotourism" then consequently have been brought together by the Cyprus Tourism Organization (CTO) in the so called "Agrotourism"-Program.

3.1.3 The Cyprus "Agrotourism" program

The Cyprus "Agrotourism" Program, launched in 1991, was designed and promoted by the Cyprus Tourism Organization (CTO). Its aim was the revitalization of villages in low mountain regions by using a multidisciplinary approach. The main goal was to renovate old village-houses and to transform them into tourist accommodation facilities, catering establishments, craft shops and exhibition areas. To initiate the program CTO cooperated with other government departments, such as the Ministry of Agriculture, but also with a big variety of non public institutions, NGO's and individuals with the aim of preserving the traditional built environment of Cyprus. To fulfil this mission the program included a financial incentive scheme to enable a partial subsidisation for restorations of traditional buildings and their transformation into accommodation units, taverns, folk art centres and museums. The subsidiary amounts to 2/3 of the interest rate for accommodation establishments, traditional craft shops, museums and exhibition areas and 1/3 for taverns. Furthermore the non-profit Cyprus Agrotourism Company was funded to promote the new product and work as a platform for all agrotourism stakeholders. Overall CTO's two million US$ investment program, backed by some financial support from the villages and district level, can after more than ten years and projects in more than 50 different villages be seen as a success.

3.1.4 The Agro-Tourist in Cyprus as a typical low-mountain range tourist

Based on the fact that agrotourism in Cyprus means to a very large extent tourism in low mountain regions and at the same time the activities of agro-tourists in Cyprus are very comparable to low mountain-tourists in other destinations as for example hiking, trekking, sight seeing etc. for the further analyses the agro-tourists in Cyprus are interpreted as typical low-mountain region tourists.

3.2 Methodology of the study

Following the approach of tourism product bundling based on geographical typesets described in section 2, the study classified in a first step the ranges of the Troodos-Mountains due to their geomorphologic situation, their climatic specifications, their low population density, their peripheral characteristics and their existing infrastructure as a typical low-mountain region. Based on this definition relevant tourism products have been identified. These are nature related tourism forms such as hiking, trekking, biking; culinary tourism options such as wine tourism, cultural potentials in the field of historic villages, several world heritage sites related to religious practices and antiquities. Furthermore the specific situation of Cyprus as an island with short distance access to the sea even from the low-mountain ranges opens up even sea related activities such as sailing. Those steps cannot be elaborated in detail due to the limitation of this article; therefore the focus is set on the two final empirical steps:

- Clarification of the demand by the identification of tourism target groups in the given geographical typeset,
- Creation of geographical typeset specific target group orientated product bundles.

In order to get an overview on the demand side given in the presented area a quantitative approach in form of a highly standardized questionnaire, addressing tourists staying in agrotourism accommodation was used. The data collection was carried out from September to November 2006, which represents the high season in this segment, in 11 different villages within all 4 government controlled districts of the Republic of Cyprus. The questionnaire covering various topics, such as interests, activities, expectations, satisfaction level and some sociodemographic data of the tourists was handed over at the reception desk. The useable amount of questionnaires turned out to be 133, which leads to the limitations of the study. On the one hand the before mentioned rather low response has to be noted, on the other hand the predominant role of the major player within Cypriot agrotourism, "Cyprus Villages", in the sample has to be mentioned, due to the share of roughly 50 % of the overall lodging capacity of this company and the poor participation of the second major player the sample consists out of around 80 % Cyprus Villages customers. Due to the presence of this company in several regions and their overall role in general the sample fulfils still all basic requirements to be considered representative.

3.3 Basic Profile of Cypriot Agro-Tourists

In order to provide the reader with a basic overview on the characteristics and interests of Cypriot agro-tourists some reflections will be presented in the following. Agro-tourists are characterised by their price insensitiveness, their quality orientation; their high education level and their relatively young age - more than 50 percent fit into the category of 20-40 years. Furthermore the low amount of domestic tourists accounting for only 9 % of the overall amount and the high share of Germans (36 %) respectively German speakers including Switzerland and Austria (45 %) amongst the interviewees has to be mentioned. The major interests of this clientele can be described in form of relaxation, enjoying local hospitality and un-spoilt landscape and last but not least the interest in local culture. As far as the mentioned aspects are concerned the profile of the group is rather homogenous, but when it comes to the activities performed a more differentiated situation appears. Based on a more detailed analysis of the performed activities a clear correlation between certain activities could be identified.

As visible in Figure 1 two groups of activities, marked in dark respectively light grey, can be identified due to a 95 % respectively 99 % correlation based on Pearson. The activities (marked in dark grey) sailing trip, mountain biking, golfing and 4WD-safari show a significant bi-variant correlation. A similar situation in form of a bi-variant correlation exists for the following activities: purchasing of local products, visiting antiquities and monasteries, culinary trips and participation in craft-courses (marked in light grey). Therefore it can be stated that there is a clear difference in everyday behaviour and activities of the, based on interests and socio-demographic aspects rather homogenous, Cypriot agro-tourists. Based on the identified strong relations within certain activities, a cluster analysis based on interests and activities was performed in order to identify different target groups within the questioned agro-tourists.

Fig. 1: Correlation matrix of activities

	sailing-trips	visit of antiquities and monasteries	purchasing of local products	culinary trips	off-road safari	mountainbiking	golfing	craft-workshops
sailing-trips	1,00	-0,13	0,07	0,10	0,23*	0,20*	0,27**	-0,02
visit of antiquities and monasteries	-0,13	1,00	0,20*	0,12	0,08	-0,03	0,06	0,31**
purchasing of local products	0,07	0,20*	1,00	0,29**	0,21	-0,19	0,03	0,37**
culinary trips	0,10	0,12	0,26**	1,00	0,44**	0,04	0,06	0,07
off-road safari	0,23*	0,08	0,21*	0,44	1,00	0,30**	0,18	0,26**
mountainbiking	0,20*	-0,03	0,19*	0,04	0,30**	1,00	0,36**	0,05
golfing	0,27**	0,06	0,03	0,06	0,18	0,36**	1,00	0,09
craft-workshops	-0,02	0,31**	0,37**	0,07	0,26**	0,05	0,09	1,00

*: significant (5 % probability of error)

**: highly signifikant (1 % probability of error)

Source: own calculations

3.4 Differentiated Activity-Groups amongst Cypriot Agro-Tourists

The on interests and activities based cluster analysis resulted in two clusters. Due to the high congruence of the given type of tourist in terms of the before mentioned socio-demographic variables, the two clusters show a rather congruence regarding those variables as well. There is no significant difference in between the clusters in terms of age, education, job or gender. But when it comes to money spent an interesting aspect appears. First of all as mentioned before the overall spending per person is with around 40 Euro per person (excluding accommodation costs) relatively high, furthermore there is a clear difference in spending between the two clusters. While the first cluster spends only around 31 Euros a day per person, the second spends 43 Euros per day per person (without accommodation costs). This difference in spending can be explained with the activities favoured respectively performed by each of the clusters. As expected, based on the high degree of correlation in between certain activities, a strong internal correlation within the two clusters of activities can be analysed. According to Figure 1 cluster 1 refers to the type of activities (dark grey) being sportier or more adventurous and at the same time more expensive to do. While the second cluster referring to the lighter grey concentrates more on calm or cultural activities like sightseeing or craft courses that are less costly. Based on those two activity-clusters the "typical" agro-tourist in Cyprus can be differentiated into the group of "Calm-Culture-Seekers" (cluster 2) and "Active Explorers" (cluster 1). The result of the cluster-analysis supports similar to the high levels of correlation in-between certain activities, the argumentation of a high compatibility of certain activities. Having the major aim of this analysis in mind to identify tourism products, which can be combined, these activities show a high bundling potential. Beside the different activities also a clear difference in the way on how those two groups want to perform their activities can be witnessed. The rather calm and observing approach of the "Calm-Culture-Seekers" combined with their strong interested in all forms of cultural expression clearly contradicts the rather active and adventurous, more experiencing approach of the "Active Explorers"

Fig. 2: Activities by Typesation

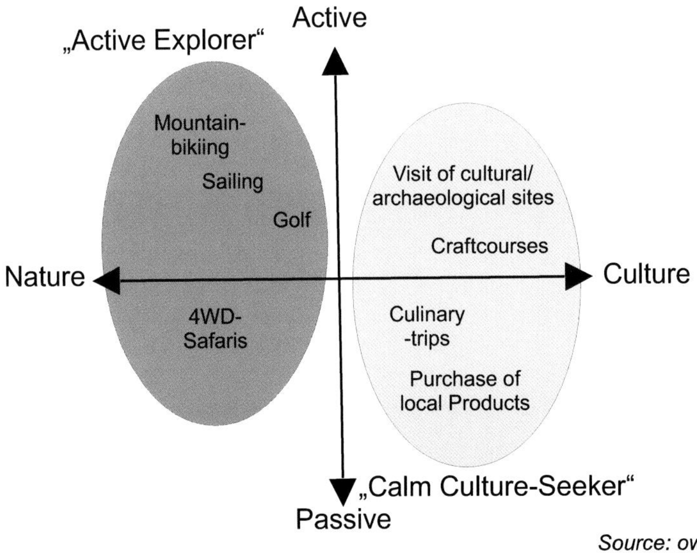

Source: own design

with their clear interest in nature. When talking about interest or orientation towards nature in the context of the "Active Explorers" it has to be clarified, that nature mainly functions as stage for their activities, the natural environment just provides an attractive framework for performing sport activities.

3.5 Possible Product Bundles for the Cypriot Low Mountain Range

The result of the cluster-analysis, in coherence with the before described high correlation in between certain activities performed by the tourists, allows the design of specific tourism products, which can be summed up in a second step into two product-bundles satisfying the needs of the identified two target groups, the "Calm-Culture-Seekers" and the "Active Explorer".
By combining the agrotourism-accommodation with the before mentioned two activity-clusters two attractive packages for the Cypriot low-mountain region can be developed. The success of such packages seems to be rather promising due to the already existing demand for the given activities and the correlation between the activities and the existing demand for this type of accommodation. Such packages could be introduced in a larger scale covering several regions within the low-mountain context and therefore become in the long term some kind of alternative to the coast based "sun & beach" tourism.

3.6 Summary of the Cypriot Case study

The presented case study clearly indicates the opportunities of the in section 2 presented approach of geographical typesettings of spatial contexts as a base for tourism product bundling. The chosen methodological approach resulted in two possible target groups, the "Calm-Culture-Seekers" and the "Active Explorers", including a specific profile for each of the two. The quantitative analysis of the demand side ensures furthermore an already existing demand for the presented activity bundles as foundation for a low-mountain-range specific tourism package.

4 Conclusion

Keeping the starting point of this paper in mind, to identify a methodology to evaluate the opportunities of low-mountain-ranges for standardised tourism packages, it has to be concluded that the applied approach based upon a geographical typesetting not just clearly showed the given potential, but furthermore even indicated the profile of the relevant target groups. The similarity of specific geographical settings furthermore ensures a rather high transferability of the results as well as of the overall methodological approach. Therefore the existing dominance of tourism packages in the "sun & beach" segment is rather a result of the strong focus of the tourism industry than the opportunities given by the geographical setting of a costal region. Specific tourism packages can be developed for several geographical settings by even having a clear market potential. A low-mountain product can work as a specific product as well as the "sun & beach" one does, the target groups exist, as well as the correlation of region-specific activities does. To conclude it can be said, that the future tourism product development should rather focus on geographical setting specific tourism product bundling than on an ongoing product diversification in order to ensure a long-term economic feasibility.

References

Beck, U. & E. Beck-Gernsheim (eds.) (1994): Riskante Freiheiten. Individualisierung in modernen Gesellschaften. Frankfurt

Berglund, K. & A. Johansson (2007): Constructions of entrepreneurship: a discourse analysis of academic publications. Journal of Enterprising Communities: People and Places in the Global Economy, Vol. 1 (No 1) pp. 77-102

Fuller-Love, N. et. al. (2006): Entrepreneurship and Rural Economic Development: a Scenario analysis approach. International Journal of Entrepreneurial Behavior & Research, Vol. 12 (No 5), pp. 289-305

Gronau W. & A. Kagermeier (2007): Key factors for Successful Leisure and Tourism Public Transport Offers In: Journal of Transport Geography, Vol. 15/7, pp. 127-135

Gronau W. & H.R. Kaufmann (2009): Tourism as a stimulus for sustainable development in rural areas: a Cypriot perspective. In: Tourismos 4 (No 1), pp. 83-95

Kaufmann, R. (1997): The Influence of Identity on Marketing– Education for Eastern German Entrepreneurs. PhD. The Manchester Metropolitan University

Komilis, P. (1994): Tourism and sustainable regional development. In: Seaton, A.V. (ed.) Tourism: The state of the art (pp. 65-73). Chichester

Lane, B. (1994): Sustainable rural tourism strategies: A tool for development and conservation. Journal of Sustainable Tourism 2 (No 2), pp. 102-111

Malach-Pines, A., H. Levy & A. Utasi (2005): Entrepreneurs as Cultural Heroes. Journal of Managerial Psychology, Vol. 20 (No 6), pp. 541-555

Morrison, A (2000): Entrepreneurship: What Triggers it? International Journal of Entrepreneurial Behaviour & Research Vol. 6 (No 2), pp. 59-71

Roden, C. (2000): Local Food and Culture, Proceedings of the Conference "Local Food and Tourism", Larnaca, Cyprus, November 2000

Roper, J.& G. Cheney (2005): The Meanings of Social Entrepreneurship Today. Corporate Governance, Vol. 5 (No 3), pp. 95- 104

Saveriades A. (2001): Developing the agrotourism (rural tourism) product: The Cyprus Experience unpublished Presentation International Conference on the Development of Ecotourism 2001

Sharpley R. (2000): Tourism and Sustainable Development: Exploring the Theoretical Divide. Journal of Sustainable Tourism, Vol. 8 (No.1), pp. 1-19

Silverman, D. (1995): Interpreting Qualitative Data. London

Thompson, J., G. Alvy & A. Lees (2000): Social Entrepreneuship- a New Look at the People and the Potential. Management Decision, Vol. 38. (No 5), pp. 328-338

Wechner, H. & H.R. Kaufmann (2006): Influencing Factors of Consumers' Perception towards Delicatessen Differentiated by Consumers' Favorite Shopping Locations. International Journal of Management Cases. Special Edition CIRCLE Conference, Vol. 9 (No 3/4)

Woehler K. (1999): Sustainibilisierung des Tourismus. Lüneburg

Andreas Kagermeier & Joachim Willms (eds.): Tourism Development in Low Mountain Ranges.
Mannheim 2010, p. 23 - 46 (= Studien zur Freizeit- und Tourismusforschung, Vol. 3)

Experience orientated staging of nature oriented and geotourism attractions – A case study from the European Geopark Vulkaneifel

Andreas Kagermeier (Trier)

Summary

The last decade has seen an experience orientation with a particular focus on leisure parks and new tourist attractions such as Urban Entertainment Centres, Brand Lands or Tropical Baths. But also in cultural urban tourism experience orientation meanwhile plays a major role. The professionalism in staging the original rough tourism product has led to a rise in the level of visitor expectation. Today, even the visitors to natural heritage sites are not satisfied by only watching or walking through the natural attractions, but expect a more sophisticated presentation. Because on-site staging has its limits, a special focus has to be laid on accompanying indoor-facilities which help to expand the experiences made during the real-world visit in the natural environment. The article analyses the factors which have to be fulfilled when aiming at successfully conceiving natural heritage sites.

Taking as an example the European Geopark Vulkaneifel (Germany), the actual presentation of the natural heritage, the needs of the visitors and options for a more state-of-the-art processing, preparation and adaptation are discussed. The presentation is based on empirical findings from a visitor survey carried out in 2008. Apart from several positive findings, different aspects which are left as a desideratum, will be presented:

- quality level and high-performance innovative ways of staging
- distinct identification of the target group
- appropriate target group orientation of the product
- the role of market-communication strategies
- supporting collateral activities.

Apart from the question of how experience orientated staging might be optimised in the study area, another focus is laid on the need to intensify cooperation in order to reach the necessary threshold and improve and increase the attractiveness of the different Geopark sites. With a more performance orientated concept that takes the audience on a thrilling journey into the spectacular geological history of our planet, an even broader public could be addressed and attracted.

1 Increasing experience orientation in geotourism

In the last years the way of presenting natural heritage for tourism purposes has seen major challenges and changes. For a long time the traditional presentation of natural (as well as cultural) heritage in museums focused on the scientific substance and a high level of scientific correctness. Therefore the image of museums is more marked by an expectation of solid scientific backing than the expectation of an attractive and entertaining presentation of interesting facts and contexts.

At the same time under the umbrella of the term "geotourism" the focus on natural attractions as generator for tourist arrivals in rural areas has risen. Especially in mountainous regions where the results of geological processes sometimes show impressing formations and situations the attention given to geological phenomenons is rising. But geotourism not only wants to turn the attention towards the aesthetic and often impressing results of geological and geomorphologial processes. At the same time the creation of an understanding for the natural processes is intended as well.

But regarding the developments in other fields of leisure and tourism where especially since the 90ies new ways of creating tourist experiences have been developed the offer of additional information on geological or geomorphological processes has to face the challenge of other offers in the tourism market with whom it has to compete if it wants to attract visitors. As *Pine & Gilmore* have expressed in their article which started the discussion on the experience economy: "Today the concept of selling experiences is spreading beyond theatres and theme parks" (1998, p. 99).

Pine & Gilmore have distinguished four approaches through which experience can be generated (cf. fig. 1). In the discussion on the experience economy dur-

Fig. 1: The four dimensions of experiences

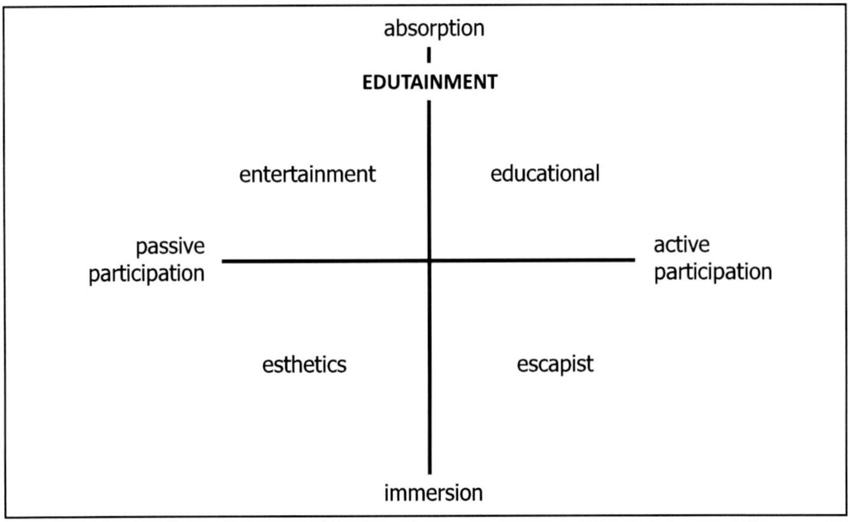

Source: Pine & Gilmore 1998, p. 102

ing the last decade (cf. for example *Smith & Onderwater* 2009 documenting the ATLAS conference on this subject) special attention has been given to only one aspect of experience, referring to passive participation and absorption of stimuli: the entertainment dimension.

This is the kind of experience most of the leisure parks are targeting at. A short-term arousal, which offers especially physical stimuli to the senses. Because roller coasters are the typical representative of this kind of entertainment sometimes its also referred to as the "roller-coaster-effect" (cf. fig. 2).

Fig. 2: Experience orientated offers of the 90ies adressing the arousal aspect

Source: www.coastersandmore.de

Apart from the traditional leisure park attractions and theme parks this concept has been widely used in thematic staging of different types, one of the most famous perhaps being the thematic orientation of hotels in Las Vegas (cf. fig. 2 above right). Apart from the fact that these stimuli wear out quite quickly and therefore always new, more exiting stimuli have to be given (a process which is sometimes called experience spiral), these types of experience are not what is headed for when looking at natural and cultural heritage. There, the dimension of active participation and absorption of information is traditionally used. The visitor should actively absorb the given information, an experience *Pine & Gilmore* are calling "educational".

The presentation of natural and cultural heritage now found itself before the background that the visitors became more and more used to exiting stimuli faced with a situation that their offers have been perceived as less and less attractive.

One way out of this dilemma has been the search for experiences that demand less effort from the visitor when acquiring the given information. Those approaches which give easier access to the information by integrating entertaining elements and approaches have come to be known as "edutainment" (cf. fig. 1).

Edutainment at the same time refers to a much more comprehensive understanding of "experience" than the Pine & Gilmore approach. Taking the five dimensions *Unger & Kerman* defined already in 1983 as determining experience:
1 Perceived freedom
2 Involvement
3 Arousal
4 Mastery
5 Spontaneity
edutainment tries to involve the visitors, to give them much more choice as a pre-defined setting in a leisure park, and let them act spontaneously in a setting that they can master according to their own interests (cf. fig. 3).

Fig. 3: Edutainment offers in museums of the European Geopark Vulkaneifel

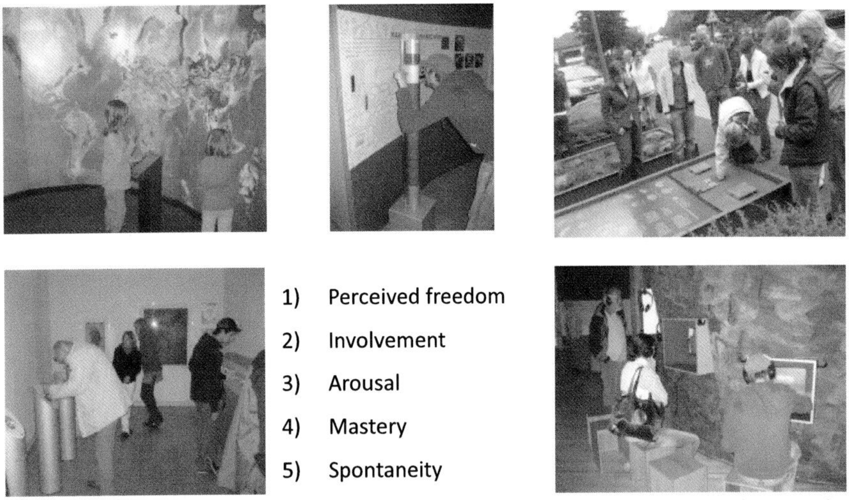

Source: own photographs

But the question remainsas to whether these approaches to activate the visitors of nature oriented tourist attractions are still sufficient to meet the expectations and demands of the visitors. Findings from culture orientated urban tourism suggest that the "experience spiral" which makes it necessary to continuously develop the offer in urban tourism may apply to nature oriented and geotourism offers as well (cf. *Kagermeier* 2009). In culture oriented tourism the activation of tourists tries to let them immerse into specific settings (to a certain extent even referring to the flow-concept of *Csíkszentmihályi*,1990) towards a more comprehensive experiencing of the historic past. Historic re-enactment as a means of creating specific longer lasting and not only superficial experiences is much easier when dealing with historic cultural aspects. But in the field of nature and geological processes this direct involvement of the tourists cannot easily be achieved. So the central question is, whether and how the tourists in nature-oriented and geotourism could be activated and integrated into the setting so that they become absorbed in the sense of a more profound experience.

2 The European Geopark Vulkaneifel

Fig. 4: National Geoparks in Germany in 2008

Source: www.geo-union.de

Geoparks are a quite new approach of trying to use geological or geomorphological phenomena to enhance the attractiveness of a tourism destination. Since the first denomination of National Geoparks in Germany according to the UNESCO-criterias in the year 2002 eleven National Geoparks have been established (cf. fig. 4; for more details see e.g. *Niklas* 2008). Covering different geological and geomorphological features that range from the meteorite crater of the Ries to the pleistocene landscape in Mecklenburg-West Pomerania most of these Geoparks are situated in German low mountain ranges. The German Geoparks are organised under the umbrella of the „Alfred-Wegener-Foundation", a geoscientific organisation, and are marketed under the brand of „planet erde" (cf. fig. 5). This organisational structure means that a main focus is put on the scientific aspects whereas tourism aspects sometimes seem to play only a secondary role in this network.

Fig. 5: Logo of the German National Geoparks

planeterde
Welt der Geowissenschaften

Source: www.geo-union.de

Apart from the national network of Geoparks in the year 2000 a European network of Geoparks was established as well. In the meantime 34 Geoparks in 13 European countries have joined this cooperation trying to promote the ideas of Geoparks and to exchange ways of promoting them for tourism purposes (cf. fig. 5).

Fig. 6: European Geoparks in 2009

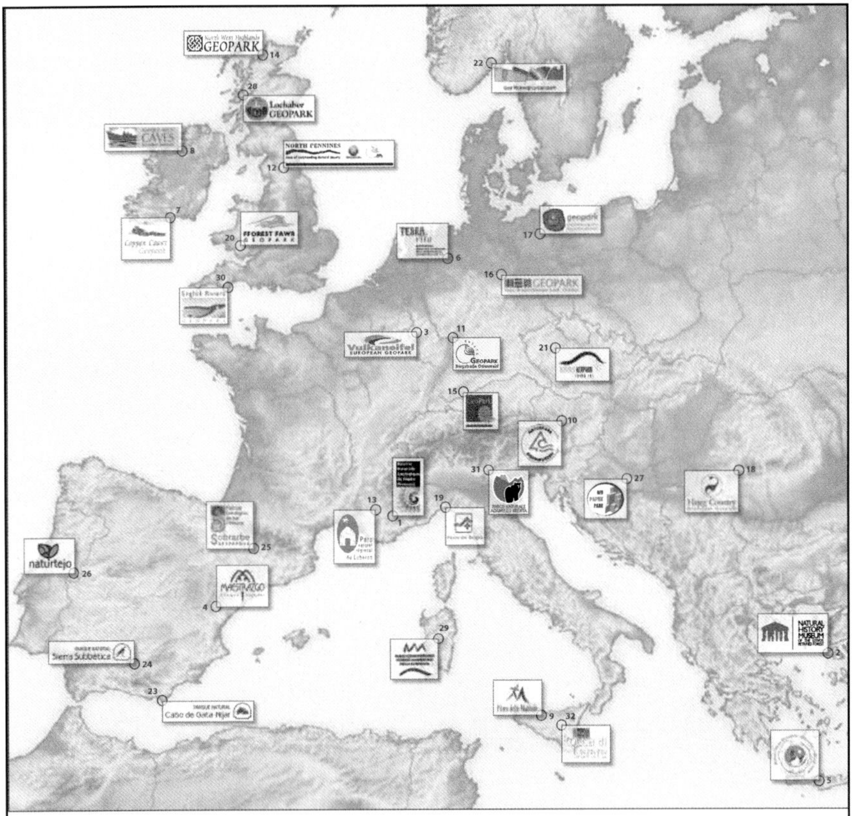

1	Réserve Géologique de Haute Provence, France	9	Parco delle Madonie Sicily, Italy	17	Geopark Mecklenburgische Eiszeitlandschaft, Germany	25	Sobrarbe Geopark Aragon, Spain
2	Lesvos Petried Forest Geopark, Greece	10	Naturpark Steirische Eisenwurzen, Austria	18	Hateg Country Dinosaurs Geopark, Romania	26	Naturtejo Geopark, Portugal
3	Vulkaneifel European Geopark, Germany	11	Geopark Bergstraße-Odenwald, Germany	19	Beigua Geopark, Italy	27	Papuk Geopark, Croatia
4	Maeztrazgo Cultural Park, Spain	12	North Pennines AONB England, Great Britain	20	Fforest Fawr Geopark Wales, Great Britain	28	Lochaber Geopark Scotland, Great Britain
5	Psiloritis Natural Park Crete, Greece	13	Park Naturel Régional du Luberon, France	21	Bohemian Paradise Geopark, Czech Republic	29	Geological Mining Park of Sardinia, Italy
6	Geo-Naturpark Terra Vita, Germany	14	North West Highlands Scotland, Great Britain	22	Gea Norvegica Geopark, Norway	30	English Riviera Geopark, Great Britain
7	Copper Coast Geopark, Ireland	15	Geopark Schwäbische Alb, Germany	23	Cabo de Gata Nijar Natural Park Andalucia, Spain	31	Parco Naturale Adamello Brenta, Italy
8	Marble Arche Cave Geopark, Northern Ireland	16	Geopark Harz Braunschweiger Land Ostfalen, Germany	24	Sierras Subbéticas Natural Park Andalucia, Spain	32	Rocca die Cerere Sicily, Italy

Source: Natur- und Geopark Vulkaneifel 2009 (www.europeangeoparks.org)

In Germany six Geoparks are part of the European Geopark network (some of them being national Geoparks at the same time):

1) Naturpark Bergstraße-Odenwald
2) Terravita Teuteburger Wald
3) Geopark Harz Braunschweiger Land Ostfalen
4) Schwäbische Alb
5) Mecklenburgische Eiszeitlandschaft
6) European Geopark Vulkaneifel.

In the Eifel there is the odd situation (due to the German federal system), that the whole Vulkaneifel belongs to the national Geopark network whereas only its western part is a member of the European Geopark network (cf. fig. 06). The European Geopark Vulkaneifel covers mainly the area of the administrative district "Vulkaneifel".

Fig. 7: Area of the European Geopark Vulkaneifel

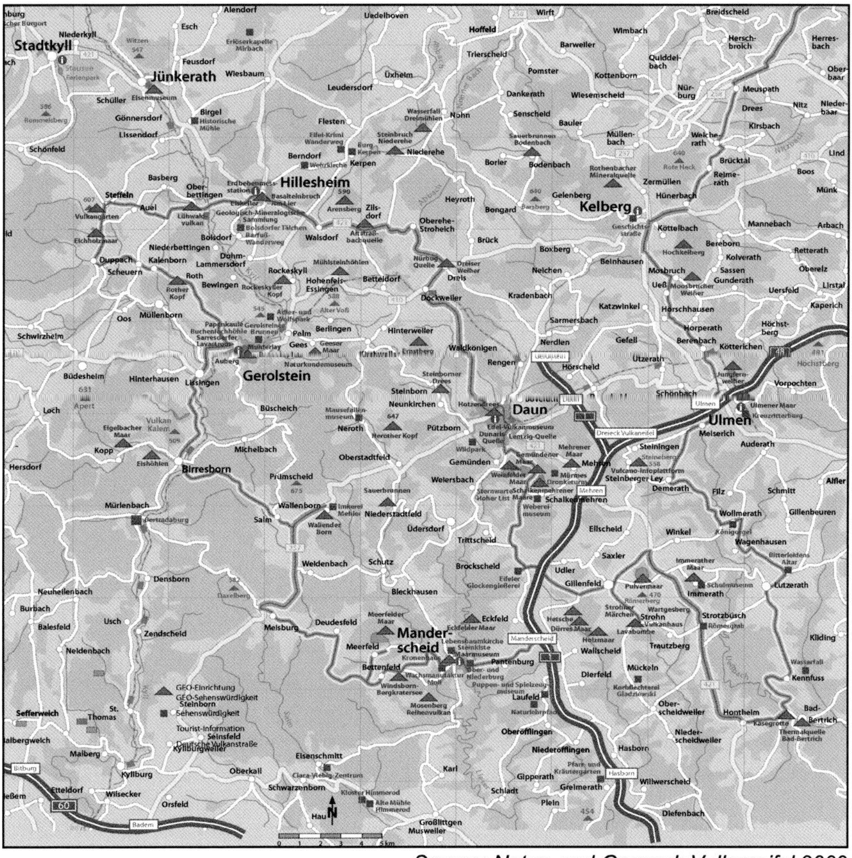

Source: Natur- und Geopark Vulkaneifel 2009

Fig. 8: Volcanos of the Eifel: the pleasant nowadays situation does not give an impression of the extreme conditions of their genesis

Source: Natur- und Geopark Vulkaneifel 2009

In the case of the European Geopark Vulkaneifel an additional challenge for communicating geological processes to the visitors and induce an understanding has to be met. The results of the volcanic past in the low mountain range of the Eifel (in the Western part of Germany near the border to Belgium) are mainly formed by maares which are lakes in the volcanic craters. These lakes are often surrounded by forests because the steep slopes are not apt for agricultural use. Thus, the situation is characterised by a certain amenity and quite pleasant atmosphere in the surrounding of the former volcanos.

So the main challenge when trying to establish a geotourism offer in the Vulkaneifel is to create opportunities where this volcanic past comes alive. Thus, apart from on-site information at the geological sites in the Vulkaneifel, supporting indoor-offers try to induce an understanding of the volcanic past of the region.

A second challenge for the marketing of the Vulkaneifel to tourists is the organisational aspect that the western part is branded as European Geopark whereas the eastern part counts as German Geopark. To tackle this separation, the so-called “Deutsche Vulkanstraße” (German volcano route) has been created in 2006 as a common tourism marketing tool that covers both parts of the Vulkaneifel (cf. fig. 9). The objective of this common marketing tool is to induce synergy between these two parts, each of which has a specific tourism potential and specific target markets. So when evaluating the presentation of the geotourism offer in the Vulkaneifel this aspect of internal cooperation was also taken into account.

Fig. 9: Deutsche Vulkanstraße (German volcano route) in the Vulkaneifel

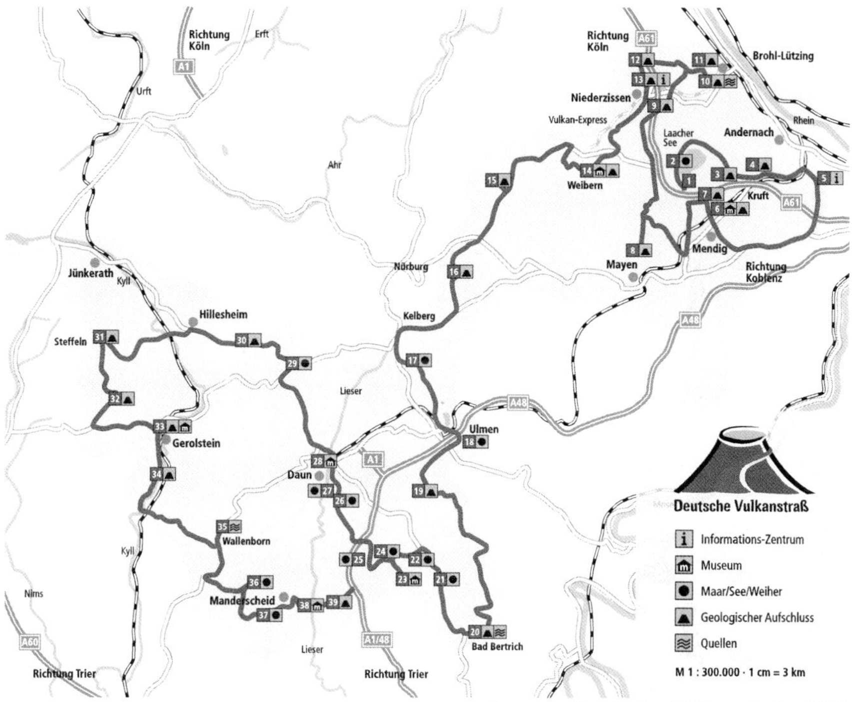

Source: Deutsche Vulkanstraße 2008

3 The methodological design

The fact that indoor information offers play a central role meant that the evaluation of the quality of the experience orientation in the European Geopark Vulkaneifel had to focus on the information offer in the museums. Therefore the study focused on three museums where information on the volcanic past of the region is provided:

1 Eifel-Vulkanmuseum Daun

2 Maarmuseum Manderscheid

3 Vulkanhaus Strohn

(number 28, 38 and 23 in fig. 9). The Eifel-Vulkanmuseum is run by the district Vulkaneifel whereas the two others have been established by the local parishes. As a fourth sample point the so called “Maarsattel” near Daun has been chosen, because it is one of the most famous spots in the Vulkaneifel where three maares can be seen at one time (number 27 In fig. 9; cf. fig. 8).

The oldest of the three museums, the Vulkanmuseum Daun (located in a former administrative building; cf. fig 10) was already founded in 1996. Today it receives about 20.000 visitors per year. Because the Vulkanmuseum Daun is the oldest of the three museums its didactic approach is the most traditional. Apart from different glass show cases only very few interactive elements are to

Fig. 10: Vulkanmuseum Daun

Photos: A. Kagermeier & I. Bradic

be found. At the same time the atmosphere in the exhibition is quite sober. One of the problems during the investigation has been that interactive elements were out of order.

The second example, the Maarmuseum Manderscheid was established in 1999. About the same number of visitors as in Daun are counted there per year (cf. fig. 11). It has to be stated that the number of visitors stagnated in the last year and that for example the opening of the German volcano route did not have

Fig. 11: Number of visitors at the Maarmuseum Manderschein

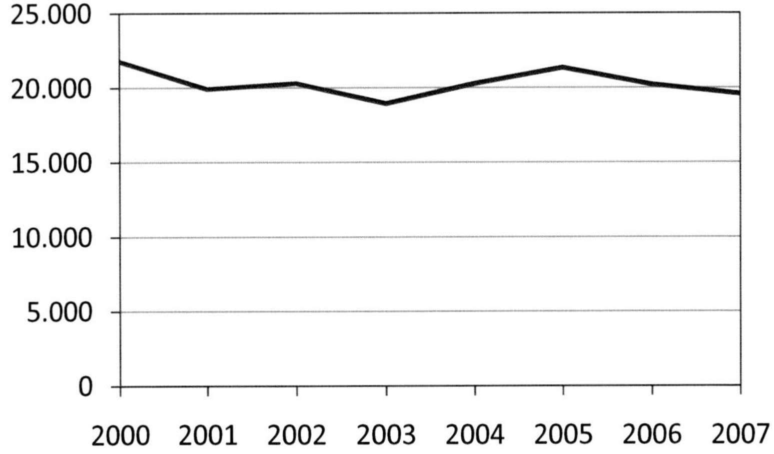

Source: Maarmuseum Manderschein

Fig. 12: Maarmuseum Manderschein

Photos: A. Kagermeier & I. Bradic

a positive impact on the number of visitors to the museum, although the number of visitors in the whole region is rising.

The Maarmuseum in Manderscheid had once been the local town hall so it offers a great space which has been equiped with a number of three-dimensional show cases and dioramas. A certain thematic emphasis is put on the aspect of succession in the former craters during the silting up process. One of the major attractions of the Maarmuseum is some kind of drilling core (above in the middle in fig. 12) which shows like a time-machine the development of the crater since the last eruption with an audio-visual animation. Other audio-visual installations show that Manderschein quite clearly follows the early ideas of edutainment offers.

The third museum in Strohn is the youngest of the three (cf. fig. 13). Opened in June 2002 in a former farmhouse it is the smallest exhibition in the sample with only limited space available.The museum is very intensively trying to convey the impression of the heat and the atmosphere of active volcanos. The intensive use of orange colours and lights as well as some interactive installations are showing quite an opposite setting compared to Daun.

In co-operation with the Vulkaneifel a visitor survey at the four selected sample points has been carried out in summer 2008. The field work has been integrated into a study course of our department (cf. *Bradic* 2009). The methodological design comprised not only face-to-face interviews with the visitors. Apart from that observations of the visitors have been carried out and some elements of Mystery Guest approaches were used as well. The mix of different quantitative methods of collecting data has been proven to produce reliable results which complement each other already in another comparable survey (cf. *Kagermeier* 2006).

Fig. 13: Vulkanhaus Strohn

Photos: Vulkanhaus Strohn

In total the students have interviewed 568 visitors at the four sample points during different days of the 2008 season (before, during and after the summer holidays, during the week as well as the week-end) to achieve a more or less representative sample.

4 Empirical findings

Almost three-quarters of the visitors were overnight guests in the region, thus showing the importance of geotourism presentations for providing attractive offers to tourists in low mountain ranges. With about one million overnight stays the district Vulkaneifel is an important destination in this part of Germany. Due to the proximity of the Netherlands and Belgium these two nationalities constitute the main incoming markets in the Eifel. The percentage of Dutch tourists (15 %) and Belgian tourists (5 %) in the sample (only overnight guests) is comparable to the share of these two nationalities in the accommodations of the district (*Statistisches Landesamt Rheinland-Pfalz*, 2009).

Recommendations are one of the most effective and at the same time cheapest marketing instruments. Their importance is supposed to rise in the next years according to a growing importance of the Social Web where recommendations of testimonials tend to have a much broader scope than the traditional word-of-mouth marketing.

The portions of visitors to whom the visit has been recommended differs significantly between the four locations. The lowest recommendation rate with only 10 % has been found in Daun, the oldest and quite "traditional" museum. Manderscheid and Strohn are achieving higher scores of recommendation. For Strohn more than one third is a quite reasonable value which signifies a good quality of the offer (cf. *Kagermeier* 2010, p. 32). But the most impressing value is achieved by the Maarsattel, where almost half of the questioned visitors said that the location has been recommended to them.

Fig. 14: Visitors coming on recommendations

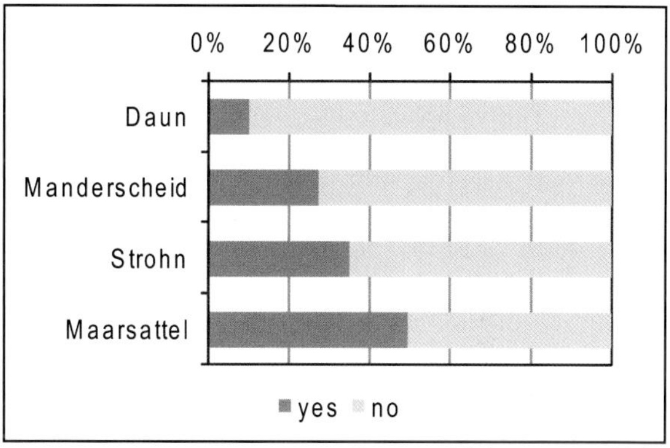

Source: Visitor survey 2008

4.1 Visitor satisfaction

This relation between the four sample points is to be found as well, when asking for the overall satisfaction with the visit. On a scale from 1 (= very good) to 4 (= very poor) the Vulkanmuseum Daun got a mean value of only 2.06. The Maarmuseum Manderscheid has been rated 1.72 and Vulkanhaus Strohn 1.61. Almost the same result (1.62) has been calculated for the visitors of the Maarsattel. This means, that the traditional concept of the Vulkanmuseum in Daun is not highly estimated by the visitors compared to a more activating setting in Strohn. Taking into account the fact that there are about 1 million overnight stays only in the district Vulkaneifel and a total of almost 10 million overnight stays in the whole Eifel (*Statistisches Landesamt Rheinland-Pfalz*, 2009) – which can be seen more or less as the catchment area for the overnight tourists – the museums in the Vulkaneifel are only attracting a very small portion of the potential market segment.

Apart from the overall satisfaction different aspects of the offer have been rated as well: the design of the information panels, the content of the given information, the quality of the interaction and the ambiance in the museum. There were no great differences from the overall rating to be found when looking at these details of the presented offer. Only the ambiance in the Vulkanhaus Strohn got an extraordinary good rating (even compared to the good score at the overall satisfaction). This means, that a good ambiance is especially appreciated and esteemed by the visitors of geotourism museums. This refers perhaps to the great contrast between the green and quiet natural surrounding and the roaring heat of liquid lava flows and lava bombs.

Another aspect giving indications on the visitors' satisfaction is the question as to whether they intend to repeat their visit at a specific site. Again the same order as for the other indicators is to be found (cf. fig. 15). But at the same time it has to be stated, that even the Vulkanhaus Strohn got only 40 % of potential repeaters. The natural landscape at the Vulkansattel produced quite contrary results. There 60 % of the visitors intend to come back again. This means, that even though the Vulkanhaus Strohn got quite positive ratings its offer is not perceived as being attractive enough to come back again. The small size of the three evaluated museums has to be seen as a constraint for a more comprehensive offer which would attract visitors to come back again. At the same time it can be assumed, that the experience orientation – even at the Vulkanhaus Strohn – is not yet as sophisticated and well developed to induce high repeater shares.

Fig. 15: Intention to repeat the visit

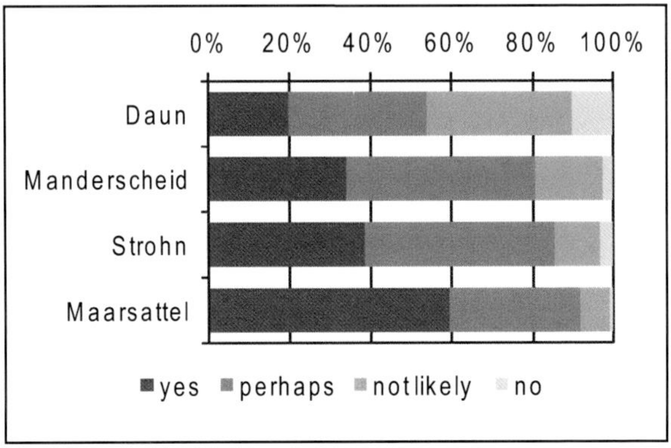

Source: Visitor survey 2008

To further identify the necessity where to take action not only the rating of overall characteristics for the museums has to be taken into account, but a more detailed evaluation of the specific parts and settings has to be carried out. Thus the visitors' rating of the particular parts and settings of the museums can be correlated with the overall satisfaction (i.e. the implicit importance) and then divided into four categories

1 high correlation with good overall ranking and a good rating of the specific setting shows the ***strength*** of a facility
2 high correlation and poor (overall and specific) ratings show an ***urgent need for changes***
3 poor ratings for a specific part of a museum but only low correlation with the overall satisfaction indicates ***need for changes*** and
4 good ratings for a specific setting but only low correlation with the overall satisfaction is called "***additional benefit***" because the good ratings do not strongly influence the general impression of a visitor (i.e. this is not a relevant salient factor).

When visualising the results for the Vulkanmuseum Daun (cf. fig. 16) it is not astonishing that most of the different parts of the museum show an (urgent) need for changes, because an overall satisfaction below average is (highly) correlated with a poor rating of the specific setting and thus showing poor experience quality. Only one interactive element (the volcano eruption) can be seen as a strength of the museum. Another element with interactive options (the geysir) which was out of order during the whole period of the survey arose expectations of the visitors and then disappointed them, because the station did not function.

But even the results for the best of the three museums at Strohn (cf. fig. 17) show, that even there not all the expectations of the visitors are met, although

Fig. 16: Ranking of relevance for taking action at the Vulkanmuseum Daun

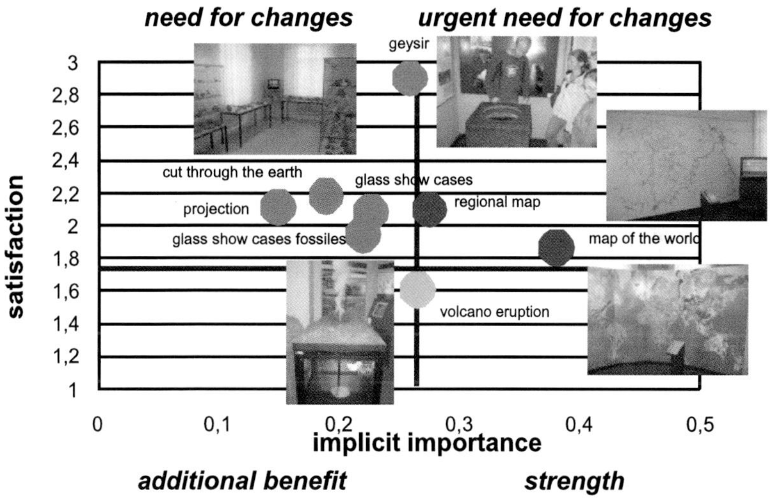

Source: Visitor survey 2008

Fig. 17: Ranking of relevance for taking action at the Vulkanhaus Strohn

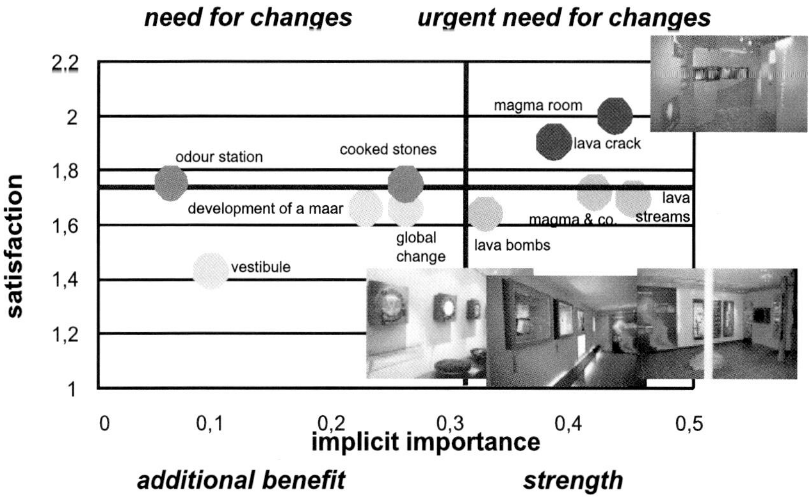

Source: Visitor survey 2008

some settings can be called "strength". This applies especially to those settings where the heat and the noise of a volcano eruption is simulated by colours and audio-visual presentations in combination with interactive elements. And again one of the interactive elements which does not work (magma room) has been positioned in the quadrant "urgent need for change". At the same time is has to be pointed out, that interaction does not automatically mean good rating. The odour station seems to be a convincing interactive setting which addresses all senses, but the visitors did not esteem this kind of interactive setting, because the experience has not been as convincing as expected.

To sum up it has to be concluded that the visitors' satisfaction at the four different sample points shows a clear differentiation in their experience quality. But even at the comparatively good museum, options and needs for amendments towards a more sophisticated experience orientation have been identified.

4.2 Results from observations and mystery guest visits

Apart from the questioning of the visitors, so called "objective" approaches (cf. *Kagermeier* 2006, p. 138) of measuring the quality of the offer in the three museums have been conducted additionally. The intention has been to identify some more details concerning the strength and weaknesses of the specific settings. Therefore the visitors and their behaviour were observed at different stations in the museums. With the same intention of identifying specific details of the presentations the students conducted mystery guest visits in the museums (before doing the visitors survey so that these results did not influence the mystery guest approach).

The two approaches focus on three aspects of the presentations in the museums which are estimated to represent their effect on the visitors:

- the ***textual*** information given (representing cognitive stimuli)
- the reactions on the ***exhibits*** (representing affective stimuli)
- the ***interactive*** opportunities dimensions (representing social stimuli).

In the following some selected results from the two museums in Daun and Strohn - which have been rated best and worst in the visitor survey - will be presented, in order to see whether additional information can be derived from the complementary approaches.

4.2.1 Vulkanmuseum Daun

At the Vulkanmuseum Daun the only exhibit that has been categorised as a "strength" (cf. fig. 16) is the model of a volcano eruption. This can be put into action by the visitors simulating the rise of the lava below the surface until the eruption takes place and smoke rises from the crater (cf. fig. 18). In the visitor survey the model of the volcano eruption got the best ratings especially from families with children. During the observations of the visitors this has been confirmed. Mainly children were fascinated and reacted enthusiastically to the animation. But it has to be stated, that only 50 % of the visitors employed this model. The reason can be seen in a lack of textual information on the model. Other visitors that were already using the model gave an idea of its functioning. But visitors

Fig. 18: Model of a volcano eruption at the Vulkanmuseum Daun

Photo: A. Kagermeier

that were alone in the room sometimes did not understand what the model was about or that it could be put into action. Adult visitors without children gave the impression that for them the setting looked too childish.

Adult visitors might have been stimulated by additional information about how to use the model. This was reflected in the results of the mystery check where the model received good ratings for "arising curiosity" and the "quality of the interaction" but poor results for the "content of the information board".

The exhibit with the worst ratings at the visitors survey has been the model of a geyser (cf. fig. 19). Thought as another interactive element of the exhibition this exhibit has been out of order during the whole summer when the survey has been carried out. But neither a note on the fact of being out of order nor an information board on the principle of the model had been installed. This of course irritated the visitors. Almost one third of the observed visitors passed the station without even taking notice. The only reaction of visitors that could be observed was wondering and irritation about what should it be about. Hence, one of the fundamental conditions of an experience-orientated presentation, the zero defect production ideal where perfection up to the last detail is the goal and which has been pointed out by *Romeiß-Stracke* (2006, p. 43), has been totally violated.

Fig. 19: Model of a geyser at the Vulkanmuseum Daun which has been out of order during the survey

Photo: I. Bradic

Fig. 20: Glass show cases with different rocks testifying volcanic activities at the Vulkanmuseum Daun

Photo: A. Kagermeier

As a third setting at the Vulkanmuseum Daun a room which contains glass show cases with different stones and rocks that were found in the region and represent the result of the volcanic activities in the past shall be discussed. Even if some explanatory information was given, these rooms were almost totally neglected by families with children. After only a few seconds most of the families left the room which offered no interesting stimuli to them. Even other visitors only looked a few moments at the exhibits, but no interactions with accompanying members of their group were registered. This poor interactive situation has been reflected by the results of the mystery check as well. The items "stimulating curiosity" and "quality of the interaction" got the poorest results from the mystery guests. But even the "design of the information boards" and the "content of the given information" were rated quite poorly. This means that the room is not attractive to visitors seeking edutainment by stimulating interactive experience settings. Equally, those being interested in educational in-depth information were not satisfied.

To sum up is has to be stated, that the poor ratings of the visitors survey have been confirmed by the two additional approaches. At the same time the observation and the mystery check delivered more detailed information about how and why the museum does not satisfy the needs of the experimental seeking visitors.

4.2.2 Vulkanhaus Strohn

The Vulkanhaus Strohn achieved quite good ratings at the visitor survey. Especially the interactive setting in the museum with its edutainment approach attracted the visitors. One of these stations was the presentation of lava bombs (cf. fig. 21). This example shows that sometimes quite simple settings which allow interaction of the visitors may be perceived as quite attractive and stimulating.

The lava bomb station supplies nothing else but different stones which flung out during volcano eruptions. Because of their specific chemical composition and the abrupt cooling during the flight they have got quite differenciated surfaces and at the same quite different specific weights. Because the different

Fig. 21: Lava bombs at the Vulkanhaus Strohn

Photo: I. Bradic

lava bombs are presented in bowls they can be touched and lifted. The simple tactile stimuli by which the visitors can experience the structure of the surface and the (sometimes astonishingly and unexpectedly high) weight of the lava bombs attracted most of the visitors. So on average the visitors spent about 5 minutes at this station. At the same time intensive communication within the group of visitors could be observed, exchanging impressions and pointing out experiences with specific lava bombs to the neighbouring visitors.

This station also got good marks during the mystery check. These referred to both the information provided and the experiences which could be made. At the same time the aptitude for different visitors from children to experts has been rated highly.

Quite the contrary has been observed at another station which is intended to be the most impressing station of the whole museum. A huge lava crack which had been discovered near the village of Strohn has been the reason for establishing the museum. The lava crack (cf. fig. 22) has been cut into pieces and reassembled within the museum (after breaking down some walls inside the building so that the entire lava crack could be exhibited).

Fig. 22: Lava crack at the Vulkanhaus Strohn

Photo: A. Kagermeier

The great effort which has been made to build up this central exhibit of the Vulkanhaus Strohn stands in contrast to the the attention the visitors are paying to it. It has been rated below average during the visitor survey (cf. fig. 17), and during the observations it had to be discovered that most of the visitors were only superficially looking at the lava crack that forms some kind of wall within the museum. Even if the explanatory textual information given was looked at by most visitors only few of them read them thoroughly. Almost no interaction between the visitors could be observed. At the same time the results of the mystery check suggest that even if the textual information shows a good quality, the curiosity of the visitor is not stimulated and no specific new experiences were to be stated. This means that the effort given to a specific exhibit does not necessarily result in a corresponding esteem of the visitors.

Fig. 23: Magma room at the Vulkanhaus Strohn

Photo: Vulkanhaus Strohn

As a third example at the Vulkanhaus Strohn the "magma room" shall be looked at. This multimedia room (cf. fig. 23) totally kept in orange colour and orange light to induce the feeling within an active volcano got one of the poorest ratings during the visitor survey. The results from the observations of the visitors show that almost all of them were attracted by the specifically coloured atmosphere and entered the room. But most of them left the room quite soon after discovering that the interactive opportunities could either not be used easily (because of missing explanatory indications) or did not work at all. The observed communication between the visitors referred mainly to the malfunction of the exhibits. During the mystery check the interactive options got outstanding rates. But this refers to visitors who are really keen on discovering the different interactive opportunities. The ordinary visitor did not show this high level of interest to discover on his own the interactive settings which lacked explanatory notes that can easily be understood.

That the time visitors are spending in a museum can to a certain extent be interpreted as an indicator for the quality of the offers is suggested by the findings in the two museums. At Daun some visitors already left after 5 minutes, with an average of 40 minutes. At the museum in Strohn – although it is smaller in size – the average duration of stay has been 58 minutes (with a minimum of 10 minutes).

4.3 Synergy effects between the the sample points

Given the fact, that the museums are part of the German volcano route their main aim is to visualise the processes which led to the appearance of the volcanic heritage in the Eifel. The visitor in the Eifel shall be able not only to experience the present-day landscape but also to get an understanding and experimental feeling of the volcanic past of the region which led to the actual landscape.

However, it has to be stated that the common marketing of the region under the umbrella brand of "Deutsche Vulkanstrasse" is not as effective as one might have expected. Only two third (69 %) of the questioned visitors at the four sample points had ever heard of the term "Deutsche Vulkanstraße". And 45 % did not know that the places where they were questioned at are part of the German volcano route.

Fig. 24: Visiting only this location

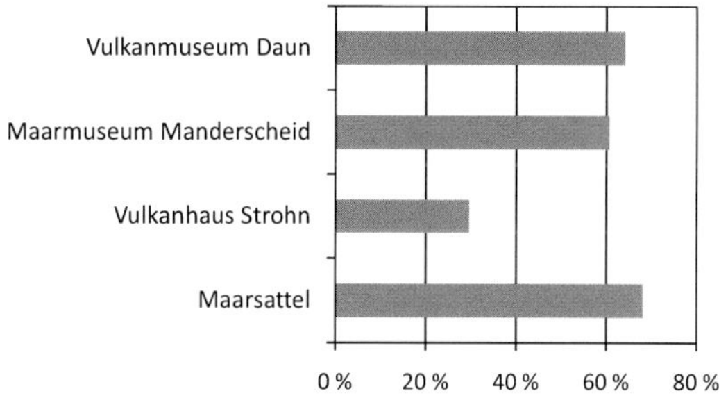

Source: Visitor survey 2008

Fig. 25: Lava bomb at Strohn

Photo: I. Bradic

At the same time the visits of attractions along the volcano route are only to a very limited extent linked with the visits of other attractions. Two thirds of the visitors at the Maarsattel said, that this was the only attraction on the volcano route they were visiting that day (cf. fig. 24). Almost the same range resulted for the Vulkanmuseum Daun and the Maarmuseum Manderschein. The rate is significantly lower in Strohn with only one third of one-stop-visits.

But this refers to the fact that only a few hundred meters away from the Vulkanhaus Strohn another attraction which is part of the German volcano route, a big lava bomb (cf. fig. 25) is visited by almost 60 % of the visitors of the Vulkanhaus.

The basic idea of the museums along the German volcano route is that some background information on the geological past of the volcano landscape is provided there. However, it has to be stated that this idea of combining visits at the natural heritage sites with visits to indoor facilities is to a great extent not followed by the visitors. From the visitors at one of the outstanding viewing points in the region, the Maarsattel, only very few visit the neighbouring museums, the Vulkanmuseum Daun (3.7 %), Maarmuseum Manderscheid (4.9 %) or the Vulkanhaus Strohn (2.5 %).

A similar result was found when questioning the visitors of the museums. Only a small part of them are combining the visit at the museum with other places along the volcano route. Those visiting other maares stayed mainly in the western part of the volcano route i.e. in the area of the European Geopark Vulkaneifel. Almost nobody in the sample has visited attractions in the eastern part belonging to the national Geopark Vulkaneifel.

At the same time only few of the visitors visit more than one museum (cf. fig. 26). Only from those questioned in Strohn about every seventh has visited or has the intention to visit one of the two other sites. Two reasons for this could be identified: One of the reasons is that in Manderscheid and Daun almost no information is to be found about the two other sites. So almost no cross-marketing activity takes place. The other reason is that the three museums do not have established a clear complementary profile. So even if the visitors know that there are other museums, they are not stimulated to go there to get further information on other fields of the volcanic past.

Fig. 26: Visiting only other museums

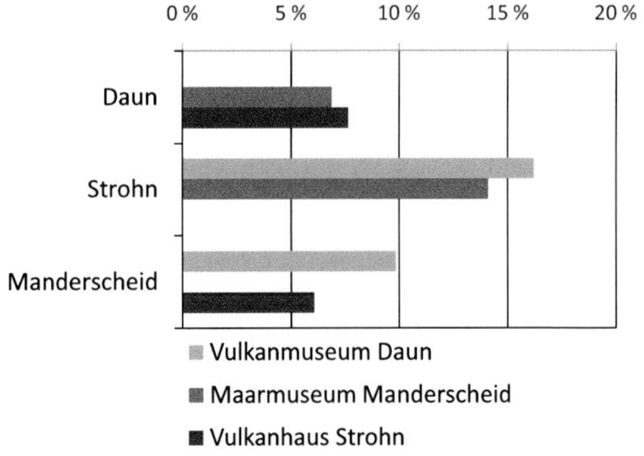

Source: Visitor survey 2008

5 Conclusion

In this article the situation for an experience-orientated staging of nature-oriented geotourism attractions has been analysed, taking as an example the European Geopark Vulkaneifel. The findings refer to two different fields of providing visitor attractions in nature-orientied and geotourism, the quality and experience orientation of the offer itself and the cooperative marketing of the product.

Experience orientation of the offer

The findings indicate that the current offer of giving an understanding of the volcanic past of the study region to the visitors has quite a few shortcomings.

1 The offer in the geotourism museums has only very limited orientation towards an experience-orientated presentation.

2 A traditional presentation is not really esteemed by the visitors which expect an up-to-date setting even when visiting natural heritage sites.

3 Apart from the ordinary experience-orientated components like the creation of imagination and the feeling for unique and exceptional attractions the zero defect challenge is often not met. Giving promises of a specific experience which cannot be fulfilled because of defects of the attractions is the most severe weakness in the studied museums.
4 The experience orientation does not necessarily mean that huge investments are necessary. To arise the interest and the curiosity of the visitors, interactive options which stimulate the communications between the visitors sometimes need only quite simple stimuli.

Cooperative marketing of the product

Apart from the quality of the offer itself the findings indicate some weaknesses in the marketing of the product and the cooperation between the different stakeholders. These aspects are quite typical of offers in low mountain ranges where the development of the structures has taken place over a long period of time and quite different stakeholders with their own interests are playing an important role. Contrary to a centrally planned and run leisure park, in rural regions usually no holistic concept of the presentation and marketing of the tourism product is to be found.

1 The small number of visitors indicates that the tourists in the Vulkaneifel are only to a limited extent aware of the edutainment offer referring to the volcanic past.
2 The very limited combination of visits to the natural sites and the museums indicates severe shortcomings in the market-communication. Low word-of-mouth recommendation rates of course are interlinked with the quality of the offer. But a more offensive indication of the different offers linked along the German volcano route should be implemented to induce more combined visits (or at least raise visitors' awareness of other attractions that are still to be seen during later visits and thus induce repeater-rates).
3 The fragmentation of the marketing activities with very differentiated responsibilities hinders a comprehensive impression of the whole volcanic offer.
4 The best solution for the Vulkaeifel might be a central information centre where the different aspects are presented in an adequate, experience-orientated way. But because this is not a realistic option due to the different responsibilities, the second best option might be a clear "division of labour" between the three museums in the region, where each of them deals with a clearly defined aspect of the volcanic past.

The findings can be seen as quite typical for low mountain ranges where traditionally a wide range of different small stakeholders are trying to promote the tourism potential of a region. The limited size of the stakeholders is often linked to limited capacity and professionalism. Thus, the challenge for low mountain ranges is to establish structures that try to integrate the different interests and raise the level of professionalism in order to produce competitive offers in low mountain ranges. But of course to a certain extent this is only wishful thinking and cannot be realised from one day to the other but is a complex process which takes a long breath.

Bibliography

Bradic, Ismir (ed.) (2009): Evaluierung touristischer Angebote in der Vulkaneifel. Trier (= unpublished report of a Leisure and Tourism Geography Forschungspraktikum)

Csíkszentmihályi M. (1990): Flow: The Psychology of Optimal Experience – Steps Toward Enhancing the Quality of Life. New York

Deutsche Vulkanstraße (ed.) (2008): Die deutsche Vulkanstraße. Erleben Sie die Faszination der Erdgeschichte. www.deutsche-vulkanstrasse.com

Kagermeier, Andreas (2006): Methoden der Messung von Besucherzufriedenheit im Vergleich – dargestellt am Beispiel einer industriekultureller Einrichtung. In: Leder, Susanne & Albrecht Steinecke (eds.): Aktuelle Themen der Tourismusforschung. Märkte – Events – Methoden. Paderborn, p. 133-152 (= Paderborner Geographische Studien, 19)

Kagermeier, Andreas (2009): Bringing the Roman times to live: Options for an experience orientated staging of the cultural heritage. In: Smith, Melanie & Leontine Onderwater (eds.): Experiencing difference. Changing tourism and tourists experiences. Amsterdam, p. 15-30 (= Atlas Reflections 2009)

Kagermeier, Andreas (2010): Erfolgsfaktoren für Events im kulturorientierten Städtetourismus – eine Evaluierung der Kaiser Konstantin Ausstellung 2007 in Trier. In: Kagermeier, Andreas. & Fanny Raab (eds.): Wettbewerbsvorteil Kulturtourismus. Innovative Strategien und Produkte. Berlin, p. 17-40 (= Schriften zu Tourismus und Freizeit, 9)

Natur- und Geopark Vulkaneifel GmbH (ed.) (2009): Vulkaneifel Magazin. Unterwegs im Land der Maare und Vulkane. Daun

Newsome, David & Ross K. Dowling (2006): Geotourism: Sustainability, impact and management. Oxford

Niklas, Susanne (2008): Potenziale im Geotourismus – Eine Analyse im Geopark Ries. Trier (= unpublished Diploma Thesis)

Pine Joseph B. & *James H. Gilmore* (1998): Welcome to the Experience Economy. In: Harvard Business Review, p. 97-105

Romeiss-Stracke, Felizitas (2006): Ist optimale Inszenierung möglich? In: Weiermair, K. & A. Brunner-Sperdin (eds.): Erlebnisinszenierung im Tourismus. Erfolgreich mit emotionalen Produkten und Dienstleistungen. Berlin, p. 35-46.

Smith, Melanie & *Leontine Onderwater* (eds.) (2009): Experiencing difference. Changing tourism and tourists experiences. Amsterdam (= Atlas Reflections 2009)

Statistisches Landesamt Rheinland-Pfalz (2009): Betriebe, Betten, Gäste, Übernachtungen, Aufenthaltsdauer, Auslastung nach Betriebsarten 2003-2008. http://www.infothek.statistik.rlp.de/lis/onlinedb/index.asp

Unger L. S. & J. B. Kernan (1983): On the meaning of leisure: an investigation of some determinants of the subjective experience. In: Journal of Consumer Research 9, p. 381–392

The "Tourism for All" approach as an option for low mountain ranges

Andreas Kagermeier & Joachim Willms (eds.): Tourism Development in Low Mountain Ranges. Mannheim 2010, p. 49 - 62 (= Studien zur Freizeit- und Tourismusforschung, Vol. 3)

Accessible tourism in Rhineland-Palatinate
– Conditions and potentials of a low mountain destination

Laura Herlitz (Trier)

Summary
Processes of social change, as for example the rising importance of leisure time, mobility and experience orientation, are factors that reduce the extent of prospects for handicapped people to participate equally in social life. Considering the imbalance of the supply of and demand for accessible tourism in Germany, the chance for mobility-limited persons to participate in tourism is slight. Especially the development of the type *provincial town* into an accessible destination assumes numerous basic conditions that must either exist or be created. Nevertheless for this type the production of the new group of mobility-limited guests can mean a chance to retain their guest amount and also to offer more comfort to their present guests.

1 The initial position
"The future competitiveness of the different destinations in Germany will be determined for a big contingent by succeeding in adapting their tourist offer during the coming years also to the needs of handicapped or mobility-limited guests" (*Ministerium für Wirtschaft und Arbeit des Landes Sachsen-Anhalt* 2002, p. 9).

Based on this citation, the aim of the project *Accessible tourism in Rhineland-Palatinate* is to determine the conditions and potentials of the city of Deidesheim in accessible tourism. The content of the citation guaranteeing the future of the competitiveness by investments in unrestricted access is – referring to the imbalance of supply and demand of accessible tourism in Germany – far from reality. Many existing possibilities of accessible tourism are put into perspective by the knowledge about retardant factors.

The extent of possibilities for handicapped people to participate equally in social life is reduced by processes of social change (the rising importance of leisure time, mobility and experience orientation). Adhering to this statement the idea that the extent of possibilities for handicapped people to participate equally depends on processes of change in society is a basic idea of the project. For some the collective leisure park is an enrichment, for others a difficulty.

1.1 Problem formulation and objective

The legislation of the German State and the supporting laws of the federal states define one aim in disability rights: Removing disadvantages for handicapped people and enabling a self-determined lifestyle. This concern encloses the establishment of accessibility in all areas of our society and therefore also the possibility of a vacation for all population groups. But accessible tourism is not a matter of course. The conception of unrestricted access and accessible tourism does not only seem to be underdeveloped on the level of the different areas of life, but also with regard to the social affiliation of the group. So there is still a deficit of an exact appraisal of the number of those who would like to take part in accessible tourism (cf. *Neumann & Reuber* 2004, p. 9).

Not only handicapped people, but also elderly people depend on unrestricted accessibility in their home town as well as at their holiday destination. The need for unrestricted accessibility increases as the demographic development of Germany proceeds.

Besides social and political dimensions, unrestricted accessibility is of economic relevancy. But for handicapped people travelling is combined with a huge number of barriers which often prevent the realisation of existing travel wishes. Even if these barriers refer only to single parts of the tourist service chain, the single parts that are accessible are only restrictedly useable, so that a trip possibly remains undone. Besides, 90% of the handicapped and mobility-limited people in Germany would be able to travel if accessible offers were available to them (cf. *Deutscher Bundestag* 2001, p. 1).

The travel intensity of the group of handicapped and mobility-limited people could be raised by the creation of an accessible offer and become an important economic factor. With a wide-spread offer in accessible tourism up to 5 billion Euros more could be generated additionally and 90.000 new full-time jobs could be created in Germany (cf. *Neumann & Reuber* 2004, p. 9).

The need of accessibility is caused by the planning of goods and services determined by persons of average measure or a healthy man of middle age. This principle of average causes the need for special solutions like *suitable for handicapped* or *appropriate for children, senior citizens and women*. The rising life expectance, the increasing number of people with mobility restrictions and the increasing self-confidence of elderly and handicapped people – caused by equalisation laws and their effects – constitute the need to replace the principle of average through unrestricted accessibility. Nevertheless, unrestricted accessibility should not only be understood as the downsizing of physical barriers. The overcoming of the barriers that exist in the heads should represent the centre (cf. *Kästner* 2007, pp. 22 and cf. *Leidner & Neumann* 2005, p. 67).

The widespread limitation of the term *accessibility* to physical barriers lead to the fact that people with walking disabilities and wheelchair users came to the fore. Nevertheless, the principle of unrestricted accessibility should not only be referred to handicapped people. Also the people for whom unrestricted accessibility is necessary to be active or mobile and people for whom unrestricted accessibility means a comfort step-up must be considered (cf. *Neumann & Reuber* 2004, p. 13).

The importance of accessible tourism has increased during the last years. But the situation of the accessible tourism market in Germany is described by *Wilken* (2002, p. 29) as paradoxical, since the underdeveloped tourist offer for handicapped and elderly people is opposed to the prospective increasing demand by handicapped and elderly people.

1.2 The group of mobility-limited people

Within this project the definition of the target group is carried out according to the definition of the ADAC. Beyond the group of handicapped people the analysis centres on mobility-limited persons in the broader sense including elderly persons, pregnant women, overweight persons and so forth (cf. *Allgemeiner Deutscher Automobil Club e.V.* 2003, p. 14). At first sight the combination of these (and other) different groups in one group with common attributes may appear politically incorrect or as a form of discrimination (cf. *Hennig* 2001, pp. 6). Nevertheless, the common characteristics which exist between putatively – and partially, nevertheless, also actually – different groups can be used for a successful addition of the core business by the potential of the demand of a marginal group. Not only people "for whom the wheelchair-symbol stands" (*Hennig* 2001, p. 7) are counted to the group, among the rest, also people who belong to the group of the senior citizens. A confrontation of the requirements of people with different mobility restrictions can show – beside strongly differentiated needs – absolute correspondence (cf. *Hennig* 2001, p. 11).

The group of mobility-limited persons consists of a lot of different groups with different needs and also different needs of assistance. This widespread differentiation means a highly complicated factor to suppliers within the realisation of accessible tourism. But the group of mobility-limited people represents an attractive audience for the here surveyed domestic tourism in Germany. Mobility limited tourists travel frequently during low season, mostly in company and often to domestic destinations. In addition, they represent a growing group: In 20 years time one in three people in Germany will be more than 60 years old (cf. *Neumann & Reuber* 2004, pp. 28).

The low season – May, September and October – is chosen increasingly as holiday time by mobility-limited travellers. This can also be ascribed to the independence from official school holidays (only every tenth of the interviewees indicated to live in a family and only 12% must follow the official school holidays). In contrast, the German total population undertakes their trips primarily in the main season – June, July and August. More than half of the interviewees travel in company. Furthermore, the destination Germany has with 41.2% a by far higher importance for mobility-limited travellers than for the German total population with only 30.5% (cf. *Neumann & Reuber* 2004, pp. 28 and cf. *Forschungsgemeinschaft Urlaub und Reisen e.V.* 2003, p. 42).

2 The project

Single hotels and other suppliers in tourism will not be able to provide accessible offers for their guests which allow a smooth vacation to them. It requires co-operative unions of suppliers and towns as well as neighbour towns to guarantee a complete tourist service chain without barriers. Nevertheless, for this purpose the consciousness about the need of the change represents the basis.

Based on this and influenced by the interaction of political objectives and the increasing attraction of the group of mobility-limited people, a Rhineland-Palatine example destination should be contemplated in connection with the focus on the group of mobility-limited persons.

Background is the consideration of the federal state Rhineland-Palatinate to support the utilisation of economic opportunities in accessible tourism in the future via a specific development of local focuses. Deidesheim is a model project whose experiences and results can be the basis for the development of a national programme for accessible tourism.

The city of Deidesheim was not selected by chance. The city attracted attention among many tourist destinations in Rhineland-Palatinate by the foundation *Bürgerhospital* which today accommodates a care facility, an accessible hotel and a café and called the attention of local tourist managers to accessible tourism.

Deidesheim is a small town with 3.700 inhabitants in the Rhineland-Palatine administrative district Bad Dürkheim and lies 1 km east of the low mountain region Haardt in the heart of the German *Weinstraße*. In Deidesheim the meaning of tourism is carried by viniculture, the viniculture festivals and by the *Pfälzer Wald* with its network of trails and hiking offer. About 150.000 guests per year spend the night in the municipality Deidesheim. Furthermore, 600.000 day visitors per year are attracted by the numerous parties and events (cf. *Verbandsgemeinde Deidesheim* 2007).

The small town of Deidesheim reflects the structures of many low mountain range destinations: Tourism is characterised by a fragmented structure, many private lodgings and few chain hotels. Tourism feeds upon the relief and climate favour of the location in the low mountain range. In fact both main economic activities of Deidesheim, tourism and viniculture, are based on this advantageous geographical position. However, consciousness about the influence of changing social processes on tourism has lead to the revision of the tourism concept with the aim of generating new guests.

2.1 The status analysis

The development potential of Deidesheim as an accessible destination was identified with the help of a status analysis that considered the whole range of tourism products such as accommodation, restaurants, wineries and the retail industry as well as the tourist infrastructure including the railway station, the town hall, public area and the local tourist information.

The customer analysis and the analysis of the self-assessment (analysis I) of the suppliers (object of investigation I) on the attribute accessibility occurred in form of a written survey. This first step also acted as a note for the choice of the suppliers that should be followed within the on-site analysis (analysis II). Analysis II revealed the elevation of the barriers which exist for people with mobility restriction. On this occasion, tourism products (object of investigation I) such as accommodation, restaurants, wineries and the retail industry as well as the tourist infrastructure (object of investigation II) with the railway station, the town hall, the public area and the local tourist information were considered. The tourist base for accessible tourism of Deidesheim could be evaluated and valued.

Figure 1: Status analysis

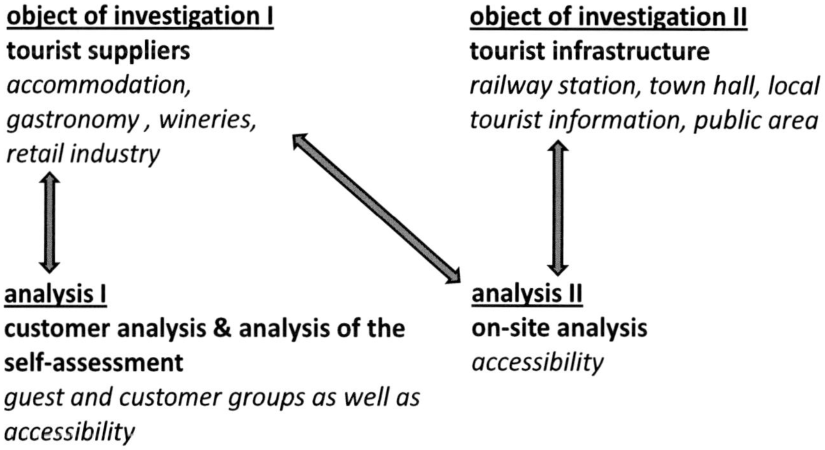

Source: own design

2.1.1 Object of investigation I

Among the object of investigation I rank accommodation, restaurants, wineries and the retail industry. The two different analyses that are concerned with object of investigation I are presented in the following.

2.1.1.1 Analysis I – customer analysis and analysis of the self-assessment

The results of analysis I enabled the identification of a principal guest group or customer group of the questioned suppliers: Elderly guests/customers and senior citizens. However, only 19% have aligned their company to a certain guest or customer group. Nevertheless, elderly guests/customers with 16% and senior citizens with 14% were named as the groups they focus on (multiple namings were possible). Elderly guests/customers and senior citizens are also estimated with 83% and 52% as the groups with the biggest future potential (multiple namings were possible). Referenced to the self-assessment of the companies, 26%

stated that their company can be used by guests/customers who are limited in their mobility and 29% said that this partially applies to their company (cf. *Herlitz* 2008, pp. 71).

2.1.1.2 Analysis II – on-site analysis

In 30 companies the barriers that exist for mobility-limited people were captured through check lists. The objects of investigation of this partial inquiry were fixed by means of a deliberate choice: The companies that took part in analysis I and stated that their company can be (partially) used by guests/customers who are limited in their mobility were selected as objects of investigation. For raising the number of the objects of investigation other companies were selected additionally according to the investigation aim.

The companies that fulfil more than 60% of the checked criteria belong to the companies of Deidesheim who can be seen as partly without barriers. Nevertheless, these companies must fulfil those criteria which are indispensable for mobility-limited people. Not fulfilling those is a reason to adjust the achieved percentage downwards. For example, the criteria of the doorway and the width of the alley to the hotel rooms. Here the fact that a higher percentage must not necessarily mean a better suitability for unrestricted access should be pointed out. The description *partly without barriers* was chosen because none of the companies fulfilled certain criteria of visual impairment (tactile leading system, a floor structure which helps to orientate or steps in contrast marked colours) and a correctly differentiated classification was only possible in the specific coherence to the type of handicap. Within the evaluation of the surveyed data a classification of the results as *without barriers*, *partly without barriers* or *not without barriers* makes sense. Furthermore the project recommends describing offers in detail and leaving the judgement on the degree of unrestricted access as much as possible to the interested traveller.

In the following the procedure of the survey and assessment of the accommodation companies is introduced exemplarily. Eight of the nine lodging businesses who indicated in analysis I to be *without barriers* (4 companies) or *partly without barriers* (5 companies) were examined. One of the companies that indicated to be without barriers declined the participation in the on site-analysis. Measured in the shown criteria from (1) to (37) hotels can fulfil 37 criteria and reach 37 points. Because the examined guesthouse does not dispose of a reception, the equipment of this drops out here, so that the guesthouse can fulfil a total of 35 criteria. Holiday apartments can fulfil 28 criteria and reach 28 points, because the equipment of reception, breakfast room/restaurant and restrooms drop out here.

Lodging business no. 1 (hotel) reached 26.5 of 37 points and can be called 72% without barriers. Lodging business no. 2 (hotel) reached 23.5 points and can be called 64% without barriers. Thus, two lodging businesses fulfil more than 60% of the criteria and belong to the companies of Deidesheim who can be called *partly without barriers*.

The procedure of the survey and assessment of gastronomy, wineries and the retail industry resembles the introduced procedure, so that subsequently only the results are introduced. Two gastronomic companies (restaurants) can be called 71% without barriers. Another gastronomic company (café) can be called 69% without barriers. None of the wineries can be called *without barriers* or *partly without barriers*, because in no case the value of more than 60% could be reached. One member of the retail industry (a supermarket) can be called 91% without barriers. Another one (a supermarket as well) can be called 82% without barriers (cf. *Herlitz* 2008, pp. 75).

Table 1: Analysis II results – lodging businesses

nr.	type	(1)	(2)	(3)	(4)	(5)	(6)	(7)	(8)	(9)	(10)	(11)	(12)	(13)	(14)	(15)	(16)	(17)	(18)	(19)
1	hotel	x		x	x		x	x	x		x	x	x	x		x	x	x	x	x
2	hotel	x		x	x	x	x	x	x			x	x			x		x	x	x
3	hotel	x		x			x	x			x	x				x		x	x	
4	holiday ap.			x	x						x					/	/	/	/	/
5	holiday ap.			x	x											/	/	/	/	/
6	holiday ap.			x	x						x					/	/	/	/	/
7	holiday ap.	x		x	x											/	/	/	/	/
8	guesthouse			x	x						x					/	/	x		

nr.	type	(20)	(21)	(22)	(23)	(24)	(25)	(26)	(27)	(28)	(29)	(30)	(31)	(32)	(33)	(34)	(35)	(36)	(37)	Σ
1	hotel	x		x		x	x	x	x	x	x	x				x	x	x		26,5
2	hotel		x	x		x	x	x		x	x		x	x		x		x		23,5
3	hotel					x				x								x		12
4	holiday ap.	/	/	/	/	x				x									x	6
5	holiday ap.	/	/	/	/	x				x									x	5
6	holiday ap.	/	/	/	/					x									x	5
7	holiday ap.	/	/	/	/	x	x			x									x	7
8	guesthouse									x										5

Source: own design

2.1.1.3 Confrontation of self-assessment and results

The self-assessment of the companies about their possibility to welcome guests or to serve customers who are limited in their mobility serves as an indicator for the businesses' consciousness about the meaning of unrestricted access. Now the results of this self-assessment surveyed within analysis I are confronted with the results of analysis II.

Altogether 23 companies claimed being *without barriers* (11 companies) or *partly without barriers* (12 companies) in the questionnaire. One of these companies rejected the participation within analysis II. In addition, eight companies who could be suitable for an unrestricted access were examined so that the confrontation is shown by answer and result of 30 companies in figure 2.

In the matrix which draws the connection between answer (self-assessment) and result (on-site analysis) the companies are shown in letters. The number of the company is given subscript and the achieved percentage elevated. The lodging business no. 1 which achieved 72% of the criteria is shown with $U_1^{72\%}$.

Five of the companies that rated themselves as *without barriers* could not be classified as *without barriers* after the surveying of the status quo, because they fulfilled less than 60% of the criteria. All 12 companies that rated themselves as *partly without barriers* were also not judged as *without barriers*. Six of the companies that did not answer the questionnaire were with less than 60% classified as *not without barriers*. Five of the companies that rated their company as *without barriers*, were judged on the basis of more than 60% of achieved criteria and the fulfilment of the criteria which are indispensable for an unrestricted access as *partly without barriers*. Two companies that did not take part within analysis I could be also classified as *partly without barriers* (cf. *Herlitz* 2008, pp. 86).

A total of 22 companies, all companies that took part in analysis I and II, assessed the degree of accessibility of their offer wrongly. This allows the conclusion that something wrong or different was understood by unrestricted access in these cases. This makes clear that there is a need of clarification which must be perceived within the attempt of a destination to develop into a destination without barriers.

Figure 2: Matrix self-assessment – results

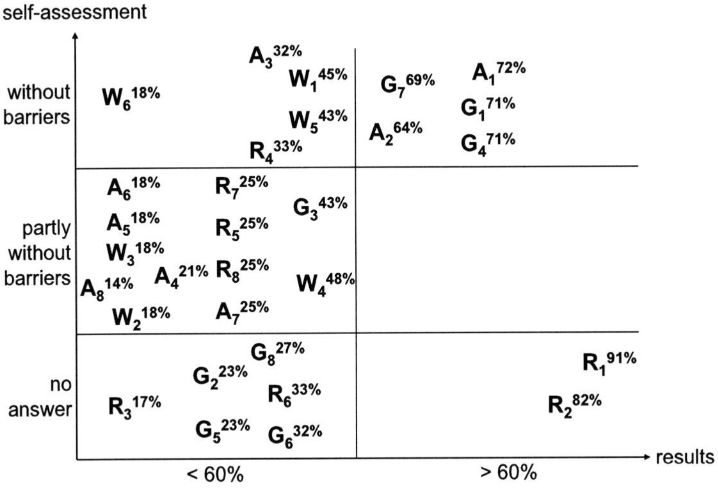

A = accommodation **G** = gastronomy **W** = wineries **R** = retail industry

Source: own design

2.1.2 Object of investigation II – Analysis II – on-site analysis

The tourist infrastructure including the railway station, the town hall and the local tourist information was examined by check lists concerning their accessibility. The public area was also examined as the connecting element.

Just like in the on site-analysis of the companies, facilities which do not reach more than 60% of the criteria or do not fulfil criteria which are indispensable for mobility-limited people and whose non-fulfilling is a reason to adjust the achieved percentage downwards, can not be called *partly without barriers*.

The railway station reached 15.5 points and could be called 65% without barriers. But the defects reduce the result clearly: Most criteria of visual impairment are not fulfilled and the weighting of the accessibility of the platform is to be reduced because of the insecurity whether the train is generally accessible to a traveller in the wheel chair. Only due to the fact that – regardless of the accessibility of the platform and the ticket machine – big insecurity insists about whether the holding train is accessible, for example to a wheel chair driver, the achieved percentage of 32.5% must be halved. This concerns the assessment of the railway station and the service which is offered here. The pure assessment of the railway station as an equipment or building would be more positive.

The town hall reached 15.5 of 28 points and fulfilled 55% of the criteria. Hence, the town hall cannot be called *partly without barriers*.

The tourist informartion only fulfilled 42.5% of the criteria and cannot be called *partly without barriers*. Decisively for this is the accessibility of the building which is not without barriers because of two steps at the entrance, and also the criteria of visual impairment which could not be fulfilled. The achieved percentage is halved for these reasons to 21.25%.

The public area (the sidewalks and their paving, the marketplace as well as parks) holds some obstacles for mobility-limited people. The sidewalks are very narrow in and around the local city centre, so that neither a wheel chair nor a mobile walking help or a person with a buggy and other people who are limited in their mobility would find enough space on it. Besides, the layers are mainly uneven. That is why the marketplace is also not without barriers.

2.2 SWOT-Analysis

In the following the results of analysis I as well as analysis II are presented as strengths, weaknesses, opportunities and threats.

Among the rest, the ascertained strengths refer on in analysis II as *partly without barriers* classified two lodging businesses, three gastronomic companies and two retail dealers that can be used by travellers with mobility restrictions to varying degrees without barriers. Nevertheless, people with visual impairments are excluded from this because the criteria of visual impairment could not be fulfilled. The barrier-free parks as well as the railway station (railway station as an equipment – not the service) also count as a strength. At this point the engagement of the lodging businesses no. 1 and 2 which distinguish themselves by thought-out planning should be accentuated.

Weaknesses turned out to be aspects of visual impairment. The criteria could not be fulfilled and besides walking disabled persons and wheel chair drivers, other impairments are hardly considered. The arrangement of the public area must be called a weakness in wide parts, because the extremely narrow sidewalks as well as the uneven pavement are barriers for people with mobility restrictions. Regrettably, even the tourist information is not barrier-free. Besides, there are no leisure offers without barriers.

Figure 3: SWOT-Analysis

strengths	**weaknesses**
2 lodging companies classified as *partly without barriers*	aspects of visual impairment
3 gastronomical companies classified as *partly without barriers*	narrow sidewalks
2 retail dealers classified as *partly without barriers*	uneven pavement
barrier-free parks	tourist information not barrier-free
railway station	no leisure offers
engagement	

opportunities	**threats**
reach a higher degree of accessibility through rebuildings	lack of interest in opening up new target groups
useable for all generations	lack of acceptance of people with mobility restrictions
consciousness about the fact that the group of the *senior citizens* has potentials	something wrong or different is understood by unrestricted access
predicate *aerial health resort*	poor consultation in the (architectural) construction of accessibility

Source: own design

The opportunities arose at companies that could reach a higher degree of accessibility through rebuilding and could thus attract other customer groups. In addition, the companies that could be marketed as useable for all generations are opportunities. The consciousness about the fact that the group of senior citizens has potentials for the future has to be valued positively. This knowledge can be ascribed to the high media presence of the topic of demographic change. The predicate aerial health resort should be used as an opportunity in particular concerning the group of the mobility-limited travellers.

As possible appearing risks mental attitude-related factors play a big role. Thus, a lack of interest in opening up new target groups or in accepting people with mobility restrictions could represent risks. Besides, clarification about the needs of the mainly unknown group is lacking, as shown in the confrontation of the results of the self-assessment surveyed within analysis I with the results of analysis II. A result of analysis II indicated another risk: Poor guidance in the (architectural) construction of accessibility (cf. *Herlitz* 2008, pp. 94).

2.3 Agenda

Based on the results of the on-site analysis and their assessment (SWOT-Analysis) the performance of Deidesheim can be valued. The existing offer in accessible tourism is poorly developed. Nevertheless, the town's, the region's and the respective companies' big interest suggests that a perceptible improvement can be achieved in the future. Above all, measures of improvement in the areas of tourist services, public area, consciousness and tolerance, consideration of hearing and visually impaired persons and leisure activities are required.

The developed agenda, which is introduced in the following, picks up these areas with measures of improvement. To develop Deidesheim into a local focus of accessible tourism in Rhineland-Palatinate, an agenda which envisions the continuous support of barrier freedom was provided. Based on the analysis, necessary measures are recommended and classified by priority in each case.

The agenda is designed as a process-accompanying guide that considers the time intensity of the conversion. Besides, the ideal of the closed tourist service chain is of course not disregarded. However, only a gradual approach to this ideal is realistic. The experiences and results of Deidesheim can still possibly flow into a project for accessible tourism in Rhineland-Palatinate and serve as a base for the development of a national model programme.

Figure 4: Agenda

priority 1 obligatory	**priority 2** essential	**priority 3** additional
1 rearrangement of the foundation Bürgerhospital	6 new signposting	11 design and development of accessible guided tours
2 redevelopment of the city centre	7 topic creation „accessible tourism“	12 coverage of accessible pathways
3 arrangement of the Schlosspark in order to be suitable for all generations	8 advancement of the presence in the publicity	13 conception of accessible spa offers
4 differentiated labelling of the tourist offers	9 new accessible design of the homepage	14 accessible conversion of the tourist information
5 training programm „accessible tourism“	10 creation of accessible information material	15 enlargement of the foundation Bürgerhospital

Source: own design

The action programme does not show a guide which treats every element of the tourist service chain: For example, public transportation will probably not be realised fast enough, so that the main focus on guaranteeing mobility must be the car. Nevertheless, within consideration of the elements of the tourist service chain in the agenda not only the feasibility plays a role. In the described case the choice of the means of transport shows a motive for the non-consideration, because means of transport concentrate with 71.6% upon the car within domestic travelling of mobility-limited persons (cf. *Neumann & Reuber* 2004, p. 28).

The projects shown in figure 4 are divided into three steps of different priority and numbered consecutively. The decision on priorities occurred by needs of the group requirements: Which conditions must be created obligatory, essential and additional to allow a vacation in Deidesheim to people with mobility restrictions? The project planning partially occurred in cooperation with the Tourist Service GmbH Deidesheim. Two of the projects are introduced in the following.

2.3.1 Project 2 *Redevelopment of the city centre*

Within the scope of the project *Redevelopment of the city centre*, Deidesheim confronts itself with problems of the pedestrian's situation in the city centre, as for example the very narrow sidewalks and mainly uneven paving as well as the marketplace. Hence, the local core is redeveloped, under special consideration of elderly peoples' and handicapped demands. Besides, the aim to raise the recreational assets of the urban centre is also pursued.

The uneven paving at many places is renewed and the sidewalks are partially widened and/or lowered, so that these can be also used with buggies, wheel chairs or a mobile walking help and crossing the streets is simplified by a ground-level connection with the roadway.

The city centre redevelopment will also increase security for pedestrians – in particular for children, senior citizens and mobility-limited people – and lead to a clear enhancement in attraction, since there are also plans for plantation, lighting, bins as well as seat opportunities.

2.3.2 Project 7 *Topic creation*

Focus of the project *Topic creation* is the aim to make accessible tourism a tourist topic of Deidesheim. Hence, the project concerns the integration of accessibility in the tourist concept of Deidesheim. Within the tourist concept the main focus is on base subjects by which the subordinated single subjects as well as the respective holiday offers are orientated. Topics which are firmly connected with Deidesheim and are suitable as signature topics should form the base of the concept. The base subjects *Wine & Gourmet* as well as *Culture* also showed subjects of the tourist concept in the past. Nevertheless they should be used in new positions. The base subject *Health & Nature* played no decisive role up to now. The predicate *aerial health resort* and the positive factors of the natural scenery and the climate should be used as a trump here. And also the biosphere reserve *Pfälzer Wald* can be positioned better in interaction with the base subject *Health & Nature*.

Six holiday offers are the result of the base subjects and four subordinated single subjects. *Holiday offers with pleasure* could imply to spend a culinary weekend in Deidesheim or *holiday offers with culture* the possibility, to get to know the history of the town.

The aim of accessibility should have a cross function in the tourist concept of Deidesheim. Figure 5 shows the structure of the concept proposal and the function of accessibility.

Figure 5: Topic creation

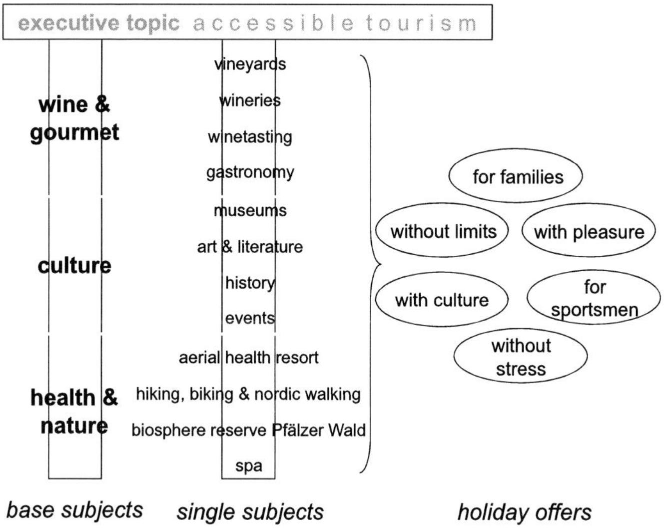

Source: own design

3 Potential, feasibility and transferability

Finally the question of the ascertained potential and the feasibility may not be absent: For the entire development of Deidesheim into an accessible destination all 15 projects would have to be implemented and the appearance of further need for action within the realisation cannot be excluded. Nevertheless, the expectation of the current implementation of all projects seems unrealistic, so that the measures which seem indispensable for a successive market development must be supported first to allow the entrance into the market.

This may leave the mark to advise against market entrance and to announce doubt in the transferability of the concept. This is not the case. Rather it became clear which basic conditions of a successful conversion must exist or be created.

First of all it should be defined for which type Deidesheim can stand and on whom the results are transferable. Deidesheim represents the type of a provincial town with approximately 100.000 overnight staying tourists per year and an older guest structure. For this type the production of the new group of mobility-limited guests can mean the opportunity to protect their guest amount and also to offer more comfort to their present guests.

The conditions which must exist to develop a destination of this type into an accessible destination are an initiative project, the support and engagement of local tourist managers and suppliers as well as of politicians. This of course is linked directly to the financial support, without which neither the tourism staff resources can be strengthened, nor can setting-related initiatives be implemented to win suppliers and citizens for the project. However, not only the financial support represents a decisive condition, also the professional consultation must be given.

References

Allgemeiner Deutscher Automobil Club e.V. (ed.) (2003): Barrierefreier Tourismus für Alle. Eine Planungshilfe für Tourismuspraktiker zur erfolgreichen Entwicklung barrierefreier Angebote. München

Deutscher Bundestag (ed.) (2001): Antwort der Bundesregierung. Hemmnisse im Tourismus für Behinderte Menschen abbauen. Drucksache 14/7217. Berlin

Forschungsgemeinschaft Urlaub und Reisen e.V. (ed.) (2003): Reiseanalyse 2003. Kurzfassung. Hamburg/Kiel

Hennig, Armin (2001): Hotelservice für Senioren und körperbehinderte Gäste. Bedarfsgerechte Hotelkonzepte ohne Barrieren und Hindernisse. Stuttgart

Herlitz, Laura (2008): Barrierefreier Tourismus in Rheinland-Pfalz. Voraussetzungen und Potentiale am Beispiel der Stadt Deidesheim. (Materialien zur Fremdenverkehrsgeographie, 67)

Kästner, Juliane (2007): Barrierefreier Tourismus. Reisen mit Mobilitätseinschränkung. Saarbrücken

Leidner, Rüdiger & Peter Neumann (2005): Chancen und Hemmnisse der barrierefreien Erschließung postmoderner Freizeiteinrichtungen und Freizeiträume in der Europäischen Union. In: *Reuber, Paul & Peter Schnell* (ed.): Postmoderne Freizeitstile und Freizeiträume. Neue Angebote im Tourismus. (Schriften zu Tourismus und Freizeit, 5). p. 65-76

Ministerium für Wirtschaft und Arbeit des Landes Sachsen-Anhalt (ed.) (2002): "Tourismus für Alle". Handbuch barrierefreier Tourismus in Sachsen-Anhalt. (Tourismus-Studien Sachsen-Anhalt, 11)

Neumann, Peter & Paul Reuber (ed.) (2004): Ökonomische Impulse eines barrierefreien Tourismus für Alle. Langfassung einer Untersuchung im Auftrag des Bundesministeriums für Wirtschaft und Arbeit. (Münstersche Geographische Arbeiten, 47)

Verbandsgemeinde Deidesheim (2007): Entstehung und Geschichte. http://www.vg-deidesheim.rlp.de/vg_deidesheim/index.phtml, 11.12.2007

Wilken, Udo (2002): Behinderte – (k)eine Chance zum Reisen und Ferien machen? In: *Wilken, Udo* (ed.): Tourismus und Behinderung. Ein sozial-didaktisches Kursbuch zum Reisen von Menschen mit Handicaps. Neuwied. p. 17-44

Andreas Kagermeier & Joachim Willms (eds.): Tourism Development in Low Mountain Ranges. Mannheim 2010, p. 63 - 72 (= Studien zur Freizeit- und Tourismusforschung, Vol. 3)

Success factors for the development of a Tourism for All approach in low mountain ranges

– possible solutions and implementation difficulties on the basis of the Thuringian pilot project "Model region for a barrier-free Tourism for All"

Markus Rebstock (Erfurt)

Summary

To design products, services and public spaces in a way that they are accessible and useable for all potential users is becoming more and more important for an inclusive society. In order to guarantee successful Design for All approaches it is required to take notice of the seven interdependent success factors of Design for All. Especially in the field of public transport stakeholders have to co-operate intensively. Concerning this matter it is advisable to implement a "coordination body for barrier-free public transport".

1 Introduction

Against the background of the demographic change and the rising share of the elderly population following from this, it will be more and more important to take care of the needs of this growing part of the population. One of the concepts which respect these requirements is "Tourism for All", an approach primarily developed for people with disabilities, which nowadays concentrates more on a holistic view of accessibility for all in tourism.

Although there seems to be a widespread general agreement that accessibility for all also has to be implemented in the tourism sector, reality clearly shows that many tourism professionals do not really know what this means. One aim of the following text is to demonstrate that the implementation of accessibility for all can only be managed by a team of people, all willing to take their individual responsibilities in their particular fields of expertise.

Various experiences across Europe have shown that certain factors emerged, which positively influence the development of a Design for All approach. Altogether seven interdependent success factors exist, which are devolved to the Thuringian pilot project "model region for a barrier-free Tourism for All". Special view is taken to measures for implementing accessibility for all in the fields of public transport and local transport infrastructure in terms of the overall target "barrier-free travel chain".

2 The Design for All approach

The European Organization EIDD – Design for all Europe declared that, "Design for All is design for human diversity, social inclusion and equality. [...] Design for All aims to enable all people to have equal opportunities to participate in every aspect of society. To achieve this, the built environment, everyday objects, services, culture and information – in short, everything that is designed and made by people to be used by people – must be accessible, convenient for everyone in society to use and responsive to evolving human diversity" (*EIDD* 2004). In other words: "Good design enables, bad design disables" (*EIDD* 2004).

There are four important demands of Design for All, which state that products and services shall be designed in a way that they

- are useable without adaption for as many users as possible,
- are adaptable, which means that they are easily adjustable to different needs,
- allow the use of individual aid and
- involve the potential users at every stage of the design process (*IDZ Design-Partner Berlin GmbH et al.* 2009, p. 37).

To put these requirements into action the success factors, which are listed in chapter 3, have to be noted.

3 The seven interdependent success factors of Design for All

The seven interdependent success factors, which have a positive influence on the development of a Design for All approach, are (*Aragall et al.* 2008, p. 18):

- decision-maker commitment
- coordinating and continuity
- networking and participation
- strategic planning
- knowledge management
- resources
- communication and marketing.

3.1 Decision-maker commitment

Generally, the implementation of Design for All processes has a better chance of success when it is of general political interest. It is the responsibility of politicians to predict future needs and to look forward to the conditions that will be necessary to protect individual rights and improve community welfare in the future. Moreover, all stakeholders and decision-makers that are responsible for the development, implementation and monitoring of policies and strategies, have responsibility for the quality of life. Thus, it can be stated that the higher the position of the decision-makers in the management structure, the greater the chances for the other success factors to have an effective impact (*Aragall et al.* 2008, p. 19).

3.2 Coordinating and continuity

Administrations typically hand over the creation of Design for All to a dedicated individual. But it is necessary to develop structures that work independently of this person. Thus it is helpful to assign a coordinator with financial resources within the administration and appoint a work unit that is financially independent. The tasks of the coordinator are mainly the organisation of network communication, following up strategies and actions defined in the master plan (*Aragall et al.* 2008, p. 20).

3.3 Networking and participation

Any stakeholders involved should take part in the process from the beginning. To identify the stakeholders that should be invited, diversity and inclusiveness have to be taken into account. Stakeholders could be users of the built environment, as well as persons responsible for preservation, legal requirements and funding sources like politicians, employees or volunteers, and other experts that can give inputs for different areas like architects, engineers, geographers, planners, craftsmen or therapists (*Aragall et al.* 2008, p. 20).

3.4 Strategic planning

The development of a Master Plan as a strategic planning tool has to include all strategies, resources, time-schedule, coordination and concrete actions with well-defined milestones. The Master Plan has to go into details and has to be evaluated at the end of the process. In order to guarantee that the content is up to date a regular update of the Master Plan is needed about every five years (*Aragall et al.* 2008, p. 21).

3.5 Knowledge management

People who have not dealed with the topic of Design for All cannot become an expert overnight. But for example the technical staff in an administrative department need to acquire the skills enabling them to participate efficiently in the process. Hence it is necessary that all stakeholders are building up a solid common knowledge base during the working process (*Aragall et al.* 2008, p. 22).

3.6 Resources

It is essential that administrations ensure the necessary resources to finish all phases of the project. These resources could be economic, human or technological. Also the reorganisation of ordinary administrative working processes can be an effective way to implement Design for All. For example the inclusion of Design for All criteria or conditions in calls for tender (construction of new streets, buildings or websites, for the purchase of vehicles, equipment or devices) is a characteristic case where administrations can achieve results without using extra resources (*Aragall et al.* 2008, p. 22f).

3.7 Communication and marketing

External communication, strategic marketing activities and continuous public relations are essential for success and external recognition. In order to underline the commitment of all partners involved and motivate other administrations it is necessary to communicate the aim of the project very early and make public the targets achieved at the project ending (*Aragall et al.* 2008, p. 23).

4 The Thuringian pilot project "Model region for a barrier-free Tourism for All"

The Thuringian pilot project "Model region for a barrier-free Tourism for All" started in 2001 an ended in 2006. Responsible body was the administration of the Association of the Thuringian Forest Natural Park. Main goal of the project was to develop a rural mountainous region in Germany into a model region for Tourism for All in order to secure a competitive advantage by implementing Tourism for All as a quality standard. The size of the model region is about 250 square kilometers and the region is part of the Thuringian Forest Natural Park. The bigger part of the model region is resided in the rural district Gotha, in particular the municipalities of Crawinkel, Gräfenhain, Georgenthal, Herrenhof, Hohenkirchen, Luisenthal and Wölfis as well as the cities of Ohrdruf and Tambach-Dietharz. Only the city of Oberhof is part of the rural district Schmalkalden-Meiningen. The population density alternates between 50 und 200 inhabitants per square kilometer (*Rebstock* 2004, p. 158).

During the term of validity about 25 part projects all along the "touristic service chain" were realised. Numerous institutions have participated in the project, including universities, consultants, tourism stakeholders and associations of people with disabilities. The Transport and Spatial Planning Institute at the Erfurt University of Applied Sciences participated in four part-projects with the focus more or less on transport issues (cf. *Gather & Rebstock* 2004, *Gather et al.* 2006, *Gather & Friedrich* 2005 and *Heiserholt* 2005).

4.1 Transfer of the success factors of Design for All to the model region

To make a rural mountainous region accessible for all is indisputably a very specific challenge (*Rebstock* 2004, p. 158). Therefore it was reasonable to check the success of the project after the end of the project on the basis of the seven interdependent success factors of Design for All (cf. chapter 3).

4.1.1 Relevance of the success factor "decision-maker commitment" for the model region

In the beginning a private organisation initiated the project. Unfortunately, it got into trouble with the formal procedure and the public law. Afterwards the association of the Thuringian Forest Natural Park adopted the project as executing organisation from the private organisation. It was responsible for the project office and the office staff as well as for the implementation of the part projects after the project end (*Rebstock* 2008, p. 48).

Due to problems with the law in the beginning of the project, the project reputation was very bad especially within the regional government. All in all the commitment outside of the involved partners definitely was too low.

4.1.2 Relevance of the success factor "coordinating and continuity" for the model region

In the beginning the private organisation coordinated the first project draft submitted for funding by the German Ministry for Research and Development. Afterwards the association of the Thuringian Forest Natural Park adopted the responsibility for coordination of future part projects, which the region had to develop. Their project office had to go along with the part projects and was responsible to give guidance to the project partners. Unfortunately, the project office was closed after the end of the project (*Rebstock* 2008, p. 48).

All in all it can be stated that continuity was a real problem, because the responsibility for the coordination changed several times during the project phase.

4.1.3 Relevance of the success factor "networking and participation" for the model region

At the starting point a private organization was established with members from the touristic sector and people with disabilities in order to formulate the first project draft. After approval of the project request a regional network named "InnoRegio-Netzwerk" was established with local stakeholders from the touristic sector and administrations as well as with all project participants. This network met several times to coordinate and vote for new part project ideas and to discuss the project preliminary and end results. After the end of the project, efforts to continue this network have been made. For this the private association BAREGIO was founded in 2007 (*Rebstock* 2008, p. 48f).

In summary networking was one of the main success factors of many part projects, because Tourism for All needs products and cooperation all along the touristic service chain.

4.1.4 Relevance of the success factor "strategic planning" for the model region

In the first project draft the overall project strategy was developed, in which all part projects had to fit. In order to get a substantiated basis for planning potentially successful part projects a master plan was produced by a professional tourism consultant. To develop part projects all along the touristic service chain the project office coordinated the part project ideas in reliance to the overall strategy. Some of the part projects continued after the official project end in order to implement the ascertained results. Also some follow-up projects especially in the field of public transport and new mobile technologies were funded (*Rebstock* 2008, p. 49).

Strategic planning recapitulatory was very important and successful in reliance not to support project ideas which had not fitted into the overall project strategy. Thus it was possible to realise projects all along the touristic service chain.

4.1.5 Relevance of the success factor "knowledge management" for the model region

Leaving aside the good overall project idea, a lack of professional knowledge existed at the beginning. Because of this organisations of people with disabilities and professional consultants briefed the "InnoRegio-Netzwerk" during the starting phase in relation to the major needs of the target groups. In addition every part project presented their preliminary and end results at the "InnoRegio-Netzwerk" meetings, so that every member had the possibility to benefit from the generated knowledge. Besides, a lot of part projects published their results in several project reports, hence every member of the local network could consult certain themes (*Rebstock* 2008, p. 49).

Altogether the publication of main project results at no charge made it possible to reach stakeholders who are active in this field all over the German-speaking countries.

4.1.6 Relevance of the success factor "resources" for the model region

At first own capital and human resources had been assembled for the preparation of the first project draft. After the approval of the project request the German Ministry for Research and Development funded the projects and the project office. All in all the ministry allocated an amount of about 7 million € for the overall project. After the project end new financial resources had to be acquired. In some thematic fields the regional government funded follow-up projects (*Rebstock* 2008, p. 49).

Altogether enough money was allocated for the project. However the funding was only deployable for research, not for implementation of the project results. For this reason only a few project results were implemented in reality.

4.1.7 Relevance of the success factor "communication and marketing" for the model region

In the pre-phase of the project the private organisation produced a map of the region to advertise the overall project idea. At the project start a professional marketing company developed a corporate design for the model region, which had to be used by all project partners. Furthermore the project office produced several press reports and conferences for local and regional newspapers. Also some part project results were officially delivered to the local stakeholders in order to implement the results. In addition a special edition of the in-house journal was produced (*Rebstock* 2008, p. 49).

In summary it can be stated that, although the marketing activities were quite successful, more activities to advertise the overall project in the region would have been good for project reputation.

5 The role of transport for a successful Tourism for All approach

First of all it can be asserted that unrestricted accessibility to the transport sector is one of the key requirements for success in Tourism for All, because at least half of the links of the touristic service chain are directly hooked on barrier-free mobility. These links are (*Rebstock* 2005, p. 82):

- journey and departure
- arrival and orientation
- locomotion on location
- leisure time and sports
- entertainment and culture
- tours and shopping.

According to this it is indispensable to develop the transport sector of a destination in a way that it is accessible for all, whenever a region wants to be successful in the field of Tourism for All.

5.1 Accessible public transport as a specific challenge

To design the public transport useable for everybody specific requirements are necessary. It is essential that the following thematic sectors were taken into consideration (*Aslaksen* 2003, p. 50):

- infrastructure
- rolling stock
- operations and services
- information.

It is very important not to forget one of these points, because "a journey is like a chain - it is only as good as its weakest link." (*European Commission - Directorate General Transport* 1999, p. 193)

Aside this complexity within one public transport system the public transport sector as a whole also is very complex and all sectors have to link to each other in an accessible way of using. Figure 1 underlines this complexity graphically.

One of the main problems is the varied responsibility in the public transport sector. For example in Germany the "Deutsche Bahn AG" is responsible for the long-distance railways and partly for short-distance trains. In reliance to the local public transport the transportation companies are accountable for the carriage with busses, trams and partly flexible public transport systems and the private taxi companies for taxi transport. Apart from that, client bodies that order the public transport performance are active on different state levels. Moreover, at the municipality level different competences are allocated in reliance to construction projects.

Fig. 1: Complexness of public transport

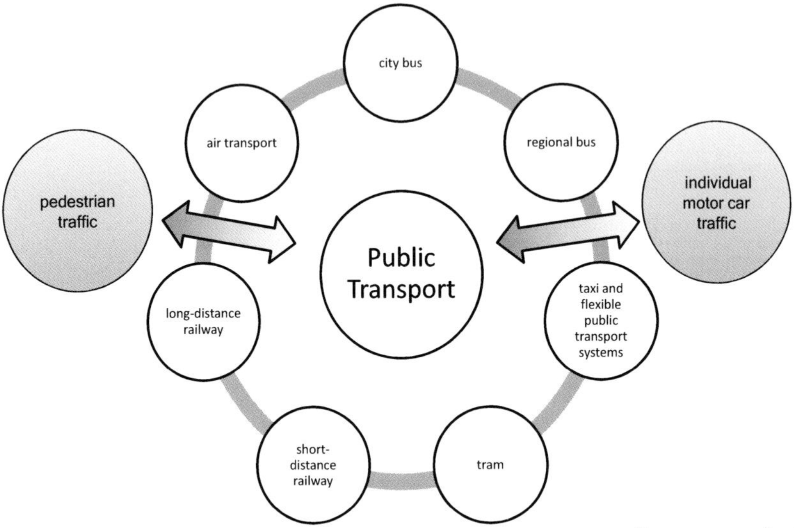

Source: own design

5.2 Centralization of coordination processes in the public transport sector

Because of the extreme complexity of public transport shown in chapter 5.1 it is indispensable to have unrestricted support from policy-makers (cf. chapter 3.1) and to establish a network (cf. chapter 3.3) with all the responsible stakeholders (*Rebstock* 2009, p. 143). In an optimal way a coordination body (cf. chapter 3.2) shall be established. Figure 2 shows the possible tasks such a "coordination body for barrier-free public transport" could take over.

Fig. 2: Coordination body for barrier-free public transport

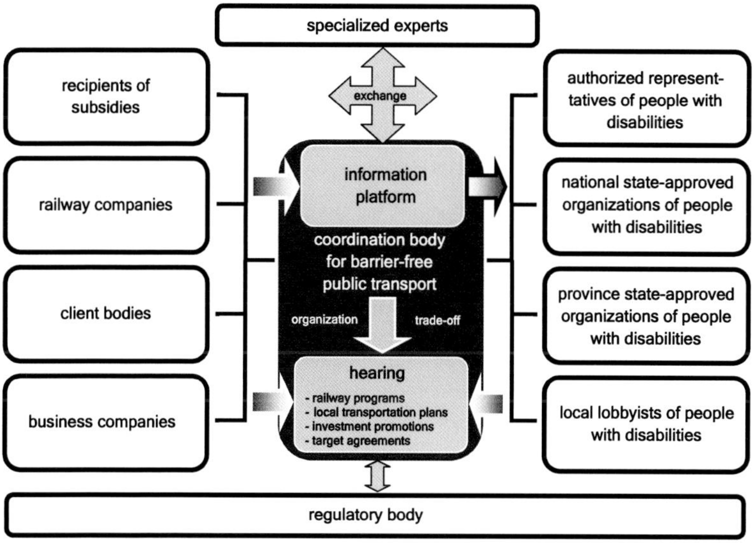

Source: Rebstock 2009 , p.137

6 Conclusions

To respect the seven success factors of Design for All it is necessary to develop an accessible tourist destination which is barrier-free for all potential guests. Only then can it be secured that the tourist offers all along the touristic service chain are accessible and useable for everybody. Therefore great efforts are required to coordinate all the different orientations held by the stakeholders from administrations, private companies and associations. Especially in the field of public transport it could be advisable to implement a coordination body in order to facilitate co-operation and to improve the quality of solutions designed for all.

References

Aragall, Francesc, Peter Neumann & Silvio Sagramola (2008): ECA for Administrations. Luxemburg

Aslaksen, Finn (2003): Barrierefreie Verkehrssysteme. In: Neumann, Peter (ed.): Barrierefreie Städte und Regionen. Münster, pp. 45-62 (= Arbeitsberichte der Arbeitsgemeinschaft Angewandte Geographie Münster, 33)

EIDD – Design for All Europe (2004): The EIDD Stockholm declaration. http://www.designforalleurope.org/upload/design%20for%20all/sthlm%20declaration/stockholm%20declaration_english.pdf, accessed September 22 2009

European Commission – Directorate General Transport (1999): COST 335 – Passengers' accessibility of heavy rail systems. Luxembourg

Gather, Matthias & Juliane Friedrich (2005): FreiRaum – Planungsleitfaden für die barrierefreie Gestaltung von Wanderwegen. Erfurt

Gather, Matthias et al. (2006): Schlussbericht Forschungsprojekt BeGiN – Behinderten-Gleichstellung im Nahverkehr. Erfurt

Gather, Matthias & Markus Rebstock (2004): Schlussbericht – InnoRegio-Projekt barrierefreie Erschließung der Talsperrenregion am Rennsteig. Erfurt

Heiserholt, Michael (2005): Events für Alle – Qualitätsstufen für barrierefreie Veranstaltungen. Erfurt

IDZ (=DesignPartner Berlin GmbH) et al. (2009): Impulse für Wirtschaftswachstum und Beschäftigung durch Orientierung von Unternehmen und Wirtschaftspolitik am Konzept Design für Alle. Berlin

Rebstock, Markus (2004): Barrierefreie Erschließung einer ländlich geprägten Mittelgebirgsregion - Vision oder Illusion?. In: *Kagermeier, Andreas* (ed.): Verkehrssystem- und Mobilitätsmanagement im ländlichen Raum. Mannheim, pp. 157-168 (= Studien zur Mobilitäts- und Verkehrsforschung, 10)

Rebstock, Markus (2005): Barrierefreie Wege in die Natur und zur Kultur – mit Auto und ÖPNV. In: *Landschaftsverband Rheinland – Umweltamt* (ed.): Barrierefreies Natur- und Kulturerlebnis. Köln, pp. 82-95 (= Beiträge zur Landesentwicklung, 59)

Rebstock, Markus (2008): Model region Tourism for All in the Thuringian forest. In: *Aragall, Francesc, Peter Neumann* & *Silvio Sagramola* (eds.): ECA for Administrations. Luxemburg, pp .48-49

Rebstock, Markus (2009): Instrumente zur Umsetzung der Barrierefreiheit im öffentlichen Personennahverkehr. Erfurt/Trier (= Dissertation an der Universität Trier)

Destination Management and Marketing as key success factors

Andreas Kagermeier & Joachim Willms (eds.): Tourism Development in Low Mountain Ranges. Mannheim 2010, p. 75 - 89 (= Studien zur Freizeit- und Tourismusforschung, Vol. 3)

The Harz Mountains as a spatial competitive unit in tourism

– Destination Governance in a German low mountain range

Andreas Lehmberg (Goslar)

Summary

The term "variety" has a positive connotation for tourism destinations. But in terms of destination management, a variety of administrative entities, everyday life regionalisation and different stakeholders cause problems. It is missing the mark to consider a tourism destination only as a spatial competitive unit and a virtual enterprise, because the relevance of social and political relations is then neglected.

The Destination Governance model, which is based on the Regional Governance approach, is a comprehensive instrument to analyse and interpret the destination's variety of interrelations.

Co-operation and self-direction are crucial factors for an effective destination management. The Harz Mountains as a tourism destination are a perfect example for the fact that, among multifaceted external interferences, trade rivalry dominates the internal relations. The protagonists within the destination complain about a lack of assistance from politics or external investors. The benefits of co-operation and self-direction for the destination's development and therefore for every single stakeholder have not yet been recognised sufficiently.

1 Introduction

Among the different aspects of a destination's competitiveness, the term "variety" is of utmost importance, even though it has an ambivalent meaning depending on the context. This ambivalence becomes apparent in regarding the Harz Mountains, Germany's northernmost low mountain range and one of the nation's leading tourism destinations, as an example. On the one hand, the Harz Mountains Tourist Board advertises the "variety of experiences" for tourists. On the other hand there is a sort of variety which causes countless problems for the destination. In the Harz region, one won't just find a variety of tourist attractions but also three federal states (Bundesländer), five administrative districts (Landkreise), dozens of municipalities (Kommunen) and a corresponding multiplicity of tourism organisations. Besides this administrative fragmentation, the "Iron Curtain", which divided the Harz region for more than 40 years, provides additional differentiation.

The Harz region does not have a singular centre or capital. Therefore the population uses the different regional centres, situated circularly around the low mountain range, for their day-to-day routine in terms of political, economical and social participation. The Harz Mountains are seen as an entity just in terms of its area of unsoiled nature.

Nonetheless the governments of the three federal states having a part in the Harz Mountains – Lower Saxony, Saxony-Anhalt and Thuringia – as well as various protagonists within the region are aiming at the region's integrative development and marketing. The guest shall not notice the borders and constraints between the different political, administrative, historical and day-to-day entities. But these borders and constraints do play a decisive role in the internal collaboration. They lead to the fact that all the protagonists characterise the co-operation within the region as problematic.

Hence the Harz Mountains are a perfect example for examining the governance of tourism destinations. In the following, firstly the Harz Mountains will be presented as a tourism destination including its stakeholders and organisational structure. Secondly the Destination Governance model will be explained and used as a conception to analyse how the destination is managed and to learn how the destination management of the Harz region could be enhanced.

The empirical data basis for the analysis are eighteen guided interviews with experts, among them representatives of the different organisations dealing with tourism, as well as politicians, representatives of the municipalities and service providers.

2 The destination

The Harz destination covers Germany's northernmost low mountain range and its immediate surroundings. Therefore the destination stretches out over 100 kilometres from east to west and 40 kilometres from north to south. The region has about 800.000 to 850.000 inhabitants.

2.1 Variety of experiences

The Harz Mountains are a year-round destination, whose touristic variety of experiences is based on different topics. Its foundation is the cultural heritage as an ancient ore mining area. The region's UNESCO world heritage sites and numerous abandoned mines tell captivating stories of the past. Its area of unspoiled nature, with the national park as a figurehead, is the second basis for the touristic variety. Culture and nature built the arena for various activities and experiences. The Harz Mountains possess some 8.000 kilometres of marked hiking trails, 1.800 kilometres of signposted mountain bike routes, a range of downhill bike parks, 500 kilometres of cross-country ski runs, some alpine skiruns, about 100 lakes and reservoirs plus spas and recreation resorts.

Fig. 1: Harz Destination

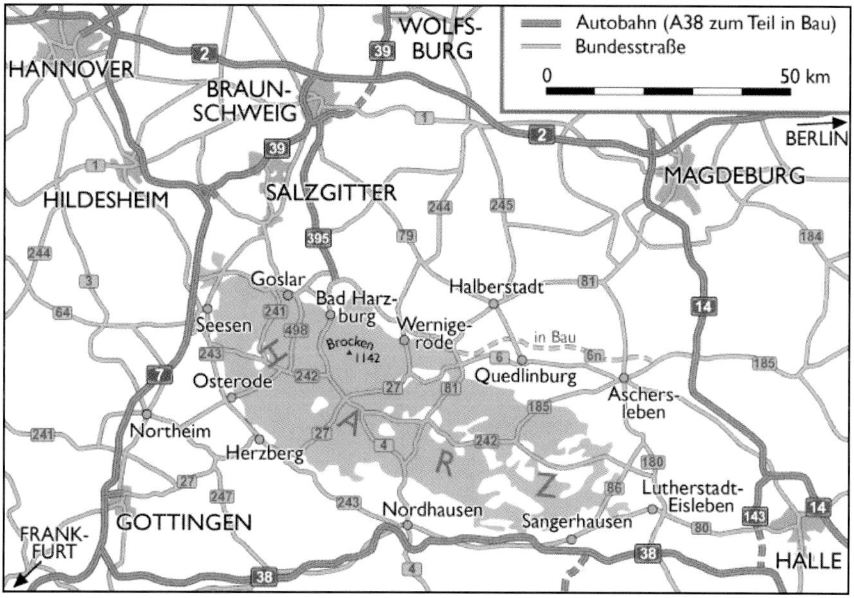

Source: Harzer Tourismusverband

2.2 Touristic characteristics and commercial relevance

In 2007, the Harz destination possessed more than 50.000 touristic beds. More than 10 million commercial overnight stays are generated per annum. Together with the private sector and the VFR-tourism (visiting friends and relatives) approximately 15 million overnight stays are estimated in total, as well as 30 million day-trippers. The economic impact on the region becomes more precise when looking at the number of employees and the tourism-generated turnover. According to the figures of the tourism board, tourism in the Harz region creates around 22,400 calculative fulltime jobs, which should be around 37,000 real jobs. Tourism generates around 1.4 billion € of turnover and an added value of 700 million € annually – accounting all administrative districts with surface belonging to the Harz region – which is 5.2 % of the regional aggregated income. In some municipalities embossed by tourism very strongly, the regional aggregated income goes up to 60 % (cf. *Zukunftskonzept Tourismus Harz 2015*, 2006: 22-24). Therefore tourism is the key economic factor in the kernel region of this low mountain range. The industry structure is, like in similar German destinations, affected by mostly family owned, small and medium sized enterprises (SMEs).

Summarising the quantitative and qualitative data about Harz-tourism, the destination fulfils all definitions' requirements to be a large low mountain destination (cf. e.g. *Bieger* 2005, *Laesser* 2002, *Becker* 2004, *Bleile* 2001, *Steingrube* 2004).

As most of the region's tourism experts agree, the destination's geographical and conceptual definition is based on the guest's perception. Both the supply chain for a complete touristic offer and a well known and marketable brand name are available. The Harz Mountains are furthermore defined independently from administrative boundaries and possess a strong profile as a self-contained cultural and natural area. The Harz has also a high commercial viability for different target groups due to the above described variety of experiences. The region has its own tourist board and with its 10 to 15 million overnight stays per annum it belongs, according to a definition of Bleile, to the large low mountain destinations (cf. *Bleile* 2001: 4-8)

3 The Harz Mountains – internal structure and external influences

Variety is, as mentioned above, an ambivalent term dealing with tourism in the Harz region. As variety of experiences, it is one of the destination's advantages of location. As variety of stakeholders and administrative entities, it complicates and partially inhibits a consistent development of the destination. It therefore leads to friction losses and to a competitive disadvantage compared to other destinations.

3.1 Institutional or political contexts

One of the most important stakeholders of a destination is politics. In the system of the Federal Republic of Germany the federal states are in charge of the economic policy and most of the other policies concerning tourism. This turns especially the economic ministries of the three federal states that have a part in the Harz Mountains – Lower Saxony, Saxony-Anhalt and Thuringia – into important stakeholders that define the framework for all regional activities. However, the Harz Mountains are situated on the outskirts of all three federal states. Regional protagonists therefore reproach the federal state governments with neglecting the region and constraining a consistent development, because the federal structure hinders any co-operation across federal state boundaries.

Within the region, the five administrative districts, the German "Landkreise", are the important local political power, which turns the chief administrative officers into the regional primary politicians. As financial supervising bodies for the municipalities, their influence reaches far within the municipalities, because most of them have a budget deficit.

The administrative districts as regions are a geographical basis for certain activities which affect tourism. The local business development for example is one of their important duties.

The significance for tourism development of the region's 60 to 70 municipalities is rated differently. The above-mentioned budget deficit is their basic challenge. It constrains their decision-making authority and often impedes necessary investment in tourism infrastructure and marketing. However, the local political bodies are important for the formation of opinions within the region.

3.2 Everyday life regionalisation

Beside the variety of political stakeholders and administrative entities, the different everyday life regionalisations of the residents account for an inconsistent view on the region. The Harz region does not have a singular centre or capital. Therefore the population uses the different regional centres, situated circularly around the low mountain range, for their day-to-day routine in terms of political, economical and social participation. This progress is often compared with the flow direction of water, which flows in different directions out of the mountains. Beyond that the German divide, which also has separated the Harz Mountains for over 40 years, is still felt in the region, even almost 20 years after the reunification.

Alongside the diffuse perception as an area of unsoiled nature, tourism is the sole link for the Harz Mountains. The different administrative boundaries, which are not sensed by the guest, play a decisive role in the peripheral orientation of all other sectors of everyday life.

4 The destination Harz – stakeholders and organisational structure

4.1. The Harzer Tourismusverband (HTV)

For the Harz-tourism, the Harzer Tourismusverband e.V. is the main stakeholder. The association was founded as Harzer "Verkehrsverband" in 1904 and has been renamed as "Tourismusverband" in January 2010. With its registered office in Goslar, it is the only Harz-wide operating organisation in tourism and therefore internationally considered as the Harz Mountains Tourist Board. The main function of the HVV is the coordinated marketing of the destination as well as the representation of stakeholder interests to outsiders, e.g. the federal states, and to other interest groups within the region. Additional to that, the HTV is responsible for the management of special projects.

The association is mainly run communally. The premium contributors, and for that reason decisive actors, are the administrative districts and municipalities, respectively their tourism organisations. Other members are touristic service providers as hotels and recreational facilities. In the fiscal year 2008 the HTV had 250 members altogether.

In principle, the existence of the HTV is appraised positively by all actors and is not questioned by anyone. The actual job done by the organisation however is criticised again and again. This criticism is almost as diverse as the structure of the members. In the interviews conducted, it stands out that every actor, which is either a member of the HTV or cooperating with it, feels that just his interests are not represented well enough.

The combination of the cumbersome structure of the association and the heterogeneous structure of its members makes the governance very complicated and leads to a very slow reaction on changes. Due to this structure the HTV also has neither pressurising means nor possibilities to impose sanctions in order to push its claims. As an association it needs to push its interests by means of persuasive power. In this context the, compared to its size, very small budget is most significant. In the past couple of years the HTV, as a marketing organisation, did not even have a free budget for marketing. The budget for marketing was bound to certain activities, mainly defined by sponsoring bodies. Therefore it is not possible for the organisation to give a financial stimulus in order to push its interests and govern the destination.

Another aspect of the criticism towards the HTV is the impact that politics have on the association and the comparably weak inclusion of the private stakeholders. In the perspective of one actor, this leads to a non-acceptance of the HTV by the local population.

4.2 Other stakeholders

Besides the HTV there are more stakeholders, whose field of activities affects tourism and which act within the whole Harz region. Three of them are worth to be mentioned. First there is the "Regionalverband Harz e.V.". Also being borne by the administrative districts, it is in charge of the regional promotion of cultural affairs and responsible for the region's nature parks and associate to the UNESCO-Geopark "Harz. Braunschweiger Land. Ostfalen". Its publicity often affects the business of the HTV. Therefore a closer co-operation between both is decided and will be implemented in 2010.

The second stakeholder worth mentioning is the Harzklub e.V., which has 92 local branches, about 15,000 members and is present destination-wide. It is the regional alliance for cultural heritage, hiking and nature conservation. It is in charge of the maintenance of more than 8,000 kilometres of hiking trails, which has a great impact on the tourism infrastructure and possesses a strong support within the regional population.

The third stakeholder is the Harzer Förderkreis e.V. Founded in the 1990s as a tourist board for the former Eastern German part of the Harz Mountains; it is now in charge of the "Typical Harz"-regional brand and the "Harz Fest", an annual regional folk festival.

In addition to these collective stakeholders, there is a multitude of private stakeholders. The largest on the destination's tourism market is the "Harzer Schmalspurbahn", a steam-driven narrow gauge railway whose route network leads through vast parts of the low mountain range. It brings about one million passengers up the "Brocken", the Harz Mountains' highest peak, 1,141 metres above sea level. As a tourist attraction, it has by any means the highest amount of customers. The administrative districts as well as the municipalities along the route network are its stakeholders. The "Harzer Highlights", a marketing alliance of the 15 largest tourist attractions, are a second important private stakeholder. Both organisations, simultaneously being networks, have an important and structurally determining impact on the destination's development.

4.3 Sub-destination structure

Below the destination one will not find a mono structured local level as described in classic destination models. The spectrum reaches from a classic bureau of the local administration, different models of privatisation up to a complete outsourcing to an external service provider. In addition, there is a range of sub-destination tourist boards trying to bring their sub-region to the market independently.

Within the municipalities you find a wide range of different, mostly family owned, small and medium sized enterprises (SMEs), as is common in German destinations.

5 The issue of governance

The structure of the stakeholders and protagonists within the destination shows a complex and heterogeneous image. But this structure is more a problem of German tourism destinations in general than an issue related to the Harz Mountains only. The special case of the Harz region is the connection of the stakeholder structure, divided into small sections, with the variety of administrative entities and everyday life regionalisation. Therefore one can assume that any issue concerning the governance of a tourist destination can be found within the Harz Mountains. Hence the region is suitable for examining these issues.
This results in two questions:

1) How is the destination governed considering the mentioned framework and stakeholders?
2) Which form of organisation seems to be adequate to govern the Harz destination?

5.1 Governing a destination

The aspect of managing or governing a destination is widely discussed within tourism studies. A destination is mostly considered as a network of offerings. The concept of destination management is broadly spread in the current scientific discussion. Grasshoff defines it as corporate planning and regulation of development, organisation and marketing of a region's touristic product, which tries to balance the interests of all touristic stakeholders (cf. *Grasshoff* 2002: 92). The destination management approach simply compares a destination to an enterprise that acts as a competitive unit providing a benefit for a customer or guest. Laesser substantiates the approach by understanding a destination as a virtual enterprise. Legally independent but economically oblique enterprises carry out a system of service provisions on the basis of common resources like cultural heritage, nature, local expertise or image (cf. *Laesser* 2002: 82).

But this perception neglects important issues concerning the management of a destination. Bieger asserts that social and political relations are not to be considered according to their relevance (cf. *Bieger* 2005: 61). Steingrube detects problems, too. The political influence in the different administrative entities with partly antipodal concerns is one of these. The orientation on administrative boundaries which are congruent to the destination is another (cf. *Steingrube* 2004: 451 et sqq.).

Further problems are up to the structure and practical orientation of the stakeholders. The private sector stakeholders in traditional German tourist destinations are mostly family owned small and medium sized enterprises (SMEs). According to the EU average, tourism enterprises have six employees. It is characteristic of such enterprises that the strategic decisions are made by the entrepreneur himself and are often strongly influenced by personal values and skills. (cf. *Raich* 2006: 168 et seq.). The missing view 'beyond one's nose' which is based upon short-term profit seeking, a lack of knowledge and fears of change is often deplored (cf. *Gustedt* 2000: 214).

A mentality of competition predominates the relations between the economic protagonists within a tourism destination, too. Implementing destination management approaches therefore is highly problematic in traditional destinations.

Although co-operation is an important element of the broadly accepted definitions of a destination, the literature characterises a lack of co-operation as a fundamental problem. Gustedt differentiates between a lack of the willingness and a lack of the ability to co-operate. The lack of willingness to co-operate is based on a timidity of innovation, conservatism, the opposition of interests and the rigidity of existing structures. The lack of ability to co-operate rests upon a deficiency of communication and information, desiderating professionalism and the dread to open up towards new stakeholders an guest structures (cf. *Gustedt* 2000: 217 and *Raich* 2006: 176).

5.2 The Destination Governance approach

The Regional Governance approach by Benz and Fürst provides a different perspective, generally dealing with the governance and coordination of protagonists' planning and activities, whose decisions and actions affect the development of a region (or in this case a destination). It relies on the constructivist definition of a region as a social construct, which could be applied to varied actualities. A region therefore is a coherent area which is homogenous in selected defined criteria and which is distinguished by these criteria from neighbouring areas. Regions exist in a socially constructed reality and become socio-politically relevant, if they have an impact on (inter)actions of persons, groups or organisations. A region becomes relevant for society, when it is built by social conventions and common perceptions (cf. *Benz* 2003: 8 et sgg.).

The borders and boundaries of a region are not drawn arbitrarily. They result from the criteria defining the region. Regions are confined unequally clear, depending on the region's function. Administrative planning regions for example need to be sharply confined, whereas tourist destinations, which are defined by the guest's perception, need to be confined more generally (*Benz* 2003: 10).

A destination consequently may be understood as a functionally and geographically confined region. According to Bieger's well known definition, a destination is a geographical space chosen by a guest or a segment of guests. It contains all facilities a guest needs for board and lodging, amusement etc. (cf. *Bieger* 2005: 56). Hence destinations have a function as guest-orientated networks of offers in areas which are defined by the guests on the base of their perceptions (cf. *Laesser* 2002: 81). The accentuation of the guest perception reveals the connection to regionalisation. The guest builds his destination by an active consumptive regionalisation.

Based on the definitions of region and destination as well as the approaches of the governance of regions, Raich developed a model of Destination Governance. The development relies on the assumption that the destination management approaches are not sufficient to govern a destination like a unit. The model does not regard a destination just as a commercially competitive unit but as a characteristic of a region. It considers all social, political and commercial elements of a destination's coordination. Raich adds the stakeholders, their practical orientation, their constellation, the way of interaction and the institutional context to these elements (cf. *Raich* 2006: 288 et sqq.)

Fig. 2: Destination Governance approach

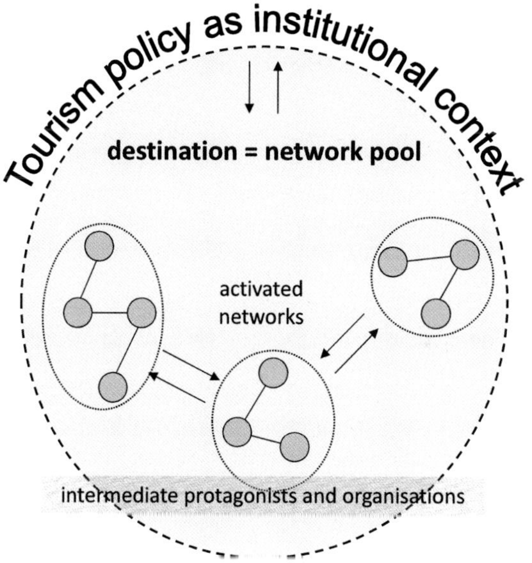

modified from Raich 2006:230

The model's control levels

Raich entitles the first control level to institutional context. The tourism policy builds an institution which affects the scope of action within the destination and governs the stakeholders' attitude. Due to the unilateral state of dependence, this connection could also be interpreted as a hierarchical structure, where politics define the overall framework supporting self governance as long as it achieves satisfying solutions (cf. *Rainch* 2006: 196 et sgg.).

The second control level is defined as latent network pool, in which all potential protagonists and stakeholders reside. Usually a network pool is not formally structured or organised. The latently existing connections between the protagonists result from geographical vicinity and guest behaviour, even if the institutional context arranges a certain structuring of the network pool within the destination to avoid parallel activities.

Self governing is the essential governing element on this level (cf. *Rainch* : 215).

Active networks, the third control level, arise from the latent network pool if protagonists believe they gain an added value from co-operation. Essential elements are mutual trust among the stakeholders and an initiator making the first move (cf. *Rainch*: 230-232).

These control levels – institutional context, latent network pool, active networks – interact and their borders have to be penetrable to get mutual exchange and co-operation, which have to be initiated and supported by intermediate protagonists or organisations. Working committees usually administer this function in a destination but it is also possible to delegate such businesses to organisations like regional tourist boards (cf. *Rainch*: 229).

5.3 Principles of achievement

The major principles of achievement in the discussion on regional (destination) governance are co-operation between regional stakeholders and self-organisation within the region.

According to Benz, co-operation is important because development-advancing contributions of regional protagonists could not be enforced (cf. *Benz* 2003: 18). For Knieling such co-operative acting is part of a policy which focuses on integration and joint responsibility. In doing so, he differentiates between five attributes of co-operation: voluntary accession, realistic exit options, consensual decision-making, marginal possibilities for sanctions and a missing ruling monopoly (cf. *Knieling* 2003: 467).

Being based on co-operation, Raich calls self-organisation the major principle for governing a destination, regarding it as public-to-private or private-to-private interaction which decentralises decision-making and governing resources. It also activates knowledge, motivation, capabilities and resources within the destination. The institutional context is supposed to set the framework for this process (cf. *Raich* 2006: 197 et seg.).

6 Co-operation within the destination Harz

The above-mentioned theoretical considerations as well as guideline-based interviews with experts are the basis for an analysis of the different forms of co-operation and organisation within the destination.

6.1 Forms of co-operation

Several interview partners consider collective protagonists like tourist boards, associations or foundations as being a form of co-operation. The members of these organisations cooperate for example through espousing common interests and aims along with using them as a networking platform.

All the above-mentioned stakeholders acting in the whole Harz region could be seen as formally structured co-operations between more or less homogeneous groups of protagonists. These groups rely on voluntary accession, have a realistic exit option and only marginal possibilities for sanctions. Especially the last point is often characterised as a major problem for the HTV.

Apart from the Harz-wide acting stakeholders, the interview partners often mentioned 'sub-regional' co-operations, which act in diverse regional subunits. Being a controversial issue, they act mostly on the basis of the administrative districts. On the one hand they are seen negatively as split-up phenomena; on the other hand, considering the local budget holes, they are the only way to retain professional tourism (marketing) structures for a lot of municipalities.

Other protagonists work closely with partners from outside the Harz Mountains on a sectoral or thematic basis. Especially the historic towns in the north of the region foster contacts to other historic towns e.g. through the UNESCO World Heritage network. The administrative districts work together with the respective regional centers on regional planning.

Public-private-partnership is an important characteristic of the governance approaches which could be detected in the Harz destination, too. Within most of the above-mentioned organisations public and private stakeholders act together. The administrative districts and municipalities as well as private protagonists are members of the Harzer Tourismusverband.

However, the interview partners complain about a missing involvement of private stakeholders in decision-making structures.

According to Raich, initiating interdisciplinary co-operations is an important task for Destination Governance. These co-operations are not in high gear within the Harz destination. Within the limits of special projects, interdisciplinary co-operations e.g. between the Hasseröder brewery and the HTV had been initiated but did not last beyond these projects.

6.2 Constraints of co-operations

The constraints of co-operations prevail in the perception of the interview partners. These problems could be explained with the practical orientation of the touristic stakeholders. The missing willingness to co-operate is up to the SME-structure in traditional German destinations.

All interview partners assess the co-operations within the destination as problematic. They explain these problems with the egoism of the stakeholders. Mainly private stakeholders or municipalities hesitate to cooperate because they fear losing customers or guests.

The municipalities hesitate to co-operate with regional structures, too, because of the fear of losing autonomy. Interview partners also notice a struggle for economic resources between the regional and local tourist boards. Both want the private stakeholders, especially the accommodation facilities, to use their marketing platforms etc. because the tourist boards finance their structures in large parts from these marketing earnings.

The structural relations within a destination rely on competition between the economic stakeholders. This perception prevails among the interview partners, too. Most of them view this internal competition on all levels within the Harz destination – between the economic as well as the political and social stakeholders. This egoism could also be seen as a driving power for the destination, but for this the co-operation has to prevail over the competition.

An interview partner whose function enables him to draw a comparison to other destinations, sees the reason for the co-operation problems in the desire to enjoy autonomy. He literally said: "If you can spend your own money the way you want, it is much easier than arranging things with somebody else, even though this might be economically much more effective. But you have to make compromises and cannot decide on your own, which seems to be quite inconvenient."

Furthermore many interview partners notice envy, jealousy and rivalry between the protagonists on the different levels.

It is controversially discussed whether these are typical problems for the Harz region or whether they apply to tourist destinations in general. For most of the interview partners, egoism and competition are not more intense than in other destinations. For the Harz Mountains, the variety of administrative boundaries – especially between the federal states – is an additional problem which complicates regional co-operations. The historical element has to be considered, too. The long time of division continues to have an impact on the region and its population. After the euphoria of the reunification in the early 1990s, envy and anger spread out from the West at the better conditions for grants due to the "Aufbau Ost" – East German recovery programme.

7 As-is analysis of governance

A tourism expert alludes to "centrifugal forces" which impede the initiation of co-operation within a destination. Egoism, internal competition and jealousy require a constant built-up of magnetism to deter the destination from breaking apart. This perception leads to the question of who is the magnet and manages or governs the destination. An interview partner's conclusion that "all is managed by the fact how much money is given for what and what is legally permitted", summarises the perception of the Harz stakeholders. Money and (political) power are recognised as important control instruments.

Private investors are the first protagonists that possess these control instruments, but they comply with the national or European Union assistance criteria to get state funding. The interview partners are of the opinion that by granting these state fundings, politics as institutional context becomes accountable for governing and developing the destination. In addition to granting financial funding, politics define the legal framework in which the destination and its stakeholders are allowed to act. Both turns politics in general and the ministries for economics of the "Harz" federal states in particular into the most powerful protagonists for the destination's development. The administrative districts and municipalities are also mentioned, but their power is limited primarily by the budget gap of local or regional administrative entities.

Therefore the governance is externalised, but self-organisation or self-direction is, besides co-operation, the second important criterion of Destination Governance. According to the interviews, self-direction does virtually not exist within the Harz destination. Some interview partners accuse the HTV of possessing a constricted self-direction. Representatives of the HTV however assess their possibilities to govern the destination as limited due to the lack of restrictive control instruments.

In summary, one could say that the centrifugal forces are very strong in the Harz destination. A region-based magnetism in terms of effective Destination Governance does not exist. The different forms and constraints of co-operation, as explained in chapter 6, play a decisive role in this context. On the one hand the stakeholders do not take sufficient advantages out of the existing co-operations. On the other hand the sensed constraints of co-operation have to get solved to develop self-direction and self-organisation which are strong enough to deploy magnetism against the structural centrifugal forces.

8 Visions of governance

Against the background of the as-is analysis the interview partners have been asked to sketch out their visions of governing the Harz destination. A pyramid structure of organisation arises from summarising the outcome.

Figure 3: Pyramid structure of destination organisation

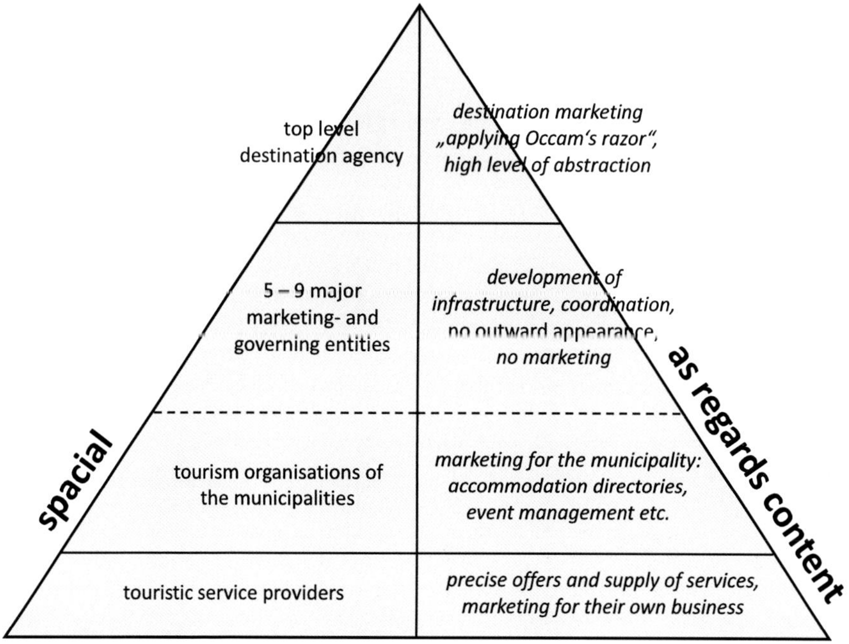

own design

A broadly accepted and invigorated form of organisation ought to govern or manage the destination. A top level destination agency, as a proposed solution, could combine functions of HTV, Harzklub and Regionalverband. The integration of Harzklub-structures would also sustain the organisations' acceptance within the population, because the widespread voluntary structures could participate in the development of the destination.

Beyond that this organisation has to possess a high degree of financial and political independence from varied political interests. This proposal focuses on a combination of financial and political independence as well as the participation of the population and combines rigorous and flexible forms of governance.

9 Conclusion

The immediate participation of the population is an innovative approach which has not yet been recognised within the discussion about governing. Beyond that the visions of governance were based on traditional approaches of hierarchical governance. The strengthening of self-organisation has only been mentioned in the margin. Solving the problems is shifted to politics or the institutional context. It is often called upon politics to finance the destination management organisation in order to gain magnetism against the centrifugal forces. A bottom-up consolidation of the organisation and the transfer of power and financial resources from the local to the regional level has never been mentioned.

This shows the structural problems of governing a destination. Overcoming the egoism of the different stakeholders expressed by envy, jealousy and rivalries remains difficult. Even though co-operation and self-organisation – as important elements for a successful Destination Governance – have been mentioned by the protagonists on a higher-level discussion, competition and rivalry prevail in the day-to-day routines.

Currently the protagonists try to organise the management of the destination more effectively, principally through the reorganisation of the Harzer Tourismusverband. The first step is the above mentioned renaming in order to create a publicity-effective start of the reorganisation process. The primary object is to build a strong magnet against the centrifugal forces which have become stronger lately. All major stakeholders are supposed to be integrated in this new organisation, primarily to create an outward impression of unity. The driving force for this process is not so much the awareness that all stakeholders benefit from an effective destination management organisation, but rather the prospect of more federal state grants.

The institutional context still plays a decisive role and the question remains as to how a co-operative self-organisation which is as independent as possible from the institutional context can be implemented. The Destination Governance approach gives a theoretical guideline for analysing procedures within the destination. Whether these exemplary perceptions could be implemented, remains an open question.

Bibliographie

Becker, C. (2004): Destinationsmanagement. In: *Becker, C., H. Hopfinger* & *A. Steinecke* (eds.): Geographie der Freizeit und des Tourismus: Bilanz und Ausblick. 2nd Edition. München, p. 465–474

Benz, A. (2003): Regional Governance. Fernuniversität Hagen. Hagen

Bieger, T. (2005): Management von Destinationen. 6th edition. München

Bleile, G. (2001): Neue Tourismus Landkarte "D". Leitfaden für Marktorientiertes Destination Management. Akademie für Touristik Freiburg (= Schriftenreihe Tourismus, 5)

Gustedt, E. (2000): Nachhaltige Regionalentwicklung durch intermediäre Organisationen? Erwartungshaltungen, Hemmnisse und Möglichkeiten, dargestellt vor dem Hintergrund intermediärer Organisationen in vier peripheren, touristisch orientierten Regionen. Stuttgart

Grashoff, C. (2002): Destinationsmanagement als neues Steuerungsmodell der Tourismusentwicklung. In: *Borghardt, J. et al.* (2002): ReiseRäume. Touristische Entwicklung und räumliche Planung. Dortmund, page 87 – 99. (= Dortmunder Beiträge zur Raumplanung, 109)

Harzer Verkehrsverband (2004): Der Harzer Verkehrsverband 1904 bis 2004. Eine wechselvolle Zeitreise. Goslar

Knieling, J. (2003): Kooperative Regionalplanung und Regional Governance: Praxisbeispiele, Theoriebezüge und Perspektiven. In: Informationen zur Raumentwicklung, Volume 8/9, p. 463–478

Laesser, C. (2002): Aufgaben des Destinationsmanagments und Herausforderungen für eine zukunftsorientierte Tourismuspolitik. In: Pechlaner, H., K. Weiermair & C. Laesser ed.): Tourismuspolitik und Destinationsmanagement. Neue Herausforderungen und Konzepte. Berlin, p. 77–121

Niedersächsisches Ministerium für Wirtschaft, Arbeit und Verkehr, Ministerium für Wirtschaft und Arbeit des Landes Sachsen-Anhalt und Thüringer Ministerium für Wirtschaft, Technologie und Arbeit (ed.) (2006): Zukunftskonzept Tourismus Harz 2015 Erfurt. (=Tourismus-Studien Sachsen-Anhalt, 22)

Raich, F. (2006): Governance räumlicher Wettbewerbseinheiten. Ein Ansatz für die Tourismus-Destination. Wiesbaden

Steingrube, W. (2004): Freizeit- und Tourismusdestinationen: Management – Struktur – Politik – Planung. In: *Becker, C., H. Hopfinger & A. Steinecke* (eds.) (2004): Geographie der Freizeit und des Tourismus: Bilanz und Ausblick. 2nd edition. München, p. 441–453

Andreas Kagermeier & Joachim Willms (eds.): Tourism Development in Low Mountain Ranges.
Mannheim 2010, p. 91 - 112 (= Studien zur Freizeit- und Tourismusforschung, Vol. 3)

Regionalmarken als strategisches Positionierungselement von Mittelgebirgsregionen
– dargestellt am Beispiel der Regionalmarke EIFEL

Frank Schaal (Berlin) & Nadine Lichter (Bickendorf)

1 Einleitung

Regionalmarken haben in den letzten Jahren an Bedeutung gewonnen. Auch im Tourismus. Welche Bedeutung diese für Mittelgebirgsregionen einnehmen können, um sich im verschärften Wettbewerb der Destinationen besser positionieren zu können, wird im Folgenden gezeigt. Als Beispiel wird hierzu die Regionalmarke EIFEL herangezogen. Sie hat es geschafft, die Region Eifel, ein Mittelgebirge im Westen von Deutschland, das sich über Nordrhein-Westfalen und Rheinland-Pfalz erstreckt, mit Hilfe von qualitativ hochwertigen Produkten aus dem Lebensmittelbereich sowie qualitativ hochwertigen Dienstleistungen aus dem touristischen Bereich effektiver und effizienter zu positionieren. Zu Beginn werden zunächst die aktuellen Entwicklungen und Problemstellungen, die zurzeit den Tourismus beherrschen, erläutert. Diese sollen den Handlungsbedarf von Regionen bzw. Destinationen verdeutlichen. Der Fokus einer effektiveren und effizienteren Marktpositionierung liegt hier auf dem Markenansatz. Hier wird zunächst das Markenphänomen und der –begriff sowie die Markengeschichte und die Evolution des Konzeptes näher beleuchtet. In einem weiteren Punkt werden die Funktionen der Marke sowohl aus Anbieter- als auch aus Nachfragersicht näher charakterisiert. Einen wichtigen Aspekt bildet auch das „Strategische Markenmanagement", was anhand verschiedener Ausführungen verdeutlicht wird. Ein weiterer Schwerpunkt des Aufsatzes liegt auf den touristischen Marken. Dabei wird vor allem darauf eingegangen, welche Stolpersteine und Problemstellungen hier für eine erfolgreiche Markenbildung überwunden werden müssen. Von besonderer Bedeutung ist dabei eine sinnvolle Gestaltung und Anwendung der Branding-Elemente, die ebenso nähere Betrachtung finden. Nachfolgend wird auf die Regionalmarkenthematik eingegangen. Als besonderes Beispiel wurde die Regionalmarke EIFEL gewählt, die mit Aspekten wie Zielen, Nutzen, Markenmanagement, Finanzierung, Marketing-Mix, Marketing-Kooperationen, Partnerschaften, Produkte und Dienstleistungen sowie den Aufgaben der jeweiligen Tourismusorganisationen charakterisiert wird.

2 Aktuelle regionale Entwicklungen und Problemstellungen

Bis Ende der 1980er Jahre orientierte sich nahezu die gesamte Tourismusentwicklung an dem Phänomen des Massentourismus. Primäres Ziel war die Erwirtschaftung möglichst hoher Skalenerträge. Die 1990er Jahre sind durch eine Verlangsamung der touristischen Nachfrage, dennoch von einem Anstieg der Reiseintensität gekennzeichnet (*vgl. Smeral* 2003, S. 144). Heute zählt der Tourismus weltweit zu den bedeutendsten Wirtschaftszweigen und stellt in vielen Ländern die wichtigste Einnahmequelle dar. Allerdings sind auch in dieser Branche die Zeiten des steilen Wachstums vorbei (vgl. *Hannemann* 2002, S. 1) und Destinationen stehen sich in einer verschärften Wettbewerbssituation gegenüber, was zu Verdrängungstendenzen führt (vgl. *Steingrube* 2004, S. 441; vgl. *Ullmann* 2000, S. 41f.). Daraus resultiert, dass die Ferienziele sich zunehmend den Instrumenten des strategischen Managements öffnen müssen, um überhaupt noch wettbewerbsfähig bzw. langfristig erfolgreich zu sein. Dafür ist es essentiell neue Trends, z. B. den Qualitätstrend und auch Gästewünsche und –ansprüche genau zu kennen und befriedigen zu können (vgl. *Scherhag & Schneider* 1998, S. 6; vgl. *Scherhag* 2000, S. 149ff.). Weiterhin nimmt die Schnelligkeit der touristischen Akteure, sich an die veränderten Branchenspielregeln anzupassen, Einfluss auf den Erfolg (vgl. *Ullmann* 2000, S. 44). Entscheidend ist jedoch, dass sich Regionen aus der Masse hervorheben, denn nur wenn sie von den Gästen wahrgenommen und als nutzenstiftend eingeordnet werden, besteht die Chance, dass sie in die Entscheidungsfindung potentieller Touristen miteinbezogen werden (vgl. *Dettmer et al.* 1998, S. 59ff.). Aufgrund dessen stellen Destinationsmarken ein beliebtes Instrument dar, um Wettbewerbsvorteile zu generieren (vgl. *Scherhag* 2000, S. 150).

3 Markenphänomen und -begriff

Marken begleiten uns im täglichen Leben und stellen ein allgemeines Phänomen dar, das in der heutigen Konsumgesellschaft einen hohen Stellenwert einnimmt (vgl. *Irmscher* 1997, o. S.; vgl. *Chandler & Owen* 2002, S. 2). Eine allgemeingültige Definition des Markenbegriffs erweist sich jedoch aufgrund der Vielgestaltigkeit als sehr schwierig (vgl. *Linxweiler* 2001, S. 51).

Im Allgemeinen stellen Marken im konsumtiven Bereich ein auf Waren angebrachtes Zeichen dar, das als das wichtigste Individualisierungsmerkmal von Produkten gilt (vgl. *Dichtl* 1992, S. 4). Als Beispiele können hier US-amerikanische Marken wie Coca-Cola oder Nike, aber auch bedeutende deutsche Marken wie Nivea oder Mercedes-Benz angeführt werden (vgl. *Chandler* & *Owen* 2002, S. 1; vgl. *Linxweiler* 2001, S. 36).

Im Jahr 1960 definierte die American Marketing Association den Begriff wie folgt: „A name, term, sign, symbol, or design, or a combination of them intended to identify the goods or services of one seller or group of sellers and to differentiate them from those of competitors" (*Keller* 1998, S. 2).

Nach *Haedrich, Tomczak* & *Kaetzke* (1997, S. 18) wird der Begriff wie folgt erläutert: „Als Marke wird jedes Angebot bezeichnet (Konsumgut, Dienstleistung, Investitionsgut), das mit einem Markennamen und zusätzlich mit festen Markenelementen gekennzeichnet ist, das den Angehörigen der Zielgruppe und weiterer Bezugsgruppen bekannt und mit einem ausgeprägten und unverwechselbaren Markenbild (Image) versehen ist".

Aus Sicht der Gesetzgebung wurde der Begriff im Markengesetz (§3, Abs. 1, MarkenG), das am 1. Januar 1995 wirksam wurde, wie folgt definiert:

„Als Marke können alle Zeichen, insbesondere Wörter einschließlich Personennamen, Abbildungen, Buchstaben, Zahlen, Hörzeichen, dreidimensionale Gestaltungen einschließlich der Form einer Ware oder ihrer Verpackung sowie sonstige Aufmachungen einschließlich Farben und Farbzusammenstellungen geschützt werden, die geeignet sind, Waren oder Dienstleistungen eines Unternehmens von denjenigen anderer Unternehmen zu unterscheiden" (*Mühlendahl* 1995, S. 7).

Die Definitionen verdeutlichen, dass der Markeneinsatz neben physischen Gütern auch bei Dienstleistungen, Personen, Unternehmen, Veranstaltungen, Landschaften, Regionen und Destinationen möglich ist (vgl. *Linxweiler* 2001, S. 51; vgl. *Keller* 1998, S. 10ff.). Weiterhin wird aufgezeigt, dass es aufgrund von verbalen oder visuellen Zeichen und damit verbundenen Aspekten, wie Werten, Ideen, Identität, Einzigartigkeit, Attraktivität und Klarheit des Auftretens etc. möglich ist, sich gegenüber anonymen Produkten besser am Markt zu positionieren (vgl. *Adjouri* 1993, S. 97; vgl. *Linxweiler* 2004, S. 17).

4 Markengeschichte und Evolution des Markenkonzeptes

Marken stellen keine neuartige Erscheinung der heutigen Wirtschaftswelt dar (vgl. *Aaker* 1991, S. 7). Die Ursprünge der Markengeschichte reichen bis in die Zeit der ältesten Kulturvölker, z. B. Ägypter, Griechen und Römer zurück (vgl. *Bruhn* 2001, S. 19). Damals wurde eine Markierung des Eigentums mit dem Ziel die Herkunft und Qualität der Produkte zu dokumentieren, vorgenommen (vgl. *Hohmeyer* 1850, S. 205ff.).

Das 13. Jh. ist aufgrund eines enormen Städtewachstums und einem Hoch im Handelsverkehr als die „Geburtsstunde" der gewerblichen Hausmarke zu charakterisieren (vgl. *Hohmeyer* 1850, S. 165f.), denn zu dieser Zeit herrschte in den Städten ein Warenüberschuss, so dass die Absatzgebiete über die Stadtgrenzen hin ausgedehnt werden mussten. Aufgrund der Distanz ging für den Handwerker der persönliche Kontakt zum Kunden verloren und wurde fortan von den Händlern übernommen (vgl. *Irmscher* 1997, S. 35). Die Entstehung der handwerklichen Hanse und Zünfte und die damit verbundenen Sanktions- und Organisationssysteme führten zu strengen Qualitätskontrollen der Produktion und Warenwirtschaft. Die eigens entworfenen Zeichen waren in der Zunftrolle zu registrieren, um bei auftretenden Qualitatsdefiziten den Hersteller zurückzuverfolgen (vgl. *Linxweiler* 2004, S. 72). Als Beispielmarke aus der damaligen Zeit ist Kölnisch Wasser zu nennen (vgl. *Mellerowicz* 1964, o. S.).

Die zweite Phase umfasst das moderne Markenwesen ab dem 18. Jh. Besonders markant ist hier die Wende vom 18. zum 19. Jh. und der damit verbundene Wandel zu einer kapitalistischen Wirtschaftsweise, die zur Auflösung der Zünfte und dem Verschwinden der Marken führte (vgl. *Dichtl* 1992, S. 24). Bedingt durch den Trend der Massenproduktion kam es zur Veränderung der Handelsstrukturen, die sich u. a. in einer Anonymisierung von Produkten und Leistungen auswirkte und sich bei den Produzenten in Unsicherheiten auswirkte. Die Markierungen ermöglichten es dem Konsumenten ein entsprechendes Vertrauen gegenüber der Ware aufzubauen (vgl. *Linxweiler* 2004, S. 74).

Der Zweite Weltkrieg brachte bedingt durch Produktionsstilllegungen bzw. -veränderungen die Markenentwicklung zum Erliegen, bevor nach Ende der Krisenzeit das Markenwesen immer bedeutender wurde (vgl. *Adjouri* 1993, S. 5). Den Ausgangspunkt der Markenbildung stellt dabei der Konsumgüterbereich dar, dem anschließend Handels- und Dienstleistungsmarken folgten (vgl. *Freyer & Dreyer* 2004, S. 85).

Nach *Bruhn* (2001, S. 19ff.) und *Meffert* & *Burmann* (1996, S. 6) kann das moderne Markenmanagement insgesamt in fünf Phasen eingeteilt werden. Dabei gelten die 1950er und 1960er Jahre als die Phase der Herstellermarken. In der daran anschließenden Phase der Handels- und Gattungsmarken (1970er Jahre) drängten auch Hersteller mit eigenen Handelsmarken auf den Markt. Die 1980er Jahre waren von zunehmenden Verdrängungsstrategien, ausgeprägten Wettbewerbsorientierungen bis hin zu „Markenpolarisierungen“ (Luxus- versus Billigmarken) geprägt. Die anschließende Dekade (1990er Jahre) ist charakteristisch für die Entwicklung der Dienstleistungs- und Investitionsgütermarken. Besonders Ökomarken und internationale Marken gewannen an Bedeutung. Diese Entwicklung ist u. a. als eine Reaktion auf die Austauschbarkeit der Leistungen sowie „ausgereifte“ Märkte anzusehen. Die fünfte Phase (ab dem Jahr 2000) kennzeichnet sich durch die Entwicklung von Stadt- und Personenmarken. Weiterhin entstand eine zunehmende Polarisierung lokaler und globaler Marken (vgl. *Linxweiler* 2001, S. 51).

5 Funktionen der Marke

Marken erfüllen sowohl für die Anbieter als auch für die Nachfrager wichtige Funktionen (vgl. *Haedrich, Tomczak & Kaetzke* 2003, S. 23). Für den Anbieter bietet die Marke eine Vielzahl von Chancen mit unterschiedlichen Zielsetzungen. Ein wesentliches Ziel besteht in der Erarbeitung von Wettbewerbsvorteilen gegenüber der Konkurrenz. Durch den Markeneinsatz ist eine Leistungsindividualisierung in den immer unübersichtlicheren Märkten möglich (vgl. *Becker* 1993, S. 162; vgl. *Adjouri* 1993, S. 100f.). So kann eine Markenbindung in Form von Wiederholungskäufen und –treue in Form von einer Stammkundschaft initiiert werden, was zu einer höheren Zufriedenheit bei den Nachfragern und zu einer absatzfördernden Wirkung sowie einem preispolitischen Spielraum bei dem Anbieter führen kann (vgl. *Freyer* 1997, S. 155; vgl. *Pepels* 1999, S. 175). Markenartikel gelten insgesamt als wettbewerbsfördernd und steigern den Grad der Innovationen, indem sie einem monotonen Angebot entgegenwirken (vgl. *Bruhn* 2001, S. 30). Die Angebotsfülle und die damit verbundene Informationsflut am Markt ziehen eine Unübersichtlichkeit und Orientierungslosigkeit für den Kunden mit sich, so dass sich daher immer häufiger auf bekannte „starke“ Marken konzentriert wird (vgl. *Ferner & Pötsch* 1998, S. 22). Für den Nachfrager stellen Marken eine Orientierungshilfe dar und helfen weiterhin bei der Entscheidungsfindung (vgl. *Becker* 1993, S. 162; vgl. *Linxweiler* 2004, S. 35f.). Marken gelten somit als „Leuchttürme in der Angebotsflut“ (*Quack* 2000, S. 170), die stressreduzierend und verhaltenssteuernd wirken (vgl. *Haedrich, Tomczak & Kaetzke* 2003, S. 23). Darüber hinaus vermitteln sie das Gefühl der Sicherheit, Vertrauen und Garantie (vgl. *Ferner & Pötsch* 1998, S. 33). Dies bedeutet, dass mit Marken bestimmte Qualitäten verbunden werden, die es seitens der Anbieter zu erfüllen gilt (vgl. *Irmscher* 1997, S. 31). Das Kaufrisiko und die Unsicherheit können insbesondere bei komplexen immateriellen und intangiblen Leistungen, wie im Tourismus, durch den Einsatz von Marken entscheidend reduziert werden (vgl. *Freyer & Dreyer* 2004, S. 85). Weiterhin können sie im sozialen Umfeld als Prestige- bzw. Imageobjekt fungieren (vgl. *Sommer* 1998, S. 3).

6 Strategisches Markenmanagement

In der Wissenschaft und Praxis ist das Strategische Markenmanagement ein weit verbreiteter Begriff und Ansatz, der durch ein vielschichtiges Aufgabenfeld geprägt ist. Dabei umfasst die Markenpolitik ganzheitliche und übergreifende Maßnahmen sowie Entscheidungen, die im Zusammenhang mit der Produktmarkierung stehen (vgl. *Bruhn* 1994, S. 17f.) Dazu gehört neben dem Aufbau, der Pflege und dem spezifischen Vertrieb der Marke auch, dass der Nachfrager von dem Angebot der überlegenen Produkte überzeugt werden kann (vgl. *Irmscher* 1997, S. 38ff.).

Die erste Phase ist die der Markenrealisierung, die sich in den Aufbau und die daran anschließende Pflege der Marke gliedert. Hier wird das primäre Ziel verfolgt, den Bekanntheitsgrad der Marke zu erhöhen und bei den Konsumenten erste Assoziationen zu wecken. Voraussetzung dafür ist eine geeignete, klar positionierte Qualität und ein für den Kunden erkennbarer Nutzen. In der Phase der Markenpflege steht eine Verbesserung und Pflege des Images im Vordergrund. In beiden Phasen spielen Brandingelemente wie der Name oder das Logo eine zentrale Rolle, da sie bei der Leistungsmarkierung eine unterstützende Funktion besitzen (vgl. *Bieger* 2006, S. 188f.; vgl. *Baumgarth* 2004, S. 160).

Die zweite Phase, die Markenpositionierung, verfolgt als zentrale Aufgabe „die strategische und aktive Steuerung der Wahrnehmung eines Leistungsangebotes durch die anvisierte Kundengruppe, mit dem Ziel, ein eindeutiges, positiv von Wettbewerbsangeboten abgrenzendes Markenimage aufzubauen“ (*Haedrich* 2004, S. 219). Damit eine deutliche und unverwechselbare Positionierung gewährleistet sein kann, ist es zunächst wichtig relevante Kernwerte, z. B. sachlich-funktionale Werte, auszuwählen und dem Produkt oder der Leistung somit einen eigenen Charakter zu verleihen. Anschließend folgt die Festlegung der Markenphilosophie, in der die Ideen, angestrebten Ziele und Visionen verankert sind (vgl. *Linxweiler* 2001, S. 68ff.; vgl. *Regionalmarke Eifel GmbH* 2007, o. S.). Eine langfristige und erfolgreiche Marktpositionierung kann nur dann erreicht werden, wenn der Lebenszyklus von Kontinuität und Dynamik geprägt ist und sich an veränderte Marktbedingungen flexibel, innovativ und qualitativ hochwertig angepasst werden kann (vgl. *Haedrich* 2004, S. 223). Die Markenführung ist ein kontinuierlicher und nie abgeschlossener Prozess, denn eine Marke sollte ähnlich einer Batterie ständig neu geladen werden, damit sie Leistung und Anziehungskraft abgeben kann (vgl. *Bieger* 2006b, S. 188f.; vgl. *Baumgarth* 2004, S. 160). Weiterhin sind die Glaubwürdigkeit, Loyalität und Sympathie einer Marke von besonderer Bedeutung (vgl. *Linxweiler* 2004, S. 78). Ein hohes finanzielles Budget ist, vor dem Hintergrund, dass der Markenaufbau und die daran anschließende Markenpflege sowie eine langfristige Kommunikationspolitik sehr kostenintensiv sind, unerlässlich (vgl. *Bieger* 1998, S. 305). Insbesondere die Kommunikation ist hier sehr wichtig, da dadurch in den Köpfen der Konsumenten, Gäste etc. konkrete Assoziationen hervorgerufen werden (vgl. *Bieger* 2006b, S. 188). Erst wenn die Marke in das Bewusstsein der Menschen eingedrungen ist, kann eine Markenloyalität und -treue initiiert werden (vgl. *Aaker* 1992, S. 57f.).

7 Touristische Marken

Die Erscheinungsformen aus dem Konsumgüterbereich können aufgrund der Intangibiltät und aufgrund des Uno-Actu-Prinzips, das bei Dienstleistungen vorherrscht, nicht identisch auf touristische Leistungen transferiert werden. Weiterhin herrscht im konsumtiven Bereich meist eine klare Trennung von Marke, Hersteller und Vertrieb, während es bei Tourismusmarken haufig zu Überschneidungen, z. B. bei Hersteller und Vertrieb, kommt. So werden z. B. Leistungen des Reiseveranstalters TUI auch über TUI-Reisebüros vertrieben. Darüber hinaus kann im touristischen Bereich eine Untergliederung in weitere Markenformen vorgenommen werden. So gibt es z. B. Beherbergungsmarken wie die Sterne-Klassifikation des Deutschen Hotel- und Gaststättenverbandes, die die Qualität der Übernachtung und die Ausstattung der Unterkunft kennzeichnet oder aber Destinationsmarken, die die Qualität der Ausstattung der Destination charakterisieren (vgl. *Freyer* 1997, S. 159ff.).

Die Markenbildung und –positionierung ist in touristischen Bereichen wie der Hotellerie, bei Airlines oder Reiseveranstaltern ausgeprägter, fortgeschrittener und weit verbreiteter als bei Destinationsmarken (vgl. *Freyer* & *Dreyer* 2004, S. 85; vgl. *Steinecke* 2001, S.10). Bereits 1991 wandte TUI als erster touristischer Konzern ein einheitliches Markenkonzept über die gesamte Wertschöpfungskette an (vgl. De *Vries* 1999 S. 255) und fasste die Unternehmen Scharnow, Dr. Tigges, Hummel und Touropa zu einer übergreifenden Dachmarke zusammen. Eine Markenpolitik verfolgen seit Mitte der 1990er Jahre auch die Reiseveranstalter Neckermann, Thomas Cook und REWE Touristik. In den letzten Jahren ist zu beobachten, dass immer mehr touristische Unternehmen ihre Leistungen mit Hilfe der Markenpolitik auf dem Markt anpreisen. Dies ist u.a. auf den Qualitätstrend zurückzuführen. Interessant ist hierbei, dass die Markenbildung früher v.a. bei qualitativ hochwertigen Produkten angewandt wurde, während heute zu beobachten ist, dass auch Qualitätsversprechen auf einem niedrigeren Leistungsniveau oder einem eingeschrankten Leistungsumfang eingegangen werden. Ein Beispiel dieser Markenbildung stellen „no frills"-airlines wie Ryanair dar (vgl. *Freyer* & *Dreyer* 2004, S. 85). Diese Entwicklung ist darauf zurückzuführen, dass der Tourismusmarkt in ein oberes, mittleres und unteres Marktsegment differenziert werden kann. In den oberen und unteren Bereichen ist ein Aufbau starker Marken möglich. Dabei wird der obere Markt von qualitätsorientierten Leistungen mit Zusatznutzen beherrscht und der untere Markt kennzeichnet sich durch preisorientierte Leistungen mit einem Grundnutzen. Im mittleren Marktsegment ist keine eindeutige Positionierung möglich, da für den Kunden kein Qualitäts- oder Preisvorteil erkennbar ist (vgl. *Haedrich* 2001, S. 45; vgl. *Haedrich* 2004, S. 224f.).

7.1 Dachmarken als Positionierungsmerkmal von Destinationen

Die Schweizer Arbeitsgruppe „Neue Strukturen im Schweizer Tourismus“ erarbeitete fünf Minimalkriterien, die funktionsfähige Destinationen von anderen abgrenzen. Dazu gehört u. a., dass diese eine eigene Marke führen sollte. Ist dies jedoch noch nicht gegeben, so sollten zumindest positive Voraussetzungen, z. B. bekannte Sehenswürdigkeiten oder landwirtschaftliche Produkte bestehen, die eine Markenbildung begünstigen. Die weiteren Kriterien beziehen sich auf Angebot, Abgrenzbarkeit und Distributionsmöglichkeiten und bleiben an dieser Stelle unbetrachtet (vgl. *Arbeitsgruppe Schweizer Tourismusdirektoren* 1998, S. 16ff.).

Aufgrund der dargestellten Veränderungen ist es unerlässlich, das sektorale Denken abzulegen und umfassendere Tourismusprodukte zu entwickeln sowie sich in Richtung effizienterer und effektiverer Destinationsmanagement-Formen zu orientieren. Daraus resultiert, dass sich insbesondere kleinere Destinationen mit geringer finanzieller und personeller Ausstattung dazu entschließen der Marke der jeweiligen Region anzuschließen bzw. eine eigene Markenstrategie zu verfolgen (vgl. *Bieger* 2006b, S. 189; vgl. *Steinecke* 2001, S. 20ff.).

Dabei besteht die primäre Aufgabe in der Bündelung des regionalen Erlebnischarakters (vgl. *Luft* 2005, S. 66). Somit kann die Definition des allgemeinen Markenbegriffes bei Regionen um diese Dimension erweitert werden. Nach *Ritchie* & *Ritchie* (1998, S. 103) lässt sich folgende Definition ableiten:

„A Destination Brand is a name, symbol, logo, word mark or other graphic that both identifies and differentiates the destination; furthermore it conveys with the promise of a memorable travel experience that is uniquely associated with the destination; it also serves to consolidate and reinforce the recollection of pleasurable memories of the destination experience”.

Weiterhin soll ein weiträumiger, einprägsamer Imagetransfer ausgelöst werden (vgl. *Luft* 2005, S. 66) und das Urlaubserlebnis durch die Marke auch nach der Reise in den Köpfen der Gäste verfestigt werden (vgl. *Scherhag* 2003, S. 44). Jedoch nur wenige Regionen haben es bisher geschafft das Thema der Markenbildung erfolgreich umzusetzen. Dies ist nicht zuletzt auf eine problematische Markenbildung im Tourismus zurückzuführen. Die Herausforderungen und Stolpersteine werden nachfolgend näher erläutert (vgl. *Steinecke* 2001, S. 20ff.).

7.2 Herausforderungen und Stolpersteine des Markenmanagements von Destinationen

Die Bildung und Führung von Destinationsmarken unterscheidet sich erheblich von dem Prozess bei Konsumgütermarken, denn hier können besondere Probleme während des Markenmanagements auftreten. Ein Stolperstein besteht darin, dass das Destinationsprodukt aus vielfältigen und heterogenen Teilleistungen zusammengesetzt wird. Dabei werden die Komponenten mehrerer Wertschöpfungsstufen in einem koordiniertem Abstimmungsprozess zu einer gesamten Leistung gebündelt (vgl. *Adjouri* & *Büttner* 2008, S. 117). Weiterhin sind bei der touristischen Markenbildung verschiedene Interessensgruppen und Unternehmen beteiligt, die es aufeinander abzustimmen gilt und deren Einzelleistungen koordiniert und aufeinander abgestimmt werden müssen. Voraussetzung für ein erfolgreiches Markenmanagement ist daher eine übergeordnete und destinationsweit agierende Organisation, die auch über ein hohes Maß an Flexibilität sowie entsprechende Kompetenzen verfügt, um die Maßnahmen durchsetzen zu können (vgl. *Scherhag* 2000, S. 150ff.). Auch hier ist wie im Konsumgüterbereich für das Markenmanagement ein hohes finanzielles Budget notwendig (vgl. *Arnold* 1992, S. 27). Dies ist jedoch aufgrund der räumlichen Zersplitterung nicht immer gegeben, da häufig finanzielle Restriktionen vorherrschen und das Budget begrenzt ist (vgl. *Bleile* 2000, S. 5).

Als problematisch erweist sich beim Markenmanagement auch, dass sich touristische Regionen nicht selten an den kommunalen Grenzen und politischen Verwaltungseinheiten, z. B. Bundesländern, orientieren und dabei nicht beachten, dass diese Grenzen für den Gast irrelevant sind, da hier meist Naturräume oder ein individuelles Vorstellungsbild in den Köpfen verankert ist. Außerdem stehen Destinationen in Konkurrenz zueinander und legen bei ihrer Arbeit ein sogenanntes „Kirchturmdenken" an den Tag. Ebenso ist auch eine mangelnde Professionalität von Leistungsträgern, eine zu starke Politisierung des Tourismus sowie das Fehlen von Kontroll- und Sanktionsmöglichkeiten zu beklagen. Gründe wie eine mangelnde Marktorientierung, ein nicht immer kontinuierliches Qualitätsniveau und unzureichende Kenntnisse über die jeweiligen Konkurrenten, den Markt oder die Gäste sollen an dieser Stelle nicht unerwähnt bleiben. Ein weiterer Aspekt, der eine Markenbildung erschwert, ist, dass nur wenige Ferienregionen auch über einzigartige Produkte verfügen, die sie von den Mitbewerbern abheben. Außerdem kann ein Erfolg nur dann gewährleistet sein, wenn sich auch die lokale Bevölkerung mit dieser identifiziert und einer Zusammenarbeit zustimmt (vgl. *Steinecke* 2001, S. 12ff.; vgl. *Scherhag* & *Schneider* 1998, S. 10).

7.3 Marken-Design im Tourismus

Der Begriff Marken-Design charakterisiert die Gestaltung der Marke mit allen marketingpolitischen Instrumenten von der Konzeption, Planung, Kommunikation, Durchführung der Vermarktung, Distribution bis hin zum Service etc. Die Instrumente können zu einem wahrnehmbaren Markenerlebnis und somit auch entscheidend zum Unternehmenserfolg beitragen (vgl. *Linxweiler* 2004, S. 140). Das Marken-Design transferiert die unternehmerischen Visionen, Ziele und Philosophie in optische und sich wiederholende Gestaltungselemente, die sich in dem Bewusstsein der wahrnehmenden Personen festsetzen und automatisch in Verbindung mit dem jeweiligen Unternehmen gebracht werden (vgl. *Freyer* 2000, S. 349; vgl. *Linxweiler* 2001, S. 76). Eine effektive Markengestaltung beinhaltet daher nicht nur das Produkt oder die Leistung, sondern auch das Konzept, die Vorstellung und das Gefühl. Das Ziel besteht also darin gegenüber den Konkurrenten ein klares, einzigartiges sowie attraktives Bild der Markeninhalte zu liefern (vgl. *Linxweiler* 2004, S. 15ff.; vgl. *Becker* 2005, S. 577; vgl. *Swoboda & Giersch* 2007, S. 11). Zu einem konsistenten Marken-Design zählen einheitlich verwendete Elemente wie Logo, Name und Slogan (vgl. *Swoboda & Giersch* 2007, S. 11). Essentiell für den Erfolg ist, dass die Elemente über eine große Wiedererkennbarkeit und eine Akzeptanz bei den jeweiligen Zielgruppen verfügen (vgl. *Bieger* 2006, S. 1189).

Logo

Das Design des Logos sollte das Markenangebot charakterisieren. Das Kennzeichnungselement ist dann einprägsam für die Gäste, wenn eine konkrete und kennzeichnende Gestaltung vorliegt. Beliebte und einprägsame touristische Logos sind beispielsweise Bauwerke oder Sehenswürdigkeiten (vgl. *Luft* 2005, S. 66; S. 220f.; vgl. *Konken* 2004, S. 329; vgl. *Freyer* 1997, S. 177).

Name

Bei vielen erfolgreichen touristischen Marken kommt nicht selten der Name des jeweiligen Unternehmensgründers zum Einsatz, z. B. Marriott-Hotel. Weiterhin werden auch Bezeichnungen nach dem Standort oder der Herkunft des Unternehmens, z. B. Air France oder aber die Kennzeichnung einer bestimmten Angebotsform, wie z. B. Inter Rail-Ticket angewandt (vgl. *Ferner & Pötsch* 1998, S. 36). Beliebt sind aber auch Phantasienamen, z. B. Phantasialand oder Robinson Club (vgl. *Meffert & Bruhn* 2006, S. 221).

Bei Destinationen bewirken Markennamen, dass die Gäste glauben, dass diese ein besseres Image als die Wettbewerber besitzen, woraus ein Prozess der Vertrauensbildung resultiert und die Basis für eine erfolgreiche Positionierung am Markt geschaffen wird. Die Namensbildung ist meist an den realen, bereits vorhandenen Namen der Regionen gebunden (vgl. *Keller* 2003, S. 30) und ist daher im Sinne des Markenrechts nicht schützbar (vgl. *Zentek* 1999, S. 61). Ein Nachteil besteht bei Namen, die negative Assoziationen hervorrufen können, z. B. Elend in Sachsen-Anhalt (vgl. *Adjouri & Büttner* 2008, S. 125f.).

Slogan

Nur selten liefert der Name einer Destination auch einen adäquaten Beitrag zur Beschreibung des Landschaftsraumes bzw. Angebotes und es ist daher nicht immer möglich die Attraktivität einer Region auszudrücken. Häufig werden Slogans zur näheren Charakterisierung des Leistungsangebotes verwendet und nehmen auf diese Weise Einfluss auf die Reiseentscheidung der Gäste. So wirbt bspw. die Eifel mit dem Slogan „Eifel – Qualität ist unsere Natur“. Bei der Formulierung des Slogans sollte jedoch darauf verzichtet werden allgemeingültige und unwirksame Zusätze wie „wunderschön“ zu verwenden. Ebenso sind Zusätze mit einseitiger Ausrichtung, wie „Einkaufsstadt“, nicht unbedingt vorteilhaft, da nur ausgewählte Angebotselemente dargestellt werden. Auf die Nutzung eines Slogans sollte dann verzichtet werden, wenn keine sinnvolle Ergänzung gefunden wird (vgl. *Luft* 2005, S. 66 & S. 220f.; vgl. *Konken* 2004, S. 329).

8 Definitorische Abgrenzungen und theoretische Bezugsrahmen zur Regionalmarkenthematik

Unter dem Begriff Region ist ein gekennzeichnetes, größeres Gebiet zu verstehen, dass aufgrund bestimmter homogener Kriterien, z. B. Geographie, Politik, Klima, Kultur etc. eine Einheit bildet. Hier stellt die innere Homogenität ein Abgrenzungsmerkmal zu anderen Regionen dar (vgl. *Hausladen* & *Heil* 2001, S. 5). *Balderjahn* (1995, S. 1) bezeichnet Regionen als „historisch gewachsene Einheiten, kulturell und wirtschaftlich verflochtene geographische Räume, die sich auch unabhängig von Landes-, Kreis- und Stadtgrenzen herausbilden und Bestand haben“. Demnach sind Regionen nicht exakt abgrenzbare und bestimmbare Territorien sind, sondern vielmehr durch Aktivitäten, Interessen, Investitionen sowie die Kultur der dort lebenden und arbeitenden Menschen entstehen. Ebenso werden sie von vorgegebenen und nicht veränderbaren Einflußgrößen, z. B. Lage etc. geprägt (vgl. *Slapa* et al. 2000, S. 5).

Auch bei Regionen wird Marketing betrieben. Der dynamische Ansatz des Regionalmarketings ist „ein marktorientiertes Steuerungsinstrument zur Entwicklung von Regionen“ (vgl. *Meyer* 1999, S. 19). Der Prozess beinhaltet neben der Entwicklung die Planung und Umsetzung von Strategien, die der Vermarktung regionaler Standorte dienen (vgl. *Hammann* 1995, S. 1167). Das primäre Ziel besteht in der Stärkung der Attraktivität einzelner Standorte für externe Zielgruppen wie potentielle Investoren, Touristen, übergeordnete poltitische Organisationen, Politiker, überregionale Medien etc. Es wird aber auch eine interne Stärkung des regionalen Bewusstseins angestrebt. Dabei stehen v. a. Unternehmen, die ansässigen Bürger, Organisationen, politische Institutionen, Verbände und Medien der Region im Vordergrund (vgl. *Wolf* 2002, S. 10; vgl. *Fehn* & *Vossen* 1999, S. 29; vgl. *Slapa* et al. 2000, S. 9). Regionalmarketing ist dann erfolgreich, wenn sich die Region konkret von anderen abgrenzen kann (vgl. *Konken* 2004, S. 76).

Bei diesem Marketingansatz stellen Regionalmarken einen wichtigen Aspekt dar (vgl. *Niedner* 1994, S. 1652). Der angestrebte Wettbewerbsvorteil besteht dabei in einer Differenzierung durch lokal erzeugte Leistungen oder Produkte, die durch die Regionalität einen Zusatznutzen für den Verbraucher stiften (vgl. *Porter* 1999, S. 37ff.). Das entscheidende Kaufkriterium stellt die Qualität dar, denn Regionalprodukte und -leistungen sind Premiumprodukte und -leistungen, die nach besonderen Richtlinien erzeugt und erstellt werden. Daraus resultieren höhere Produktionskosten für den Anbieter und weiterführend höhere Preise für den Konsumenten. Aufgrund dessen wird auch seitens der Verbraucher ein entsprechender immaterieller Zusatznutzen, z. B. beim Geschmack oder das Gefühl, etwas Gutes zu tun etc. erwartet. (vgl. *Kullmann* 2007, S. 32ff.; vgl. *Dehne* 2002, S. 9). Die damit verbundene Einmaligkeit ermöglicht es dem Anbieter aufgrund einer niedrigeren Preisempfindlichkeit der Konsumenten einen höheren Ertrag zu erzielen und den Abnehmer an die Marke zu binden. Darüber hinaus werden für die Konkurrenten durch die Einzigartigkeit der Produkte bzw. Leistungen Eintrittsbarrieren geschaffen (vgl. *Porter* 1999, S. 37ff.).

Um eine erfolgreiche Regionalmarke implementieren und auch langfristig erfolgreich führen zu können, sollte eine Region zunächst eine ausgeprägte Marketingkompetenz bei den Akteuren aufweisen können. Dazu zählt u.a. die Fähigkeit, Marketingstrategien formulieren zu können, die sich von den Wettbewerbern unterscheiden. Weiterhin sollte die Region über eine breite und qualitativ hochwertige Produkt- und Leistungspalette verfügen. Hier ist es wichtig, dass besondere Produktionsrichtlinien definiert werden und die Mindestanforderungen auch mit Hilfe eines effektiven Kontrollsystems überwacht werden. Der Vertrieb regionaler landwirtschaftlicher Produkte wird meist über Bauern- und Hofläden organisiert, aber auch die Gastronomie von Tourismusregionen sowie der Einzelhandel stellen wichtige Distributionskanäle für regionale Produkte dar. Weiterhin ist es wichtig, dass neben einem positiven regionalen Image auch eine bestimmte Kaufkraft bei Einwohnern und Touristen erreicht wird. Die Abgrenzung der Region sollte beim Markenansatz mit den landschaftlichen, kulturhistorischen und sozioökonomischen Grenzen der Einwohner und Zielgruppen übereinstimmen und sich nicht an politischen Räumen orientieren. Von besonderer Bedeutung sind auch ein abnehmergerechtes Preis-Leistungsverhältnis sowie eine professionelle Kommunikationspolitk (vgl. *Dehne* 2002, S. 9ff.).

9 Die Eifel – Portrait einer Destination

Die Eifel erstreckt sich über die beiden Bundesländer Nordrhein-Westfalen und Rheinland-Pfalz sowie über Ostbelgien und Luxomburg. Im Norden wird die Eifel durch die Maas und die Niederrheinische Bucht, im Osten durch das Mittelrheintal, im Süden vom Moseltal und im Westen durch die Landesgrenze begrenzt. Aus naturräumlicher Sicht betrachtet ist das Mittelgebirge durch verschiedene, mannigfaltige und kontrastreiche Landschaften gekennzeichnet. Bereits in den 1950er Jahren war die Eifel, auch bekannt als „Das Grüne Herz Europas", aufgrund der Nähe zu den Großstädten und Industriegebieten an Rhein und Ruhr sowie nahe der Zechen von Lüttich, Charleroi und Esch eine beliebte Erholungslandschaft (vgl. *Schramm* 1963, S. 9f.). In den 1960er Jahren setzte ein agrarstruktureller Wandel ein, der dazu führte, dass es zu einer räumlichen Verflechtung mit den nahe gelegenen städtischen Zentren kam. Diese boten neue Arbeitsplätze mit besseren Verdienstmöglichkeiten. Die Reduzierung der Agrarwirtschaft stellte eine Chance für den Tourismus in der Eifel dar (vgl. *Erdmann* 1998, S. 41f.). Zu den touristischen Attraktionspunkten zählen u. a. die Maare in der Vulkaneifel, die Moorlandschaft Hohes Venn, eine vielfaltige Flora und Fauna, mächtige Eifelburgen sowie Klöster (vgl. *Schramm* 1963, S. 10). Weiterhin gelten die Ebenheiten der Westeifel, die Täler der Our und Rur oder historische Stadtbilder wie in Monschau sowie Teile des Bitburger Gutlandes als touristisch sehr interessant (vgl. *Christians* 1998, S. 31).

Die zentrale touristische Dachorganisation stellt die Eifel Tourismus GmbH dar. Diese verfolgt primär das Ziel der regionalen Tourismusförderung. Konkrete Aufgaben bilden diverse Marketingaktivitäten (z. B. Prospektwerbung, Messebesuche, etc.), die Produktentwicklung, die Reisevermittlung und –buchung etc. In den Kompetenzbereich fallen ebenfalls sämtliche Aufgaben im Rahmen der touristischen Dienstleistungen der Regionalmarke EIFEL.

Die wichtigsten touristischen Kennzahlen bestätigen den Erfolg der Arbeit der Eifel Tourismus GmbH sowie untergeordneter touristischer Verkehrsämter und Tourist-Informationen. So besuchten im Jahr 2007 rund 45,7 Tagestouristen und mehr als 1,3 Mio. Gäste (mit mehr als 4,5 Mio. Übernachtungen) die Eifel. Dabei lag der Schwerpunkt der Reisenden mit über 830.000 Ankünften und 3,1 Mio. Übernachtungen in der rheinland-pfälzischen Eifel. Die tourismusbedingten Bruttoumsätze lagen bei insgesamt ca. 338.117.000 €. Daraus resultieren eifelweit Nettoumsätze von rund 303.543.500 € (vgl. *Regionalmarke Eifel GmbH* 2008, o. S., vgl. *Eifel Tourismus GmbH* 2008, o. S.).

10 Regionalmarke EIFEL

„Ein gutes Zeichen, wenn das Einfache wieder zum Besonderen wird."

(vgl. *Regionalmarke Eifel* o. J.)

Diese Philosophie steht hinter der Regionalmarke EIFEL, deren Geburtsstunde im Jahr 2001 liegt. Damals initiierte das Bundesministerium für Verbraucherschutz, Ernährung und Landwirtschaft den regionalen Wettbewerb „REGIONEN AKTIV – Land gestaltet Zukunft". Damit verbunden war eine finanzielle Förderung von 2002 bis 2007. Das primäre Ziel bestand darin, den ländlichen Raum durch innovative und neue Perspektiven zu stärken und eine höhere Wertschöpfung zu erreichen. Hier wurde insbesondere auch das Schaffen neuer Einkommensquellen angestrebt. Weiterhin stand auch eine verbraucherorientierte und umweltfreundliche Lebensmittelerzeugung und Landbewirtschaftung sowie eine Stärkung der Beziehung zwischen Stadt und Land im Vordergrund (vgl. *Regionen Aktiv* 2008a, o. S.; vgl. *Hannemann* 2003, S. 3; vgl. *Hannemann, Popp* 2005, S. 2).

Bundesweit wurden von über 200 Bewerbern insgesamt 18 Modellregionen anhand der regionalen Entwicklungskonzepte ausgewählt, darunter auch der Eifelkreis Bitburg-Prüm mit dem Naturpark Südeifel (vgl. *Regionen Aktiv* 2008a, o. S.; vgl. *Widera & Hannemann* 2004, S. 100; vgl. *Hannemann* 2003, S. 3). Die regionalen Schwächen liegen hier in dem verschärften drastischen landwirtschaftlichen Strukturwandel, mit dem auch ein Rückgang der Beschäftigungszahlen einhergeht sowie in der schlechten Verkehrsanbindung. Dem gegenüber stehen Stärken wie ein hoher Imagewert, die Nähe zu den Niederlanden, Belgien und Luxemburg sowie Kooperationen zwischen Landwirtschaft, Handel und Tourismus (vgl. *Regionen Aktiv* 2008a, o. S.).

Das Dachmarkenkonzept der Regionalmarke EIFEL wurde 2004 gegründet und gilt als Qualitätszertifikat für hochwertige regionale Produkte und touristische Dienstleistungen (vgl. *Popp* 2004, S. 4; vgl. *Regionen Aktiv* 2008a, o. S.). Dieses Vorhaben sollte grenzüberschreitend umgesetzt werden. Die Modellregion wird dabei in Rheinland-Pfalz im Süden durch das Moseltal, im

Osten durch das Rheintal und im Westen durch die luxemburgischen und belgischen Staatsgrenzen begrenzt. Dem Norden sind die nordrhein-westfälischen Gemeinden Bad Münstereifel, Mechernich, Kall, Schleiden, Hellenthal, Dahlem, Blankenheim und Nettersheim des Kreises Euskirchen und die Gemeinden Heimbach, Hürtgenwald, Nideggen, Kreuzau und Vettweis des Kreises Düren sowie die Gemeinden Monschau, Roetgen, Simmerath und Stolberg des Kreises Aachen und die Städte Rheinbach und Meckenheim des Kreises Rhein-Sieg zugehörig (vgl. *Regionalmarke Eifel GmbH* 2008, o. S.; vgl. *Widera & Hannemann* 2004, S. 101).

10.1 Ziele und Nutzen Eifeler Qualitätsprodukte und -dienstleistungen

Mit der Schaffung und Umsetzung der Regionalmarke EIFEL werden diverse Zielsetzungen verfolgt. Das Markenkonzept strebt u.a. das Ziel an, die attraktiven sowie traditionell gewachsenen Kultur- und Urlaubslandschaften durch die Gewährleistung einer naturrelevanten Bewirtschaftung und Verarbeitung zu erhalten. Dadurch kann insbesondere die Wettbewerbsfähigkeit der landwirtschaftlichen, handwerklichen und touristischen Betriebe im Klein- und Mittelstand erhalten werden. Ebenso ist es möglich, regionale Arbeitsplätze sowie Steuereinnahmen zu wahren bzw. zu sichern. Die Intention der Anbieter und Dienstleister der qualitativ hochwertigen Produkte und Leistungen besteht darin, den zunehmend qualitatsorientierten Erwartungen sowie dem Verlangen nach nachvollziehbaren Herkunftsgarantien gerecht zu werden und somit zusätzliche Erwartungen zu erfüllen. Daraus ergibt sich für sie eine Möglichkeit, die Leistungen und Produkte durch Kooperationen besser am Markt zu positionieren und die Wertschöpfung auf allen Erzeuger- und Verarbeitungsebenen zu steigern, denn Kunden und Gäste sind dazu bereit einen höheren Preis, der sich aufgrund eines Zusatznutzens, wie z. B. hohe Qualität, Erlebniselemente, Genuss, kontrollierte Transparenz etc. rechtfertigt und so einen Mehrwert gegenüber dem eigentlichen Grundnutzen, z. B. Erholung oder Ernährung, darstellt, zu zahlen (vgl. *Hannemann* 2006, S. 6; vgl. *Eifel Tourismus GmbH* 2007a, S. 10; vgl. *Popp* 2004, S. 4). Weiterhin soll die Regionalmarke dazu beitragen, dass die Bewohner stärker für eine Identifizierung mit ihrer Region sensibilisiert werden und ein „Wir-Gefühl" aufbauen. Ohne deren Kooperation und Akzeptanz ist der Erfolg nicht gewährleistet (vgl. *Regionalmarke Eifel GmbH* 2007c, S. 2). Demnach wird mit der Markenbildung in der Eifel eine gemeinsame Identifikation sowie ein gemeinsames Dach für vielfältige zukunftsorientierte Kooperationen angestrebt (vgl. *Hannemann* 2003, S. 3).

10.2 Markenmanagement - Von der Idee, Umsetzung und Organisation

Das Markenmanagement der Regionalmarke EIFEL wurde von der Idee bis zur Umsetzung von der Umwelt-, Tourismus- und Regionalberatung FUTOUR GmbH & Co. KG in München begleitet. Die erste Phase umfasste die Grundlagen der typischen Markenbildung, die von einem einheitlichen Markenauftritt,

-schutz, -präambel, -nutzungsordnung und -verträgen bis hin zu vorläufigen Lizenzgebühren reichten. Der festgelegte Markenkern der Produkte und Dienstleistungen besteht aus den Werten der Qualitätsgarantie, einer kontrollierten Transparenz in der gesamten Produktions- bzw. Dienstleistungskette sowie der regionalen Herkunft. In der zweiten Phase wurden die Kriterien und Mindestanforderungen für die Produkte und Dienstleistungen festgelegt. Danach erfolgte die Markteinführung und der Aufbau zentraler Vermarktungs- und Vertriebsstrukturen sowie eine daran angeschlossene umfassende produktunabhängige Bewusstseinskampagne zur Markenpositionierung (vgl. *Hannemann* 2006, S. 6, vgl. *Regionalmarke Eifel GmbH* 2007, S. 2ff.).

Geführt und getragen wird die Marke von dem Markengeber Naturpark Süd-Eifel. Dieser gründete die Regionale Entwicklungsgruppe, die aus rund 30 Institutionen des ländlichen Raums (u. a. aus Land- und Forstwirtschaft, Tourismus, Naturschutz, Handel, Verbraucherschutz, Bildung) besteht und sich um alle Grundsatzentscheidungen für den Markenaufbau und die –weiterentwicklung kümmert. Als Markennehmer wurde die Regionalmarke EIFEL GmbH mit Zuständigkeitsbereichen wie operatives Geschäft, Marketing und Vertrieb sowie Abwicklung der Markennutzungsverträge gegründet. Als Gesellschafter der Organisation gelten zu je 25% der Kreisbauernverband Bitburg-Prüm, die Kreishandwerkerschaften Mosel und Hunsrück-Region sowie die Eifel Tourismus GmbH. Zu je 12,5% sind der Naturpark Südeifel e. V. und der Naturpark Nordeifel e. V. beteiligt (vgl. *Regionalmarke Eifel GmbH* 2007, S. 6ff.). Dadurch sind mit den Organisationen aus Landwirtschaft, Handwerk, Tourismus und Naturschutz alle wichtigen Säulen des ländlichen Raumes vertreten (vgl. *Regionalmarke Eifel GmbH* 2008, o. S.).

Markennutzer können Erzeuger und Verarbeiter aus dem land- und forstwirtschaftlichem Gewerbe sowie Anbieter touristischer Dienstleistungen werden. Dafür wird zwischen dem Nutzer und der Regionalmarke EIFEL GmbH ein Markennutzungsvertrag abgeschlossen. Voraussetzung ist dabei, dass die definierten Qualitätskriterien für die jeweiligen Produkte oder Dienstleistungen zu erfüllen sind. Die entsprechenden Ziele und die dahinter stehende Philosophie sind in einer Markenpräambel verankert. Die Markennutzer sind dazu verpflichtet sich einer Prüfgemeinschaft anzuschließen, die jährlich die Kontrollen für den Bereich durchführt und die Ergebnisse dokumentiert (vgl. *Regionalmarke Eifel GmbH* 2007, S. 2ff.).

10.3 Finanzierung

Regionalmarken finanzieren sich zu Beginn primär durch staatliche oder andere externe Förderungen, z. B. durch Agrarbehörden, Naturschutzverbände, Stiftungen, Sponsoring etc. (vgl. *Dehne* 2002, S. 17). Noch bis 2011 hat die Regionalmarke EIFEL Zeit sich ökonomisch zu profilieren. Danach entfällt die Förderung durch Drittmittel aus den beteiligten Ländern, Kreisen und Kommunen (vgl. *Hannemann* 2006, S. 6). Die Marke finanziert sich bis dato außerdem durch die Mitgliedsbeiträge, Lizenzgebühren, Umsatzprovision etc. der Markennutzer (vgl. *Dehne* 2002, S. 17). Die Höhe der Gebühren richtet sich bei den Produkten nach dem Umsatzvolumen (vgl. *Popp* 2007, S. 128) und im touristischen Bereich nach der Bettenanzahl (vgl. *Qualitätsoffensive Eife*l 2008, S. 1).

10.4 Marketing-Mix

Die Marketingaktivitäten der Regionalmarke EIFEL gliedern sich in die vier Marketingfelder Kommunikations-, Produkt-, Preis- und Distributionspolitik und finanzieren sich über die soeben erläuterten Markennutzungsgebühren.

Produktpolitik

Die Regionale Entwicklungsgruppe definiert und beschließt die Qualitätskriterien für die Produkte und Dienstleistungen. Die Vorarbeit sowie Vorschläge dafür werden von den Mitgliedern der branchenbezogenen Qualitätsausschüsse geleistet (vgl. *Regionalmarke Eifel GmbH* 2007, S. 16). In den Kriterienkatalogen wird definiert, welche Bedingungen zu erfüllen sind. Die Markennutzer sind dazu verpflichtet sich der jeweiligen Prüfgemeinschaft anzuschließen, die jährlich die Mindestanforderungen kontrolliert (vgl. *Regionalmarke Eifel GmbH* 2008, o. S.).

Kommunikationspolitik

Während der Einführungsphase bestand das primäre Ziel darin die Markenwerte und -philosophie zu kommunizieren sowie die Produkte und Leistungen zu positonieren. Die Produkte werden z. B. auf Veranstaltungen, Messen, Events, Wochenmärkten und bei Gastronomieaktionen beworben (vgl. *Eifel Tourismus GmbH* 2007a, S. 19). Weiterhin werden in regelmäßigen Abständen aktuelle Presseartikel in diversen Print- sowie Online-Medien zu aktuellen Themen veröffentlicht (vgl. *Regionalmarke Eifel GmbH* 2007, o. S.).

Eine besondere Bedeutung kommt der Präsenz im Internet zu, denn neben der Darstellung auf der Homepage www.regionalmarke-eifel.de sind die Markennutzer auch dazu berechtigt auf Partnerplattformen, z. B. den Homepages der Eifel Tourismus GmbH, des Deutschen Tourismusverbandes oder der Straße der Römer, zu werben. So genießen die zertifizierten touristischen Betriebe im Gegensatz zu den nicht-zertifizierten Betrieben einen Vorrang bei den Marketingmaßnahmen der Eifel Tourismus GmbH. Die Markennutzer werden dabei in diversen Medien besonders hervorgehoben (vgl. *Eifel Tourismus GmbH* 2007b, S. 2).

Vertriebspolitik

Die Produkte und Leistungen der Regionalmarke EIFEL kennzeichnen sich durch gemeinsame Qualitätskriterien, ein hochwertiges Erscheinungsbild der Produkte, die wiedererkennbare Gestaltung sowie eine gemeinsam abgestimmte Preispolitik. Dadurch ist eine Einheitlichkeit am Markt gewährleistet. Die zertifizierten Produkte werden über Handelsketten, auf Märkten und Veranstaltungen etc. an den Endkunden vertrieben. Eine weitere Vertriebssäule bilden der Handel und die Gastronomie. Hier verpflichten sich die Lizenznehmer, einen bestimmten Anteil der Produkte im Wareneinsatz zu verwenden. Außerdem bieten sie die Produkte zum Kauf an. Der Vertrieb der Tourismusleistungen erfolgt durch Eigenvertrieb oder über die lokalen Tourismusorganisation bzw. die Eifel Tourismus GmbH (vgl. *Regionalmarke Eifel GmbH* 2008, o. S.).

Preispolitik

Die qualitativ hochwertigen Produkte und Leistungen der Regionalmarke EIFEL werden im Höher- bis Hochpreissegment angeboten, da hier seitens der Konsumenten eine niedrigere Preisempfindlichkeit besteht. Weiterhin würde eine Positionierung im Niedrigpreissegment nicht mit den kommunizierten Markenwerten übereinstimmen und die landwirtschaftlichen Strukturen sind nicht auf eine Massenproduktion mit einer verbundenen Stückkostendegression ausgerichtet. Eine Stärkung des Wirtschaftsraumes ist nur möglich, wenn alle Beteiligten für ihre Leistungen einen fairen Mehrerlös erhalten. Damit diese Strategie langfristigen Erfolg hat, ist eine Abstimmung von Mindesterlösen ebenso wichtig wie die Bewahrung einer konstanten Preisstabilität und eine einheitliche Preispolitik gegenüber Handel und Gastronomie (vgl. *Regionalmarke Eifel GmbH* 2007, S. 18f.).

10.5 Co-Branding und Marketing-Kooperationen

Zahlreiche, bereits seit Jahren eigenständige, etablierte und sehr bekannte Eifeler Marken- Unternehmen – vorrangig aus der Lebensmittelbranche - unterstützen die Regionalmarke EIFEL und bilden tragende Säulen im Markenkonzept (vgl. *Regionalmarke Eifel GmbH* 2008, o. S.). Das Ziel des Co-Brandings besteht darin, durch einen gemeinsamen Auftritt die Potentiale auszuschöpfen und positive Synergieeffekte zu erzielen. Durch die Zusammenarbeit wird die Marke bekannter gemacht und kann somit auf weiteren Märkten neue Zielgruppen erschließen. Außerdem soll in den Bereichen Werbung, PR- und Öffentlichkeitsarbeit ein Beitrag für die Region geleistet werden und diese gestärkt werden. Zudem können im Distributions- und Kommunikationsbereich Kosten eingespart werden. Voraussetzung für ein erfolgreiches Co-Branding sind ähnliche Images und Markenkulturen (vgl. *Haedrich, Tomczak & Kaetzke* 2003, S. 134ff.).

Kooperationen von renommierten Betrieben mit der Regionalmarke EIFEL sind durchführbar, wenn eine Verbundenheit des jeweiligen Betriebes zur Eifel besteht, z. B. durch Schaffung und Erhalt regionaler Arbeitsplätze, Firmensitz in der Region oder eine Wertschöpfung in der Eifel vorhanden ist. Das EIFEL-Logo kann jedoch nur dann zu Marketingzwecken verwendet werden, wenn die notwendigen Mindestkriterien in dem jeweiligen Produkt- und / oder Leistungsbereich erfüllt werden. Als Beispiel für Co-Branding-Partner können Mineralwasserunternehmen wie Dauner Sprudel, Gerolsteiner Sprudel und Rhodius Mineralquellen genannt werden (vgl. *Eifel Tourismus GmbH* 2007a, S. 19; vgl. *Eifel Tourismus GmbH* 2007b, S.6; vgl. *Regionalmarke Eifel GmbH* 2008, o. S.).

10.6 Partnerschaften

Hinter der Regionalmarke EIFEL steht eine Strategie, die nicht nur beabsichtigt, starke regionale Produzenten als Kooperationspartner zu gewinnen, sondern die u.a. auch das Ziel verfolgt Institutionen, Behörden, Verbände und Vereine zu akquirieren. Diese Partner identifizieren sich mit der Philosophie sowie deren Zielen und haben eine unterstützende und fördernde Wirkung. Dadurch ist es den Partnern möglich für sich selbst und für die gesamte Region einen Vorteil zu erlangen. Zu den Partnern gehören Institutionen und Organisationen wie beispielsweise die einzelnen Stadt-, Verbandsgemeinde- bzw. Kreisverwaltungen sowie Sparkassen und Volksbanken. Komplettiert wird die Liste der Partner durch einzelne Institutionen, wie dem Trierischen Volksfreund oder dem Wochenspiegel (vgl. *Eifel Tourismus GmbH* 2007a, S. 10, vgl. *Regionalmarke Eifel GmbH* 2008, o. S.).

10.7 Produkte

Die Regionalmarke EIFEL umfasst ein breites Produktportfolio. Anfangs gehörten dazu auch Holzprodukte, z. B. Möbel aus zertifiziertem Eifel-Holz, die jedoch auf wenig Interesse stießen. Daher wurde die Serie wieder eingestellt. Im Bereich der Lebensmittel hingegen kam und kommt es zu kontinuierlichen Erweiterungen des Programms (vgl. *Regionen Aktiv* 2008b, S. 3). Die Produkte gliedern sich in 12 konventionelle Gruppen und 9 Bio-Produktgruppen. Dazu gehören Produkte wie Wurstwaren, Apfelsaft, Käse, Edelbrände, Honig etc. (vgl. *Regionalmarke Eifel GmbH* 2007, S. 17).

10.8 Touristische Dienstleistungen

Zu den touristischen Dienstleistungen, die sich mit der Regionalmarke EIFEL zertifizieren lassen können, zählen Ferienwohnungen und Pensionen sowie Hotelbetriebe. Auch hier sind Mindestanforderungen zu erfüllen (vgl. *Popp & Hannemann* 2005, S. 2ff.). Als essentielle Zugangsbedingung gilt dabei für alle Betriebe die Lage im Naturraum Eifel. Durch die Unterzeichnung der Markenpräambel verpflichten sich die Teilnehmer die Markenphilosophie und deren Zielen zu verfolgen. Die Ferienwohnungen und Privatzimmer müssen bei der Klassifizierung des Deutschen Tourismusverbandes mindestens drei Sterne erlangen. Dies gilt ebenso für die Hotellerie- und Gastronomiebetriebe, die durch den Deutschen Hotel- und Gaststättenverband klassifiziert werden. Bei rein gastronomischen Betrieben wird auch VIABONO-zertifizierten Betrieben eine Teilnahmemöglichkeit gegeben. Als weitere Voraussetzung gilt es die Anforderungen im Bereich der ServiceQualitat Deutschland zu erbringen. Darüber hinaus ist auch die Teilnahme an den Seminaren der Qualitätsoffensive EIFEL sowie Treffen zwecks Erfahrungsaustausch Pflicht (vgl. *Regionalmarke Eifel GmbH* o. J.a, o. S.; vgl. *Regionalmarke Eifel GmbH* 2008, o. S.).

Von den zertifizierten Betrieben wird gewünscht, dass sie die Corporate Identity in ihren Aktivitäten positionieren. Mit Hilfe von Kundenbewertungskarten werden aktuelle Trends und Gästebedürfnisse erfragt und es wird offen mit Lob und Kritik umgegangen. Weiterhin sollte in der hauseigenen Werbung auf die Mitgliedschaft hingewiesen werden und mit Hilfe von Gästemappen über Aspekte wie die Philosophie, Lieferanten und gastronomischen Betriebe informiert werden. Im Bereich der Hotellerie und Gaststätten zählt darüber hinaus als Kriterium die Ausstattung des Hauses mit einer Verkaufs- und Informationsecke über die Regionalmarke EIFEL. Bei kleineren Betrieben, in denen aufgrund der Betriebsgröße keine Präsentation möglich ist, sollten ein Informationsverweis und Bestellmöglichkeiten in der Gästemappe aufgeführt sein. Die zertifizierten Betriebe verpflichten sich weiterhin dazu, einen bestimmten Anteil regionaler Qualitätsprodukte in ihren Wareneinsatz zu integrieren und jährlich mindestens eine kulinarische Veranstaltung durchzuführen bzw. daran teilzunehmen (vgl. *Popp* 2004, S. 4; vgl. *Regionalmarke Eifel GmbH* o. J.a, o. S.). Durch diese Rahmenbedingungen wird den Gästen ein hohes Qualitätsniveau mit einem besonderen Service sowie regionaltypischer Küche als Erlebniselement geboten (vgl. *Popp & Hannemann* 2005, S. 1f.). Darüber hinaus wird eine Qualitätssicherung, z. B. durch Checklisten der hauseigenen Qualitätsanforderungen, durchgeführt. Im Bereich des Vertriebs ist es notwendig, dass der Betrieb dem Reservierungssystem der Eifel Tourismus GmbH angeschlossen ist. Nicht zuletzt verpflichten sich die teilnehmenden Betriebe dazu, sich aktiv in der touristischen Angebotsgruppe zu beteiligen und mit anderen Akteuren zu kooperieren. Die zu erfüllenden Anforderungen werden von einem Q-Teammitglied der dafür zuständigen Tourist-Information überprüft (vgl. *Regionalmarke Eifel GmbH* o. J.a, o. S.).

10.9 Aufgaben der Eifel Tourismus GmbH und der lokalen Tourist-Informationen im Markensystem

Die EIFEL Tourismus GmbH hat sich das Ziel gesetzt, die Qualitätsoffensive kontinuierlich weiterzuentwickeln und umzusetzen. Dabei wird die Organisation bei Aufgaben wie der Definition und Umsetzung der Qualitätskriterien, der Bildung und Schulung des Q-Teams, bei der Organisation der Zertifizierung der Betriebe sowie bei der Planung und Durchführung von Lehrfahrten und Weiterbildungsveranstaltungen für die Leistungsträger tätig (vgl. *Qualitätsoffensive Eifel* 2007, S. 5; vgl. *Eifel Tourismus GmbH* 2007b, S. 4).

Auch Vertreter der lokalen Tourist-Informationen nehmen in dem System eine wichtige Rolle ein, denn sie bilden gemeinsam mit Vertretern der Eifel Tourismus GmbH das Q-Team. Das Q-Team besitzt die Aufgabe das Regionenprofil in den einzelnen Themenbereichen durch eine permanente Weiterentwicklung zu schärfen. Dabei sind auch hier von den Mitgliedern bestimmte Kompetenzen zu erbringen. So ist neben einer kontinuierlichen sowie strukturierten Betriebsberatung und -betreuung auf partnerschaftlicher Ebene, die fachliche Kompenente sehr wichtig. Die Kenntnisse sollten dabei über eine Ausbildung zum Qualitätscoach über Grundkenntnisse der Dachmarke VIABONO und die Klassifizierungsysteme bis hin zu Kenntnissen über die festgelegten Kriterien der Marke EIFEL reichen. Weiterhin ist es wichtig, an den Q-Teamsitzungen teilzunehmen (vgl. *Qualitätsoffensive Eifel* 2007, S. 3f.).

11 Fazit

Der Aufsatz hat aufgezeigt, dass das moderne Markenwesen im Tourismus in Form von Destinations- und Regionalmarken im zunehmenden Wettbewerb ein potentielles Instrument darstellt, um sich gegenüber den Mitkonkurrenten mit Hilfe eines einzigartigen Profils effektiver und effizienter am Markt zu positionieren (vgl. *Irmscher* 1997, S. 30; vgl. *Becker* 1993, S. 162; vgl. *Adjouri* 1993, S. 100f.). Hier entsteht jedoch auch ein Vorteil für die Nachfrager (vgl. *Haedrich*, *Tomczak* & *Kaetzke* 2003, S. 23). Um erfolgreiches Markenmanagement zu betreiben, ist es notwendig, dass bestimmte Voraussetzungen erfüllt werden. Im touristischen Bereich ist die Markenbildung und -positionierung in anderen Bereichen wie Hotels oder Airlines ausgeprägter als bei Destinationen (vgl. *Freyer* & *Dreyer* 2004, S. 85). Dennoch sind sich die Verantwortlichen regionaler Organisationen durchaus bewusst, dass Marken eine hohe Bedeutung einnehmen (vgl. *Scherhag* 2000, S. 153). In diesem Zusammenhang und im Rahmen des 2001 gestarteten Modellvorhabens „REGIONEN AKTIV – Land gestaltet Zukunft" entstand die Regionalmarke EIFEL. Die Implementierung ist erfolgreich gelungen und die Eifel nimmt eine Vorreiterrolle bei der Postionierung von qualitativ hochwertigen Produkten und Dienstleistungen ein. Den Erfolg des Konzeptes haben bereits andere Wettbewerbsregionen, z. B. die Nachbarregion Mosel, erkannt und streben an, eine ähnliche Marke zu etablieren. Es bleibt also mit Spannung abzuwarten, wie sich die Regionalmarke EIFEL, insbesondere im touristischen Bereich, entwickeln wird.

Literaturverzeichnis

Aaker, David A. (1992): Management des Markenwerts. Frankfurt am Main

Adjouri, Nicholas (1993): Die Marke als Botschaft. Die kommunikative Funktion der Marke und ihre Interdependenzen zur Werbung. Berlin

Adjouri, Nicholas & *Tobias Büttner* (2008): Marken auf Reisen Erfolgsstrategien für Marken im Tourismus. Wiesbaden

Arnold, David (1992): Modernes Markenmanagement. Wien

Arbeitsgruppe Schweizer Tourismusdirektoren (1998): Neue Strukturen im Schweizer Tourismus – das Konzept. In: *Bieger, T.* & *C. Laesser* (Hrsg.): Neue Strukturen im Tourismus. – Der Weg der Schweiz. Bern / Stuttgart / Wien. S. 16-50

Balderjahn, Ingo (1995): Marketing für Regionen. Ein Konzept für die Neuen Bundesländer? Potsdam

Baumgarth, Carsten (2004): Markenpolitik. Markenwirkungen – Markenführung – Markencontrolling. 2., überarbeitete und erweiterte Auflage. Wiesbaden

Becker, Jochen (1993): Marketing-Konzeption. Grundlagen des strategischen Marketing-Managements. 5. verbesserte und ergänzte Auflage. München

Becker, Jochen (2005): Einzel-, Familien- und Dachmarken als grundlegende Handlungsoptionen. In: *Esch, Franz-Rudolf* (Hrsg.): Moderne Markenführung. Grundlagen –Innovative Ansätze – Praktische Umsetzungen. 4., vollständig überarbeitete und erweiterte Auflage. Wiesbaden. S. 381-402

Bieger, Thomas (1998): Dienstleistungsmanagement – Einführung in Strategien und Prozesse bei persönlichen Dienstleistungen. Mit Fallstudien verschiedener Praktiker. Bern/Stuttgart/Wien

Bieger, Thomas (2006): Management von Destinationen. 6., unwesentlich veränderte Auflage. Bern/Stuttgart/Wien

Bleile, Georg (2000): Management des Wandels – Plädoyer für eine neue Tourismusorganisation. Heft 4. Akademie für Touristik Freiburg. Schriftenreihe Tourismus. Freiburg

Bruhn, Manfred (1994): Begriffsabgrenzungen und Erscheinungsformen von Marken. In: *Bruhn, Manfred* (Hrsg.): Handbuch Markenartikel. Band 1. Stuttgart. S. 3-41

Bruhn, Manfred (2001): Begriffsabgrenzungen und Erscheinungsformen von Marken. In: Bruhn, Manfred (Hrsg.): Die Marke. Symbolkraft eines Zeichensystems. Bern/Stuttgart/Wien. S. 13-53

Chandler, Jon & *Mike Owen* (2002): Developing Brands with Qualitative Market Research. London

Christians, C. (1998): Von der Agrarlandschaft zur Erholungslandschaft. In: *Naturfreunde-Internationale* (Hrsg.): Landschaft ohne Grenzen Eifel-Ardennen. Geschichte – Kultur – Radtouren – Wanderungen. 2. Auflage. Köln/Bachem. S. 28-34

Dehne, Peter (2002): Regionale Entwicklungskonzepte – Begriffsbestimmung und Funktionen. In: *Keim, Karl-Dieter* & *Manfred Kühn* (Hrsg.): Regionale Strategien und Steuerungskonzepte. Arbeitsmaterial der Akademie für Raumforschung und Landesplanung. Nummer 287. Hannover. S. 24-33

Deichsel, Alexander (1998): Namensfindung und Namensgestaltung. In: *Tomczak, Torsten, Marcus Schögel* & *Eva Ludwig* (Hrsg.): Markenmanagement für Dienstleistungen. St. Gallen. S. 94-104

Dettmer, Harald (1998) (Hrsg): Tourismus-Marketing-Management. München/Wien.

De Vries, Jomique (1999): Marketing Joint Venture zur Ausdehnung der Markenpräsenz. In: *Bastian, Harald, Karl Born* & *Axel Dreyer* (Hrsg.): Kundenorientierung im Touristikmanagement. München/Wien. S. 245-262

Dichtl, Erwin (1992): Grundidee, Varianten und Funktionen der Markierung von Waren und Dienstleistungen. In: *Dichtl, Erwin* & *Walter Eggers* (Hrsg.): Marke und Markenartikel als Instrumente des Wettbewerbs. München. S. 1-24

Eifel Tourismus GmbH (2007): 2. Marketingsitzung der Betriebe Regionalmarke EIFEL-Ferienwohnungen und Privatzimmer. Prüm. (*Unveröffentlichtes Ergebnisprotokoll*)

Eifel Tourismus GmbH (2008a): Homepage der Eifel Tourismus GmbH. Prüm. Abrufbar unter: http://www.eifel.info.

Eifel Tourismus GmbH (2008b): Die Wertschöpfung im Tourismus für den Bereich der Eifel Tourismus GmbH im Jahr 2007. Prüm

Erdmann, Claudia (1998): Die Eifel heute: Trends, Probleme und Chancen. In: *Naturfreunde-Internationale* (Hrsg.): Landschaft ohne Grenzen Eifel-Ardennen. Geschichte – Kultur – Radtouren – Wanderungen. Köln. S. 40-44

Fehn, Monika & *Klaus Vossen* (1999): Stadtmarketing. Trends und Konzepte. Stuttgart

Ferner, Fritz-Karl & *Walter Pötsch* (1998): MarkenLust und MarkenFrust im Tourismus. Wien

Freyer, Walter (1997): Tourismus-Marketing. München

Freyer, Walter (2000): Tourismus-Marketing – Marktorientiertes Management im Mikro- und Makrobereich der Tourismuswirtschaft. München

Freyer, Walter & *Axel Dreyer* (2004): Qualitätszeichen im Tourismus – Begriffe und Typen. In: *Weiermair, Klaus* & *Birgit Pikkemaat* (Hrsg.): Qualitätszeichen im Tourismus – Vermarktung und Wahrnehmung von Leistungen. Berlin. S. 63-92

Graumann, Jens (1983): Die Dienstleistungsmarke. Charakterisierung und Bewertung eines neuen Markentypus aus absatzwirtschaftlicher Sicht. Bamberg/München

Haedrich, Günther, Torsten Tomczak & *Philomela Kaetzke* (1997): Strategische Markenführung. Stuttgart

Haedrich, Günther (2001): Branding und Positionierung von Destinationen. In: *Bieger, Thomas; Harald Pechlaner* & *Albrecht Steinecke* (Hrsg.): Erfolgskonzepte im Tourismus. Marken – Kultur – neue Geschäftsmodelle. Wien. S. 41-50

Haedrich, Günther, Torsten Tomczak & *Philomela Kaetzke* (2003): Strategische Markenführung. Planung und Realisierung von Markenstrategien. 3., vollständig überarbeitete, erweiterte und aktualisierte Auflage. Bern/Stuttgart/Wien

Hammann, Peter (1995): Kommunales und regionales Marketing. In: *Tietz, Bruno, Richard Köhler* & *Joachim Zentes* (Hrsg.): Handwörterbuch des Marketing. Stuttgart. S. 1166-1176

Hannemann, Tobias (2002): Die Positionierung der deutschen Nationalparke als Destinationen am touristischen Markt. Trier

Hannemann, Tobias (2003): Ein gutes Zeichen. Gemeinsam mehr erreichen. München. Abrufbar unter http://www.futour.com/pdf/zeitung/2003.pdf

Hannemann, Tobias (2006): Eine Regionalmarke auf Erfolgskurs. München. Abrufbar unter http://www.futour.com/pdf/zeitung/2006.pdf

Hausladen, Helmut & *Martin Heil* (2001): Regionalmarketing. Herausgegeben vom Auswertungs- und Informationsdienst für Ernährung, Landwirtschaft und Forsten. Bad Honnef

Hohmeyer, Carl Gustav (1850): Die Haus- und Hofmarken. Berlin

Irmscher, Markus (1997): Markenwertmanagement. Aufbau und Erhalt von Markenwissen und -vertrauen im Wettbewerb. Eine informationsökonomische Analyse. Frankfurt am Main (= Europäische Hochschulschriften. Reihe V. Band 2081)

Keller, Peter (1998): Destinationsmarketing. Strategische Fragestellungen. St. Gallen

Keller, Kevin Lane (2003): Strategic brand management: building, measuring, and managing*brand equity*. 2nd edition. New Jersey

Kohl, Manfred (2006): Neue Herausforderungen im Qualitätsmanagement des alpinen Tourismus. In: *Pechlaner, Harald* & *Elisabeth Fischer* (Hrsg.): Qualitätsmanagement im Tourismus. Kundenorientierung – Kundenbindung – Kundenzufriedenheit. Wien. S. 3-11

Konken, Michael (2004): Stadtmarketing – Kommunikation mit Zukunft. Meßkirch

Kullmann, Armin (2007): Regionalvermarktung in den deutschen Biosphärenreservaten aus Sicht der wirtschaftlichen Akteure. Frankfurt am Main

Linxweiler, Richard (2001): BrandScoreCard – Ein neues Instrument erfolgreicher Marken- Führung. Groß-Umstadt

Linxweiler, Richard (2004): Marken-Design – Marken entwickeln, Markenstrategien erfolgreich umsetzen. 2. erweiterte Auflage. Wiesbaden

Luft, Hartmut (2007): Destination Management in Theorie und Praxis. Organisation und Vermarktung von Tourismusorten und Tourismusregionen. Destinationsmanagement. Meßkirch

Margreiter, Josef (2001): Die Marke Tirol: Ziele – Strategien – Maßnahmen. In: *Bieger, Thomas, Harald Pechlaner* & *Albrecht Steinecke* (Hrsg.): Erfolgskonzepte im Tourismus. Marken – Kultur – neue Geschäftsmodelle. Band 5. Wien. S. 29-34

Meffert, Heribert & *Christoph Burmann* (1996) Identitätsorientierte Markenführung. Grundlagen für das Management von Markenportfolios. Arbeitspapier 100. Wissenschaftliche Gesellschaft für Marketing und Unternehmensführung e. V. Münster. Münster

Meffert, Heribert & *Manfred Bruhn* (2006): Dienstleistungsmarketing: Grundlagen – Methoden – Konzepte; mit Fallbeispielen. 5. Auflage. Wiesbaden

Mellerowicz, Klaus (1964): Markenartikel. Die ökonomischen Gesetze ihrer Preisbildung und Preisbindung. München/Berlin

Meyer, Jörn-Axel (1999): Regionalmarketing. Grundlagen, Konzepte, Anwendungen. München

Mühlendahl, Alexander von (1995): Deutsches Markenrecht. München

Niedner, Manfred (1994): Markenpolitik für Städte und Regionen. In: *Bruhn, Manfred* (Hrsg.): Handbuch Markenartikel. Band 3: Markenerfolg – Markenrecht – Markenumfeld. Stuttgart. S. 1646-1658

Pepels, Werner (1999): Kompaktlexikon Produktmanagement. München/Wien

Popp, Dieter & *Tobias Hannemann* (2005): Qualitätsoffensive für Eifel-Hotellerie und -Gastronomie. München

Popp, Dieter (2004): Die Eifel setzt ein gutes Zeichen – Qualität im Tourismus setzt sich durch. München. Abrufbar unter http://www.futour.com/pdf/zeitung/2004.pdf

Popp, Dieter (2007): Regionale Dachmarke als Nachhaltigkeitskonzept: Erfahrungen mit der Regionalmarke EIFEL für eine Dachmarke Rhön. München

Porter, Michael E. (1999): Wettbewerbsvorteile: Spitzenleistungen erreichen und behaupten. 5. durchgesehene und erweiterte Auflage. Frankfurt am Main/New York

Quack, Heinz-Dieter (2000): Nachfrageentwicklung in Deutschland. In: *Fontanari, Martin L.& Klaus Scherhag* (Hrsg.): Wettbewerb der Destinationen. Erfahrungen – Konzepte – Visionen. Wiesbaden. S. 164-173

Qualitätsoffensive Eifel (2008): Gebührenordnung zur Lizenzvergabe. Prüm

Regionalmarke Eifel GmbH (2007): Markenbericht für 2006 und 2007. Prüm

Regionalmarke Eifel GmbH (2008): Homepage der Regionalmarke EIFEL GmbH. Abrufbar unter www.regionalmarke-eifel.de

Regionalmarke Eifel GmbH (o. J.): Ein gutes Zeichen, wenn das Einfache wieder zum Besonderen wird. Imageflyer. Bitburg

Regionen Aktiv (2008a): Homepage von Regionen Aktiv. Hürth. Abrufbar unter: www.modellregionen.de

Regionen Aktiv (2008b): Erfolgsgeschichte regionale Wertschöpfungspartnerschaft. Regionalmarke EIFEL: Qualität vom Stall bis an die Theke. Hürth

Ritchie, B. J. R. & R. J. B. Ritchie (1998): The Branding of Tourism Destinations: Past Achievements and Future Challenges. In: *Keller, Peter* (Hrsg.): Destination Marketing – Scopes and limitations. Publikationen der AIEST, Volume 40. St. Gallen. S. 89-116

Scherhag, Klaus (2000): Profilierungsstrategien für touristische Regionen. In: *Fontanari, Martin L. & Klaus Scherhag* (Hrsg.): Wettbewerb der Destinationen. Erfahrungen – Konzepte – Visionen. Wiesbaden. S. 149-162

Scherhag, Klaus (2003): Destinationsmarken und ihre Bedeutung im touristischen Wettbewerb. Lohmar / Köln

Scherhag, Klaus & Stefan Schneider (1998): Strategische Herausforderung an ein zukunftsweisendes Kooperationsmanagement. In: Jahrbuch für Fremdenverkehr. München. S. 5-30.

Schramm, Josef (1963): Im grünen Herzen Europas. In: *Schramm, Josef* (Hrsg.): Die Eifel – Land der Maare und Vulkane. Essen. S. 9-13

Slapa, Sabine et al. (2000): Regionalmarketing. Das Instrument Regionalmarketing im Überblick. Drei Fallbeispiele für Regionalmarketing-Initiativen in den Neuen Bundesländern. Zusammenfassung der Ergebnisse der Tagung „Überregionaler Erfahrungsaustausch Regionalmarketing“. DSSW-Materialien. München

Smeral, Egon (2003): Die Zukunft des internationalen Tourismus. Entwicklungsperspektiven für das 21. Jahrhundert. Wien

Steinecke, Albrecht (2001): Markenbildung von Destinationen: Erfahrungen – Herausforderungen – Perspektiven. In: *Bieger, Thomas, Harald Pechlaner & Albrecht Steinecke* (Hrsg.): Erfolgskonzepte im Tourismus. Marken – Kultur – neue Geschäftsmodelle. Band 5. Wien. S. 9-27

Steingrube, Wilhelm (2004): Freizeit- und Tourismusdestinationen: Management – Struktur – Politik – Planung. In: *Becker, Christoph, Hans Hopfinger & Albrecht Steinecke* (Hrsg.): Geographie der Freizeit und des Tourismus. 2. Auflage. München/ Wien. S. 441-453

Swoboda Bernhard & Judith Giersch (2007): Internationales Corporate Brand Management. Das Beispiel Henkel. Düsseldorf

Wolf, Klaus (2002): Einführung zum Symposium am 9. November 2001. In: *Wolf, Klaus* (Hrsg.): Stadt- und Regionalmarketing – Vermarktung von Stadt und Region. Frankfurt am Main. S. 9-13 (= Rhein- Mainische Forschungen, 122)

Widera, Christiane & Tobias Hannemann (2004): Die neue Regionalmarke EIFEL: gemeinsam mehr erreichen – unter einem Dach. Trier/Prüm

Zentek, Sabine (1999): Produktprozesse – Entwicklung und Rechtsgeschichten bekannter Deutscher Marken. Ludwigsburg

Searching for innovative products

Andreas Kagermeier & Joachim Willms (eds.): Tourism Development in Low Mountain Ranges. Mannheim 2010, p. 115 - 134 (= Studien zur Freizeit- und Tourismusforschung, Vol. 3)

Natur- und Aktivtourismus in deutschen Mittelgebirgsregionen
– Produktinnovationen für das Destinationsmanagement

Kathleen Lumma & Sven Groß (Wernigerode)

Summary

In einer von Stress und Hektik geprägten Zeit, in der Erholung und Kontraste zum Alltag immer bedeutender im Tourismus werden, sind die deutschen Mittelgebirge trotz ihres natürlichen Potenzials von rückläufigen bzw. stagnierenden Gästezahlen geprägt. Um vom Trend zu mehr Ruhe und Entspannung sowie der steigenden Nachfrage nach naturtouristischen Produkten zu profitieren, muss das Image von Mittelgebirgsregionen durch innovative, moderne Produkte verjüngt werden. Die dafür notwendigen Produktinnovationen müssen strukturiert entwickelt werden, um in Zukunft mit neuen Angeboten Touristen in die Mittelgebirge zu locken.

1 Einleitung

In der gegenwärtigen Arbeits- und Alltagswelt, die häufig durch Stress und Hektik sowie durch eine zunehmende Urbanisierung geprägt ist, werden Aspekte wie Erholung, Ruhe und Natürlichkeit in der Freizeit und auf Reisen immer bedeutender (vgl. *F.U.R.* 2010, S. 90f.). Um dem alltäglichen Leben kurzzeitig zu entfliehen, nutzen Tagesausflügler und Übernachtungsgäste touristische Angebote, die im Kontrast zum Alltag stehen und damit die genannten Bedürfnisse erfüllen. Dazu zählen beispielsweise der Nationalpark- und Naturparktourismus, der Landurlaub aber auch Formen der aktiven Entspannung wie Wandern, Radfahren oder Reiten, wobei alle diese Reiseformen in einer der Alltagswelt gegensätzlichen, natürlichen Kulisse stattfinden. Auf Grund der weiter fortschreitenden Globalisierung, welche den wirtschaftlichen Wettbewerb weltweit verstärken wird, ist auch in Zukunft kaum mit Änderungen der Lebens- und Arbeitsbedingungen sowie der Work-Life-Balance zu rechnen, so dass der heute schon zu erkennende Nachfragetrend nach naturtouristischen Produkten weiter Bestand haben wird. So hat z. B. die University of Cambridge Besucherzahlen (1996-2006) von 280 Naturschutzgebieten in Australien, Kanada, Chile, China, Ecuador, Ghana, Indien, Indonesien, Japan, Korea, Madagaskar, Peru, Philippinen, Ruanda, Südafrika, Sri Lanka, Tansania, Uganda, Großbritannien und den USA untersucht und dabei festgestellt, dass die Besucherzahlen in den meisten Ländern und Kontinenten gestiegen sind (vgl. *Balmford et al.* 2009, S. 1f.).

Folglich können Destinationen, die diesen Trend berücksichtigen, profitieren und sich im Wettbewerb profilieren. In Deutschland bieten besonders die Mittelgebirgsregionen durch ihre abwechslungsreichen Landschaftsformen und eine meist geringere Bevölkerungsdichte als in anderen Teilen Deutschlands das natürliche Potenzial für Naturtourismus, welches teilweise in den Nationalparks bereits genutzt wird. Während in Deutschland durchschnittlich 230 Einwohner auf einem Quadratkilometer leben, sind es z. B. im Landkreis Harz nur 56 Einwohner/km², in Altenberg im Erzgebirge 65 Einwohner/km², in Masserberg im Thüringer Wald 74 Einwohner/km², in der Schwarzwaldgemeinde Baiersbronn 83 Einwohner/km², in Bischofsheim a. d. Rhön 72 Einwohner/km², in Medebach im Sauerland 64 Einwohner/km² und in der Gemeinde Cham im Bayerischen Wald 112 Einwohner/km² (vgl. *Statistisches Bundesamt* 2009). Zudem bieten die meisten dieser Regionen bereits aktivtouristische Angebote, welche ideal mit dem Naturtourismus verbunden werden können. Demnach können die Mittelgebirge vom Trend zum Naturtourismus in besonderer Weise profitieren und im Deutschlandtourismus an Bedeutung gewinnen.

Aus diesem Grund beschäftigt sich der folgende Beitrag mit dem Natur- und Aktivtourismus in deutschen Mittelgebirgsregionen und zeigt auf, wie Regionen Produktinnovationen in diesem Bereich entwickeln können.

„[…] Naturtourismus bietet Natur – zumindest als Kulisse – für eine Vielzahl touristischer, insbesondere auch sportlicher Aktivitäten, z. B. Tauchen, Klettern, Luftsport, Survival, Expeditions- und Abenteuertourismus. Ein Schutz- oder Erhaltungsziel ist nicht zwangsläufig impliziert […].“ (*BFN* 2009)

Aktivurlauber sind Reisende, „[…] die zu einem wesentlichen Teil sportliche Aktivitäten im Urlaub ausüben. Dabei konzentrieren sich Aktivurlauber nicht auf eine bestimmte Sportart, sondern widmen sich verschiedenen Sportaktivitäten.“ (*Dreyer* 1995, S. 33)

Dazu wird zunächst auf die derzeitige Situation dieser Regionen kurz eingegangen. Im Anschluss daran werden theoretische Grundlagen zu Innovationen und zum Innovationsprozess ausgezeigt, bevor deren Anwendung an einem Praxisbeispiel aus dem Harz erklärt wird.

2 Aktuelle Situation der deutschen Mittelgebirge

Die meisten deutschen Mittelgebirge leiden seit Jahren unter ihrem „angestaubten“ Image, zudem waren sie bis etwa 2006 von einer rückläufigen Übernachtungsentwicklung gekennzeichnet und erholen sich seitdem nur langsam (vgl. *Ostdeutscher Sparkassenverband* 2009, S. 42ff.), was v. a. daran liegt, dass diese Regionen in den letzten Jahrzehnten weniger Touristen mit ihren Produkten anziehen konnten als andere deutsche Destinationen. Bis in die 1970er Jahre wurden mehrheitlich inländische Regionen von deutschen Touristen nachgefragt, wovon auch die Mittelgebirge profitierten. Weiteren positiven Einfluss erzeugten die steigende Bedeutung des Erholungsaspekts sowie die Bedeutung des Wanderns während der Urlaubsreise. Mit Zunahme des Outbound-Tourismus und dem Abklingen der Wanderbegeisterung ging allerdings auch die Bereitschaft der deutschen Touristen, ins Mittelgebirge zu reisen, zurück. Während andere deutsche Regionen (z. B. Küsten, Alpen) den Wettbewerb im globalen Destinationsnetz annahmen und trotz eines rückläufigen Anteils an Inlandstouristen in Deutschland weiterhin innerdeutsche Reisende mit ihren Produkten anzogen, konnten die deutschen Mittelgebirgsregionen kaum mit modernen Produkten überzeugen (vgl. *DTV* 2002, S. 4ff.; *Krüger* 2010, S. 15ff.; *Neumann* 2005, S. 144f.).

In Anlehnung an das Destinationslebenszyklusmodell von *Butler* (2006, S. 4ff.) befinden sich deutsche Mittelgebirge demnach in der Phase des Niedergangs, in der die touristische Wertschöpfung abnimmt und Neuprojekte auf Grund von Besitzstanddenken verhindert werden (vgl. Abb. 1).

Abb. 1: Destinationslebenszyklus nach Butler

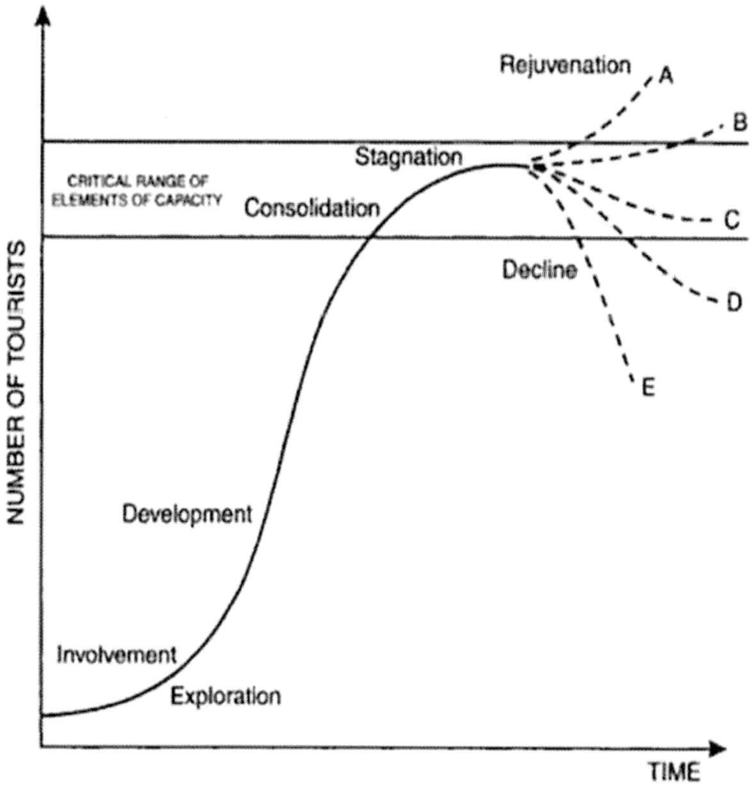

Quelle: Buttler 2006, S. 4ff.

Um diesen Trend umzukehren und wieder mehr Touristen anzuziehen sowie eine steigende Wertschöpfung zu erreichen, muss ein Relaunch bzw. eine Verjüngung stattfinden, die v. a. von den angeboten touristischen Produkten ausgeht. Aus diesem Grund sind Produktinnovationen für Mittelgebirge von besonderer Bedeutung, wenn in naher Zukunft ein Wiederaufleben der Mittelgebirgsregionen anstrebt wird.

Neben der besonderen Eignung für den Naturtourismus begünstigen außerdem Reisetrends wie die Tendenz zu kürzeren, individuellen, gesünderen und klimafreundlichen Reisen die nahen, inländischen Reiseregionen allgemein und naturbelassene Mittelgebirgsregionen im Speziellen (vgl. *Opaschowski* 2008, S. 338ff.). Es fehlt in den deutschen Mittelgebirgen folglich nicht an den grundsätzlichen Voraussetzungen für den Tourismus (natürliches Angebot, Infrastruktur etc.) und der Attraktivität der Region, sondern an einer ansprechenden Angebotsgestaltung (vgl. *Menzel* et al. 2008, S. 30ff.). Demnach müssen die angebotenen Produkte im Bereich Natur- und Aktivtourismus innovativ sein, um sich damit die Aufmerksamkeit der Touristen zu sichern und vom Wettbewerb abzusetzen.

3 Innovationen im Tourismus

Zunächst soll jedoch erläutert werden, was unter dem Begriff Innovation allgemein zu verstehen ist und wie Produktinnovationen in diesem Beitrag zu verstehen sind. Darüber hinaus wird kurz auf die besondere Bedeutung von Innovationen für den Tourismus allgemein und für Mittelgebirgsregionen im Speziellen eingegangen.

3.1 Begriffliche Abgrenzung von Innovationen

Eine allgemeingültige Definition des Begriffs Innovation existiert in der Wissenschaftstheorie bisher nicht. Stattdessen ist eine Vielzahl unterschiedlicher Definitionsversuche vorhanden, die auf jeweils unterschiedliche Charakteristika einer Innovation abzielen (vgl. Tab. 1).

Barnett (1953) und *Aregger* (1976) verstehen Innovationen als neuartige Prozesse oder Produkte, stellen dabei jedoch auf den Grad der Neuigkeit ab. Demnach ist von Innovationen immer nur dann zu sprechen, wenn es sich tatsächlich um eine signifikante Veränderung des bisher Vorhandenen handelt. *Schmookler* (1966) und *Vedin* (1980) hingegen stellen auf die Erstmaligkeit der Nutzung bzw. Einführung eines Produkts oder Prozesses ab, wodurch Innovationen nur diejenigen neuen Produkte und Prozesse sind, die erstmalig am Markt auftreten. Ein wahrnehmungsorientierter Definitionsansatz findet sich bei *Rogers* (1983) sowie *Zaltman, Duncan & Holbeck* (1984), die als Innovation lediglich die Produkte und Prozesse verstehen, die vom Nutzer als neuartig erkannt werden. Der tatsächliche Neuigkeitswert spielt hierbei keine Rolle. Darüber hinaus existieren weitere Begriffsbestimmungen, bei denen für die Definition von Innovationen auf die Erfüllung von Bedürfnissen oder die Möglichkeiten der Problemlösung durch neue Produkte abgestellt wird. Des Weiteren werden prozessorientierte Begriffsauslegungen genutzt, bei denen nicht allein auf die Erfindung neuer Produkte oder Prozesse abgestellt wird, sondern auf deren Verwertung bzw. auf den gesamten Prozess von der Ideenfindung bis zur Markteinführung (vgl. u. a. *Hauschildt* 2004, S. 3ff.; *Pleschak, Leschak & Sabisch* 1996, S. 1ff.).

Tab. 1: Ausgewählten Definitionen des Begriffs „Innovation"

Name des Autors (Jahr)	Ansatz der Definition
Barnett (1953) Aregger (1976)	***produktorientierter Ansatz:*** Neuigkeitsgrad von Produkten/Prozessen
Schmookler (1966) Kieser (1969) Vedin (1980)	***marketingorientierter Ansatz:*** Erstmaligkeit von Produkten/Prozessen
Rogers (1983) Zaltman/Duncan/Holbek (1984)	***kundenorientierter Ansatz:*** Wahrnehmung als Neuheit
Pfeiffer/ Staudt (1975) Moore/ Tushman (1982) Rickards (1985)	***bedürfnisorientierter Ansatz:*** Problemlösungseignung/Grad der Bedürfnisbefriedigung
Roberts (1987) Brockhoff (1992)	***konsumorientierter Ansatz:*** Verwertung von Neuheiten
Uhlmann (1978) Goldhar (1980) Dosi (1988)	***prozessorientierter Ansatz:*** Entwicklungsprozess von Neuheiten

Quelle: in Anlehnung an Hauschildt 2004, S. 4ff.

Trotz der unterschiedlichen Ansätze haben alle Definitionen gemeinsame Kernpunkte, die zur Abgrenzung des Begriffs „Innovation" für diesen Beitrag genügen. Innovationen werden generell als merkliche Veränderungen von Produkten oder Prozessen verstanden, mit deren Hilfe Unternehmensziele besser erfüllt werden sollen.

Für den Tourismus sind Produktinnovationen von besonderer Bedeutung, weil diese durch die Integration des externen Faktors Kunde bei der Dienstleistungserstellung im Vergleich zu Prozessinnovationen direkt vom Kunden wahrgenommen werden. Aus diesem Grund beschränken sich die folgenden Ausführungen zu Innovationen in deutschen Mittelgebirgsregionen auf Produktneuerungen.

Bei den Produktinnovationen werden im Allgemeinen vier verschiedene Stufen unterschieden, gemessen am Neuigkeitsgrad bzw. Innovationsrisiko und dem Wettbewerbsvorteil, den sie schaffen (vgl. Abb. 2). Die höchste Stufe der Innovation stellen dabei die „wahren" Produktinnovationen dar. Darunter wird die Markteinführung tatsächlich neuer Produkte verstanden, die sich an bestehenden Kundenwünschen orientieren oder eine neue Nachfrage kreieren. Ziel ist es, die Wettbewerbsposition zu verteidigen oder auszubauen. Allerdings ist

Abb. 2: Formen von Produktionsinnovationen

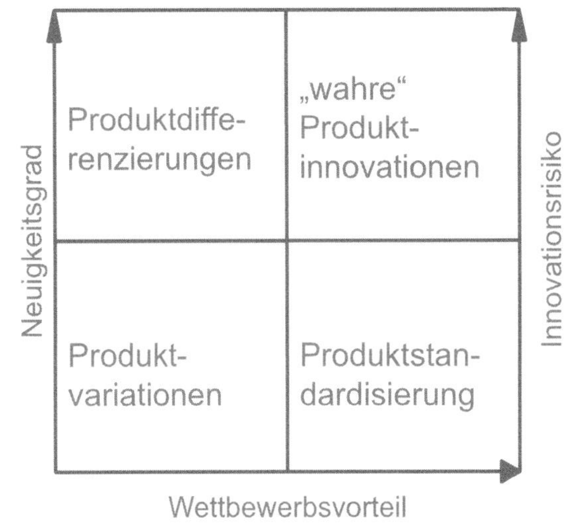

Quelle: eigene Darstellung nach Vahs & Burmester 2005, S. 72ff..

eine solche Neuentwicklung auch mit einem hohen Investitionsrisiko verbunden, da nicht genau vorhergesagt werden kann, ob sich tatsächlich ein Erfolg einstellt. Je neuartiger Produkte im Allgemeinen sind, desto schwieriger ist die Abschätzung der Akzeptanz des Produktes und umso höher ist das Investitionsrisiko. Bei Produktdifferenzierungen werden im Gegensatz zu wahren Produktinnovationen lediglich einzelne oder mehrere Produktbestandteile eines bereits bestehenden Produkts variiert, so dass das bestehende Angebot ergänzt wird.

Damit kann schnell auf veränderte Kundenwünsche reagiert bzw. eine Erweiterung der Zielgruppe erreicht werden. Allerdings ist der Wettbewerbsvorteil geringer, da die Veränderungen schneller von konkurrierenden Unternehmen adaptiert werden können, als bei tatsächlich neuen Produkten. Ähnlich verhält es sich mit Produktvariationen, bei denen lediglich geringfügige Änderungen an existierenden Produkten vorgenommen werden, die jedoch trotz der Geringfügigkeit den Nutzen des Produkts steigern. Auf Grund der einfachen Imitierbarkeit ist der Wettbewerbsvorteil jedoch gering. Durch Produktstandardisierungen, die ebenfalls eine Form der Produktinnovationen darstellen, wird der zunehmenden Individualisierung von Produkten mit der Gestaltung von einheitlichen Einzelproduktkomponenten, die in einem Baukastensystem zusammengefügt werden, entgegengewirkt. Dadurch entstehen Kostenvorteile im Wettbewerb (vgl. *Vahs & Burmester* 2005, S. 72ff.).

In diesem Beitrag werden unter Produktinnovation demnach jegliche merkliche Veränderungen eines Produkts (Differenzierungen, Variationen, Standardisierungen) sowie die Neuerfindung von Produkten („wahre“ Innovationen) verstanden, die die Erfüllung des Unternehmensziels unterstützen. Damit muss eine touristische Produktinnovation nicht zwangsläufig ein langwieriger und kostenintensiver Prozess sein, da auch kleinere Veränderungen dazu beitragen können, das Unternehmensziel – Steigerung der Wertschöpfung – zu erreichen.

3.2 Bedeutung von Innovation für den Tourismus

Die oben beschriebenen Produktinnovationen sind im Tourismus von besonderer Bedeutung, da das touristische Produkt unter starkem Druck steht. Durch die weitreichende Vernetzung der Tourismuswirtschaft mit anderen Bereichen wie Politik, Ökologie, Technologie, Soziales und Ökonomie bedingen Änderungen in diesen Bereichen Veränderungen des Reiseverhaltens der Touristen bzw. fordern direkt Änderungen des touristischen Produkts (vgl. *Freyer* 2009a, S 45ff.). In einem sich ständig wandelnden Umfeld steht folglich auch das touristische Produkt unter dem Druck sich regelmäßig zu verändern und sich den Bedürfnissen der Kunden sowie gesetzlichen, technologischen und ökologischen Gegebenheiten anzupassen. Folglich sind Innovationen im Tourismus von immenser Bedeutung.

4 Der Innovationsprozess am Beispiel einer Produktentwicklung im Harz

Die Entwicklung und Einführung solcher innovativer Produkte sollte mit Hilfe eines organisierten Prozesses erfolgen, damit wichtige Entwicklungsschritte nicht übergangen werden. Daher ist es eine Möglichkeit, das theoretische Innovationsprozessmodell der Entwicklung von zeitgemäßen Produkten für den Aktiv- und Naturtourismus zu Grunde zu legen und in die touristische Praxis zu übertragen.

4.1 Der Innovationsprozess in der Theorie

In der Wissenschaftstheorie sind, ähnlich den Begriffsdefinitionen, unterschiedliche Prozessmodelle existent, die jeweils unterschiedlichen Anforderungen gerecht werden. Gemeinsamer Ausgangspunkt aller Modelle ist jedoch die Gliederung des Entwicklungsprozesses in drei Stufen gemäß *Schumpeter* (vgl. Abb. 3).

Demnach beginnt eine Innovation mit der Invention, die die eigentliche Idee oder Erfindung darstellt. Darauf folgt der Schritt der Innovation, worunter die Verarbeitung der Idee zu einem detaillierten Konzept verstanden wird. Zum Abschluss folgt mit der Diffusion die Verbreitung und Markteinführung der Produktidee (vgl. *Hipp* 2000, S. 25ff.).

Abb 3: Stufen des Innovationsprozesses

Quelle: Walder 2007, S. 78

Tab. 2 Übersicht zu Modellen des Innovationsprozesses im Dienstleistungssektor

Name des Autors (Jahr)	Prozessmodell
Freiling/Weißenfells (2003)	***3 Phasen:*** Inkubationsphase – Realisierungsphase – Abschlussphase ***Besonderheit:*** Orientierung an Phasen der Dienst-leistungserstellung
Bruhn (2003)	***3 Phasen:*** Voreinführungsphase – Markteinführungsphase – Nachprüfungsphase ***Besonderheit:*** Orientierung an Phasen der Dienst-leistungserstellung
Scheuring/Johnson (1989)	15 Phasen ***Besonderheit:*** Integration von Partnern
Cooper (1988)	5 Phasen ***Besonderheit:*** Zielorientierung
Zeitlhaml/Bitner (1996)	7 Phasen ***Besonderheit:*** Zielorientierung
Alam/Perry (2002)	10 Phasen ***Besonderheit:*** Überschneidung einzelner Phasen
Johnson/Menor/Roth/Chase (2000)	4 Phasen ***Besonderheit:*** Integration aller möglichen Beteiligten

Quelle: Walder 2007, S. 79ff.

Dieses Grundmodell wurde für die Sachgüter- sowie für die Dienstleistungsentwicklung weiterentwickelt und detailliert. Bei den Prozessmodellen für Produktinnovationen im Dienstleistungssektor wird v. a. vom siebenstufigen Modell von *Booz, Allen & Hamilton* (1982) zur Entwicklung von Sachgüterinnovationen ausgegangen und entsprechend auf Dienstleistungen adaptiert. Speziell für den Dienstleistungssektor existieren beispielsweise Prozessmodelle von *Freiling & Weißenfells* (2003), *Bruhn* (2003) sowie *Scheuing & Johnson* (1989), die Besonderheiten der Dienstleistung berücksichtigen, aber – wie in Tab. 2 dargestellt – jeweils unterschiedlich detailliert sind. Darüber hinaus bestehen weitere Modelle, die den Anforderungen von Dienstleistungen in besonderer Weise gerecht werden (vgl. *Walder* 2007, S. 78ff.).

Trotz aller Unterschiede der genannten Prozessmodelle bestehen auch Gemeinsamkeiten zwischen den theoretischen Ansätzen, die zusammengefasst ein Grundschema zur Entwicklung von Dienstleistungsinnovationen widerspiegeln. Dabei handelt es sich um einen sechsstufigen Prozess (vgl. Abb. 4), der auf Grund seiner Eigenschaft als Basisschema je nach Gegebenheiten des Einzelfalls ergänzt werden kann.

Abb. 4: Grundschema eines Innovationsprozesses

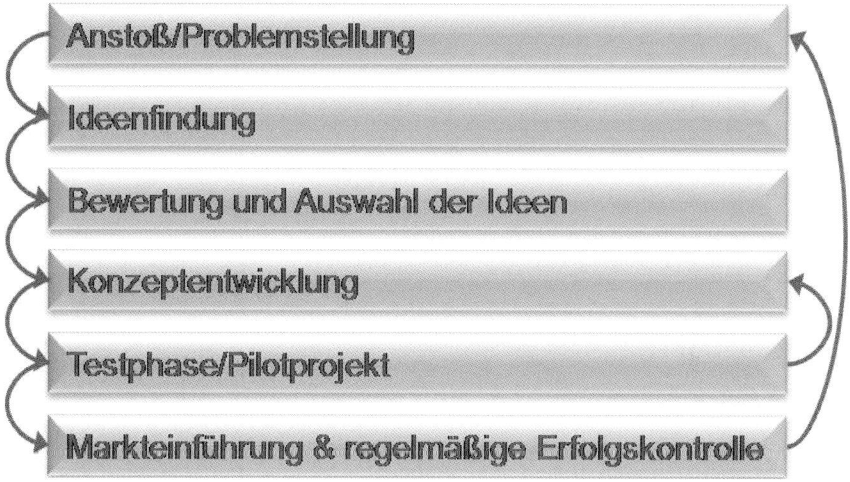

Quelle: eigene Darstellung, in Anlehnung an Vahs/Burmester 2005, S. 132ff.

Auf Grund seiner Übersichtlichkeit und Flexibilität ist dieses Modell besonders für die Praxis als Leitfaden für Produktentwicklungen geeignet. Im Folgenden werden daher Details dieses Prozesses erklärt und auf das Destinationsmanagement angewandt.

Anstoß der Innovation

Der Prozess zur Entwicklung neuer Produkte oder zur Veränderung bestehender Produkte muss zunächst angestoßen werden. Ein Anlass dafür liegt in der Regel in einem Abweichen der erzielten Ist-Ergebnisse von den Soll-Vorgaben, wodurch angezeigt wird, dass das bestehende Produkt die geplanten Zielvorgaben nicht erreichen kann. Um das Problem genauer zu lokalisieren, ist es notwendig zu analysieren, woher die Abweichungen stammen. Beispielsweise können neue Konkurrenten und Produkte den eigenen Absatz schwächen oder neue Technologien können z. B. das Umfeld verändern (vgl. *Vahs & Burmester* 2005, S. 136ff.).

Dieser Prozess wird in einem Unternehmen folglich oft durch das Controlling angestoßen, aber auch andere Abteilungen können auf Probleme aufmerksam machen und so einen Innovationsprozess auslösen. In touristischen Betrieben sind dies oftmals Bereiche, die im direkten Kundenkontakt stehen, wie das Beschwerdemanagement oder der Vertrieb. Zudem werden Anstöße für Neuentwicklungen von Produkten auch durch Projekt- und Arbeitsgruppen gegeben, die sich mit übergeordneten touristischen Themen beschäftigen (z. B. Leitbildentwicklung, Foren für Tourismus, touristisches Stadtmarketing).

Destinationen nehmen hierbei jedoch eine Sonderstellung ein, da sie keine Unternehmen im eigentlichen Sinne sind, sondern ein Netz aus Einzelunternehmen, die gemeinsam die Destination charakterisieren und über deren Ausgestaltung bestimmen. In einer Destination besteht daher für den Anstoßprozess der Vorteil, dass durch Beteiligung vieler Akteure Probleme schneller erkannt und bekannt werden und damit schneller reagiert werden kann. Destinationen besitzen also generell eine hohe Innovationskraft auf Grund der Beteiligung vieler Akteure.

Allerdings führt diese Beteiligung auch dazu, dass möglicherweise zu oft und zu viele Probleme angesprochen werden, wodurch die Gefahr besteht, dass der Blick für die wirklich wichtigen Probleme verloren geht.

Ideenfindung

Nachdem das Problem identifiziert ist, müssen Ideen zur Problemlösung gefunden werden. Bezogen auf Produktinnovationen müssen demnach mögliche Produktneuerungen oder -veränderungen entwickelt werden, die dazu beitragen die Abweichungen zwischen Ist und Soll zu beheben (vgl. *Vahs & Burmester* 2005, S. 141ff.).

Dazu kann man sowohl bereits bestehende Ideen aus unterschiedlichen Quellen (z. B. Lieferanten, Kunden, Wettbewerber etc.) sammeln, als auch durch Kreativitätstechniken neue Ideen gewinnen. Zu diesen Kreativitätstechniken zählen u. a. das Brainstorming und -writing, die 6-3-5-Methode sowie die Entwicklung von morphologischen Kästen (vgl. *Walder* 2007, S. 90).

Bei der Entwicklung der Produktideen ist es von besonderer Bedeutung, den Kunden und seine Wünsche im Auge zu behalten, da der Tourismussektor durch die Integration des externen Faktors Tourist ein besonders stark ausgeprägter Käufermarkt ist.

Destinationen haben hier wiederum den Vorteil, dass sie aus vielen Akteuren bestehen und daher viele mögliche Ideengeber vorhanden sind. Allerdings können diese sehr unterschiedliche Vorstellungen haben und verschiedenste Ideen entwickeln, so dass unter Umständen eine unüberschaubare Anzahl an Ideen entsteht, wodurch auch gute Ideen verloren gehen können.

Bewertung und Auswahl der Produktideen

Aus den gesammelten Anregungen müssen im Anschluss die Ideen herausgefiltert werden, die für die Problemlösung besonders gut geeignet sind. Zur Bewertung der Eignung bestimmter Ideen eignen sich sowohl qualitative wie auch quantitative Bewertungsverfahren. Bei den qualitativen Verfahren kommen v. a. Checklisten sowie Ressourcen- oder SWOT-Analysen in Frage, während sich Verfahren zur Wirtschaftlichkeitsrechnung besonders für eine quantitative Bewertung eignen (vgl. *Vahs & Burmester* 2005, S. 187ff.).

Bei Dienstleistungen ist oftmals eine Kombination aus beiden Methoden von Vorteil, da im Tourismus stets der Kunde und seine Wünsche im Auge behalten werden sollten und nicht nur auf den messbaren, wirtschaftlichen Erfolg abgestellt werden kann.

Die Bewertung sollte nicht durch alle Beteiligten der Produktentwicklung vorgenommen werden, sondern durch ein Gremium aus Fach- und Führungskräften, um fachlich richtige Entscheidungen zu treffen und diese auch durchsetzen zu können. Werden hingegen alle Akteure an der Ideenbewertung beteiligt, kann es dazu kommen, dass der Entscheidungsprozess mehr Zeit in Anspruch nimmt und die Beteiligten von anderen (operativen) Tätigkeiten abgehalten werden.

In Destinationen ist eine solche Gremienbildung schwierig, da im Gegensatz zu Einzelunternehmen innerhalb einer Destination keine hierarchischen Strukturen bestehen anhand derer die Zugehörigkeit zum Gremium bestimmt werden kann. Vielmehr müssen aus der Vielzahl an Akteuren der Destination fachlich kompetente und führende Unternehmer sowie ggf. externe Berater in ein solches Gremium gewählt werden.

Konzeptionierung

Nach der Auswahl kann für die einzelnen Produktideen ein Konzept entwickelt werden, das eine detaillierte Produktbeschreibung, weitere Bereiche des Marketings sowie die Beschreibung sonstiger relevanter Managementaufgaben enthält. Dazu gehören z. B. ökologische Aspekte, rechtliche Aspekte (Patente, Namensrechte), Finanzierungskonzepte etc. (vgl. *Freyer* 2009a, S. 327).

Hierfür sollten Mitarbeiter gewählt werden, die das entsprechende allgemeine touristische Know-How sowie Spezialkenntnisse des jeweiligen Themengebietes besitzen. Allerdings stellt sich die Frage, in welcher Arbeitsform sie dieses Konzept gemeinsam entwickeln. Es ist sowohl als befristete Gremienarbeit möglich als auch als institutionalisierte Gremienarbeit oder Projektarbeit. Während bei der befristeten Gremienarbeit interne Mitarbeiter für einen begrenzten Zeitraum zusammen an der Produktkonzeptionierung arbeiten, ist die institutionalisierte Gremienarbeit auf Dauer angelegt, wodurch eine rollierende Produktentwicklung möglich ist. Die Projektarbeit bietet die Chance, neben den internen Mitarbeitern auch externe Fachkräfte an der Entwicklung zu beteiligen und externes Know-how anzuwerben (vgl. *Vahs & Burmester* 2005, S. 226ff.).

In Destinationen sind generell alle Arbeitsformen denkbar. Allerdings ist es auf Grund der Einbindung vieler Akteure besonders wichtig, bei Meinungsverschiedenheiten einen Interessenausgleich zwischen den einzelnen Beteiligten anzustreben, damit keine Widerstände gegen die neuentwickelten Produkte entstehen. Zudem müssen, wie in Unternehmen üblich, Zuständigkeitsbereiche für bestimmte Akteure und Aufgaben festgelegt werden. Beides kann in Destinationen jedoch je nach Größe der Destination und der Anzahl der Beteiligten sehr umfangreich und herausfordernd sein.

Darüber hinaus ist es im Tourismus allgemein wichtig, dass bei einer Produktentwicklung stets beachtet wird, dass touristische Produkte wie andere Dienstleistungen einfach zu imitieren sind (vgl. *Freyer* 2009b, S. 94). Dadurch sollte ein Hauptaugenmerk der Produktentwicklung darauf liegen, die Produkte durch bestimmte Produktbestandteile unverwechselbar zu machen. Hierfür eignen sich besonders regionale Eigenheiten, die nicht ohne Authentizitätsverlust nachgeahmt werden können.

Testphase

Nachdem das Konzept erarbeitet und akzeptiert ist, kann ein Produkttest stattfinden. Dieser ist notwendig, damit der Markterfolg getestet und bei einem möglichen Misserfolg der finanzielle Schaden begrenzt werden kann (vgl. *Woratschek* et al. 2004, S. 401). Dabei gehört zum Pilotprojekt sowohl die erstmalige Dienstleistungserstellung als auch das Innovationsmarketing. Dies beinhaltet v. a. die Kommunikation und den Vertrieb des zu erprobenden Produktes. Um die Kommunikation und den Vertrieb effektiver zu betreiben, ist es ratsam bereits während der Konzeptionsphase mit der Vermarktung des Testproduktes zu beginnen, so dass die beiden Phasen ineinander übergreifen (vgl. *Vahs & Burmester* 2005, S. 271ff.).

Im Gegensatz zu Sachgütern ist es für einen Produkttest von Dienstleistungen auf Grund des uno-actu-Prinzips unabdingbar, den Kunden als externen Faktor in die Produktion einzubeziehen (vgl. *Walder* 2007, S. 139). Dadurch kommt dem Kunden auch hierbei eine wichtige Rolle zu. Gleichzeitig besteht jedoch auch die Möglichkeit das Produkt direkt am Kunden zu testen und ein Feedback zu erhalten, während Sachgüter, die ohne Kundeneinbindung getestet werden, nur auf ihre allgemeine Gebrauchsfähigkeit und nicht auf ihre Kundenfreundlichkeit untersucht werden können.

Während und nach der Testphase muss der Erfolg des neuen Produkts gemessen werden, was sowohl qualitativ als quantitativ erfolgen kann (vgl. *Vahs & Burmester* 2005, S. 283ff.). Im Tourismus gehören dazu u. a. Zufriedenheitsbefragungen und Beschwerden, die Aufschluss darüber liefern, warum die Produkte die Bedürfnisse der Touristen nicht befriedigen. Darüber hinaus ist auch im Tourismus eine Erfolgsrechnung erforderlich, die das finanzielle Ergebnis ausweist.

Dabei ist zu beachten, dass die quantitative Messung in Destinationen schwierig sein kann, da viele Einzelakteure eingebunden sind und damit sowohl jeder Einzelne den Erfolg messen muss, als auch die Destination als Gesamtheit.

Markteinführung

Ist die Testphase erfolgreich, kann das Produkt, unter Umständen nach weiteren Anpassungen, am Markt endgültig eingeführt werden. Dabei wird die langfristige Dienstleistungserstellung aufgenommen und das Innovationsmarketing fortgeführt. Zudem muss eine regelmäßige, kontinuierliche Erfolgskontrolle stattfinden, wobei die gleichen Probleme auftreten können wie in der Testphase (vgl. *Vahs & Burmester* 2005, S. 256ff.).

Mit Markteinführung ist dieser Innovations- und Produktentwicklungsprozess abgeschlossen. Bei schnelllebigen Produkten oder solchen, die leicht imitierbar sind, ist es jedoch meist notwendig schnell wieder von Neuem mit der Entwicklung von Produktinnovationen zu beginnen. Damit wird die Entwicklung von innovativen touristischen Produkten zur Daueraufgabe, was speziell auf Destinationsebene an seine Grenzen stößt. Der große personelle und finanzielle Aufwand ist auf Grund geringer Kapitalausstattung vieler Destinationen kaum zu handhaben. Lediglich Destinationsorganisationen, die gewinnbringend arbeiten, können dies wie beschrieben durchführen. Alle übrigen Destinationen müssen neben der eigentlichen Aufgabe der Produktentwicklung auch die Generierung von finanziellen Mitteln aus Fördermitteln oder durch Beteiligung Externer (wie im Falle des Praxisbeispiels) betreiben.

4.2 Der Innovationsprozess am Beispiel des Harzes

Nachdem Details des Innovationsprozesses erklärt und Besonderheiten von Destinationen dabei berücksichtigt wurden, kann nun gezeigt werden, wie Mittelgebirgsregionen mit Hilfe dieser Struktur neue Produkte entwickeln können. Dabei wird auf ein Beispiel aus dem Harz zurückgegriffen, bei dem neue Produkte im Bereich Natur- und Aktivtourismus entwickelt werden.

Im Harz existieren diverse Hütten und Häuser in Waldgebieten, die lediglich temporär für Freizeitzwecke (z. B. Jagd) genutzt werden. Da diese Unterkünfte allerdings Instandhaltungskosten verursachen und damit die finanzielle Situation des Eigentümers belasten, steht ein Verkauf oder aber die dauerhaft gewinnbringende Verwendung der Unterkünfte zur Debatte. Da der Harz die wichtigste touristische Destination in Sachsen-Anhalt darstellt, ist eine touristische Nutzung der Unterkünfte eine Möglichkeit, die genannten Häuser zukünftig gewinnorientiert zu nutzen. Das Angebot solcher naturnahen Hüttenunterkünfte existiert derzeit in deutschen Mittelgebirgen allgemein nur in Ausnahmen (z. B entlang des Rennsteigs; *o. V.* 2009) und würde die Entwicklung einer Produktinnovation erfordern.

Der Innovationsprozess wurde in diesem Beispiel von den Eigentümern der Gebäude und folglich durch eine nicht-touristische Institution initiiert. Daran zeigt sich die Stärke eines Destinationsnetzwerkes bei der Ideengenerierung, da auch ein nicht-touristisches Unternehmen und Privatpersonen Initiatoren einer Produktinnovation in einer Destination sein können.

In den meisten Fällen können tourismusfremde Unternehmen die Produktentwicklung jedoch nicht allein betreuen, da häufig das fachliche Know-how und personelle Kapazitäten fehlen. Daher wurde im Harz bei der weiteren Bearbeitung eine im Tourismussektor tätigte Beratungsinstitution einbezogen – das Kompetenzzentrum für Informations- und Kommunikationstechnologien, Tourismus und Dienstleistungen der Hochschule Harz (Wernigerode), Arbeitsbereich Tourismus. Die Mitarbeiter des Kompetenzzentrums wurden damit beauftragt, ein Konzept zur touristischen Nutzung von Hütten zu entwickeln und damit die Produktentwicklung in ihren einzelnen Schritten zu leiten.

Das Kompetenzzentrum begann zunächst mit der Entwicklung von Ideen, in welcher Art und Weise die Hütten und Forsthäuser touristisch genutzt werden könnten. Dazu wurden Ideen sowohl durch bestehende Quellen und Praxisbeispiele (z. B. Neuseelands Great Walks, Wildnis-Trail im Nationalpark Eifel) als auch durch Brainstorming generiert. In dieser Phase wurde zum einen analysiert, in welcher Weise andere touristische Destinationen Hütten für ihre Zwecke nutzen. Zum anderen wurden durch Brainstorming Produktideen auf Basis potenzieller Zielgruppen entwickelt. Als Ergebnis dieser Ideenfindung konnte festgehalten werden, dass die Hütten im Allgemeinen als Unterkünfte z. B. für den Ski- und für den Aktivtourismus sowie als Ausflugslokale genutzt werden. Es entstanden zudem Produktideen für den Wander-, Rad- und Reittouristen sowie für Familien, Kinder/Jugendliche und Incentive-Reisende. Alle Ideen berücksichtigten in besonderer Weise die Nähe zur Natur und Outdoor-Aktivitäten, wodurch eine generelle Tendenz zu Produkten im Natur- und Aktivtourismus erkannt wurde.

Die Bewertung der möglichen Produktideen wurde durch die Leitung des Kompetenzzentrums und der Eigentümer der Gebäude vorgenommen. Damit konnte von Beginn an sichergestellt werden, dass bei der Umsetzung der Produktideen auf allen Ebenen für Akzeptanz gesorgt ist. Die Bewertung wurde auf Basis einer detaillierten Zielgruppenanalyse (Analyse des Reiseverhaltens, des Nachfragevolumens sowie zielgruppenspezifischer Besonderheiten), einer Marktanalyse (Daten zum Harztourismus) sowie einer Angebotsanalyse durchgeführt. Dabei konnte festgestellt werden, dass reittouristische Produkte beispielsweise nur schwer umzusetzen sind, da das Nachfragevolumen sehr begrenzt ist, die entsprechende Infrastruktur im Harz fehlt sowie die Konkurrenz im reittouristischen Markt sehr stark ist. Touristische Produkte für Kinder- und Jugendgruppen scheiden zudem aus, weil die vorhandenen Hütten und Forsthäuser zu klein sind. Wander-, rad- und familientouristische Angebote sowie Incentives sind hingegen mögliche Produkte, die das Angebotsportfolio des Harzes ergänzen können.

Da bereits bei der Ideenfindung eine klare Ausrichtung auf Produkte des Natur- und Aktivtourismus deutlich wurde, wurde diese Tendenz auch für die weitere detaillierte Produktentwicklung beibehalten. Auf Grund der Tatsache, dass mit den Hütten eine besonders naturnahe Beherbergungsform vorliegt, sollen auch die weiteren Produktbestandteile dem Motto „Natur pur“ entsprechen und demnach einen Gegensatz zur Alltagswelt darstellen. Unter diesen Voraussetzungen wurde z. B. ein Produkt für den Themenbereich „Hiking & Biking“ entwickelt, denn für diese naturnahen Outdooraktivitäten können die Hütten und Häuser sowohl für Touren von Hütte zu Hütte genutzt werden als auch als Unterkunft, von der aus Standortwanderungen und -radtouren unternommen werden können. Als Besonderheit im Harz werden die Hütten nicht nur einfache Unterkünfte sein, wie sie aus dem Alpenraum oder z. B. aus anderen Destinationen wie Neuseeland oder Skandinavien bekannt sind (vgl. *DAV* 2009; *NZRTI* 2009). Vielmehr sollen die Unterkünfte so ausgebaut und ausgestattet werden, dass eine einheitliche Qualität auf Niveau eines Ferienhauses oder einer Ferienwohnung gegeben ist, ohne aber das Bild der natürlichen Umgebung zu beeinträchtigen. Daher sollen die Hütten beispielsweise mit Kaminen, Holzmöbeln, volleingerichteten Küchen, Bädern und Schlafräumen ausgestattet werden (vgl. Abb. 5).

Abb. 5: Beispiel einer Hütte im Harz

Quelle: Fotos: Lumma 2009

Es ist zudem angedacht, dass einige Unterkünfte mit besonderen Komfort-Einrichtungen wie Saunen oder Dampfbädern ausgestattet werden, um die Exklusivität deutlich zu machen und den Wanderern und Radfahrern entsprechend ihren Vorlieben nach einem langen Tag Erholung zu garantieren (vgl. *Bremer* 2007, S. 47; *Trendscope* 2009, S. 89). Unabdingbar ist des Weiteren eine gemütliche, urige Atmosphäre, die durch die oben genannten Holzmöbel und Kamine sowie Lagerfeuer- oder Grillplätze vermittelt wird.

Für Wander- und Radtouristen müssen die Unterkünfte mit Hilfe des bestehenden, gepflegten und ausgewiesenen Wegenetzes so miteinander verbunden werden, dass verschiedene mehrtägige sowie halbtägige und eintägige Strecken begangen bzw. befahren werden können.

Ein zusätzlicher Aspekt bei der Gestaltung dieses Hiking- und Biking-Produkts ist die Betonung des Mottos „Natur pur“, indem die Touren so unternommen werden können, dass dabei nicht ein Ort oder eine Stadt betreten werden muss und demnach ein „Ausstieg auf Zeit“ ermöglicht wird.

Neben der Wegeführung ist auch eine thematische Aufbereitung für die Einzigartigkeit des Produkts unabdingbar. Dabei werden im Harz ausschließlich regionalspezifische Themen wie beispielsweise die Harzer Hexen und Sagen oder der traditionelle Bergbau und das Hüttenwesen gewählt, um eine Unique Selling Proposition zu erhalten.

Zur Umsetzung der Inszenierung ist der Einsatz eines mobilen Guides, wie es ihn z. B. am Feldbergsteig bereits gibt, vorgesehen (vgl. *Tourist Information Feldberg* 2009). Damit können regionale Besonderheiten herausgestellt und zugleich eine Wegweisung vorgenommen werden, ohne dass die Natur mit Wegweisern und Informationstafeln überfrachtet wird.

Abrundung findet ein solches Produkt mit regionaler Identität durch eine regionale Küche. Dabei könnten zum einen die Produkte, die für die Selbstversorgung auf Bestellung in der Hütte bereitgestellt werden, aus der Region stammen. Zum anderen könnten zusammen mit einem Profikoch regionaltypische Gerichte in der Hütte gekocht werden. Zudem wäre auch eine Selbstversorgung, wie sie in Ferienwohnungen üblich ist, möglich.

Darüber hinaus wird im Harz auch ein Produkt entwickelt, das speziell auf die Bedürfnisse von Familien ausgerichtet ist. Für Familien gelten hinsichtlich der Ausstattung der Hütten dieselben Anforderungen nach Gemütlichkeit und Atmosphäre wie für Wanderer und Mountainbiker. Allerdings ist neben diesen Standards v. a. die Kinderfreundlichkeit von Bedeutung, so dass die Hütten in wesentlichen Belangen kindgerecht ausgestattet werden. Das bezieht sich sowohl auf Bäder und Schlafzimmer als auch auf Utensilien wie Kinderstuhl und -bett sowie Kindesicherungen für Steckdosen.

Des Weiteren gilt zu beachten, dass Familien auf Reisen zugleich Erholung und Zeit füreinander suchen als auch Kontakt mit anderen Familien (vgl. *Antz & Schreiber* 2004, S. 11ff.). Daher sollte darauf geachtet werden, dass Unterkünfte gewählt werden, die durch ihre ruhige Lage im Wald Erholung für die Eltern und Abenteuer für die Kinder bieten, gleichzeitig aber groß genug sind, um mehrere Familien zu beherbergen. Hier setzt man im Harz auf größere Häuser, in denen mehrere Ferienwohnungen oder Familienzimmer bereitgehalten werden.

Zudem ist es notwendig, adäquate Freizeitangebote in der Umgebung anzubieten, die familiengerecht sind und zudem zum Gesamtkonzept mit dem Motto „Natur pur“ passen. Dazu zählen z. B. Wanderungen, die auf Grund der Thematisierung und Inszenierung auf Familien zugeschnitten sind. So sind v. a. die Mythen des Harzes für Familien relevante Themen. Aber auch lehrreiche Themen wie die Köhlerei sorgen entsprechend aufbereitet für Abwechslung und Erlebnisse für die ganze Familie. Wiederum hilfreich bei der Inszenierung sind mobile Guides, die die Familien, aber v. a. die Kinder, auf den Touren begleiten, leiten sowie informieren. Damit sind auch GeoCaching-Applikationen möglich wie z. B. moderne Schnitzeljagden oder RätselCaches, bei denen Kindern ihren natürlichen Forscherdrang ausleben können.

Neben den naturverbundenen Outdoor-Aktivitäten müssen besonders für Familien zusätzliche Schlechtwetter-Angebote vorhanden sein. Dabei kommt die Bereithaltung der klassischen Spielzeuge (z. B. Gesellschaftsspiele, Bausteine etc.) in Betracht, aber auch eine vollkommen andere Denkweise. Da es im deutschen Mittelgebirge regelmäßig regnet und windig ist, könnte man den Gästen vermitteln, dass diese Wetterlagen dazugehören und zum Aussehen der Region maßgeblich beitragen. Es gibt demnach kein schlechtes Wetter, sondern nur typische Wetterlagen, die die touristischen Aktivitäten nicht unterbinden, sondern lediglich leicht beeinträchtigen. Mit entsprechender Kleidung und Ausrüstung kann die Natur bei regnerischem Wetter ebenso erkundet werden, wie bei strahlendem Sonnenschein (vgl. Abb. 6).

Abb. 6: Positiver Umgang mit „schlechtem" Wetter am Beispiel Baiersbronn

Regen in Baiersbronn

Im Gemeindegebiet Baiersbronn fallen im langjährigen Mittel etwa 2000 Millimeter Niederschlag pro Jahr. Das ist mehr als doppelt so viel wie beispielsweise in Hamburg (700 mm) oder auch Freiburg (900 mm). Dabei wirkt der Waldboden des Schwarzwaldes als Filter wie Wasserspeicher gleichermaßen, wodurch das Wasser gleichmäßig übers Jahr verteilt zur Verfügung steht. Auch wenn Flüsse heute ihre Bedeutung als Transportwege für das Holz verloren haben, so spielt das Wasser doch eine wichtige Rolle als Energielieferant und Lebensspender: Fast 50 Prozent des Trinkwasserbedarfs bezieht Baiersbronn aus dem eigenen Gemeindegebiet, etwa zehn Prozent des verbrauchten Stromes wird aus nachhaltigen Quellen wie Wasserkraft gewonnen.

Quelle: BAIERSBRONN TOURISTIK 2008, S. 4

Des Weiteren können die Hütten für Incentive-Reisen genutzt werden, die zur Erholung dienen oder bei denen Teambuilding-Aktivitäten in der freien Natur stattfinden sollen. Für Incentives müssen die Hütten unbedingt mehrere Einzelzimmer enthalten und entsprechende sanitäre Einrichtungen (z. B. separate Toilette), da es sich bei den Incentive-Reisenden um Kollegen handelt und nicht wie bei den vorhergehend beschriebenen Zielgruppen um Familienmitglieder und enge Bekannte. Aus diesem Grund können im Harz v. a. große Hütten oder mehrere Hütten, die beisammenstehen, genutzt werden.

Da Incentives wie beschrieben häufig nicht nur reine Belohnungsreisen sind, sondern meist mit Gruppenaktivitäten kombiniert werden, um gleichzeitig die Teamfähigkeit zu stärken, müssen entsprechende Möglichkeiten in der Umgebung vorhanden sein oder geschaffen werden (vgl. *Kirstges* 2000, S. 3f.). Dazu zählen Teambuilding-Aktivitäten, bei denen gemeinsame sportliche Herausforderungen gemeistert werden müssen, oder aber Rätsel, die gemeinsam zu lösen sind. Solche können z. B. wieder als spezieller RätselCache als Form des GeoCachings angeboten werden. Aber auch das Hineinschlüpfen in die Rolle eines Försters nach dem Motto „Ranger for a day!“ inklusive Nutzholzgewinnung oder Aufforstung sowie Navigation durch den Wald könnte eine solche Incentive-Maßnahme darstellen. Auch hier richtet sich die genaue Ausgestaltung nach dem abgeleiteten touristischen Angebot vor Ort.

Da Incentive-Reisende wie andere Geschäftsreisende eher keine Selbstversorgung bevorzugen und generell das Besondere suchen, wäre es ratsam auch hierbei neue Wege zu beschreiten. Eine Möglichkeit besteht darin, am Abend einen Kochkurs unter professioneller Anleitung zu veranstalten, bei dem nur Produkte des Waldes bzw. der Region, die vielleicht vorher beim GeoCaching gesammelt wurden, verarbeitet werden. So lernen die Teilnehmer etwas über die regionalen Produkte und das Gemeinschaftsgefühl wird durch das gemeinsame Kochen und Essen gestärkt.

Für die Umsetzung der Projektideen im Harz soll zunächst ein Pilotprojekt mit insgesamt sechs Hütten gestartet werden, die vorrangig für Wanderer und Radfahrer bereitgehalten werden, da dies die größten und vielversprechendsten Zielgruppen sind. Es wird dabei zunächst eine mehrtägige Wanderung oder Radtour von Hütte zu Hütte gestaltet und angeboten. Neben einer Erfolgsrechnung wird außerdem die Zufriedenheit der Kunden befragt, damit das Produkt im Laufe und nach der Testphase an die Kundenwünsche angepasst werden kann.

Nachdem diese Pilotphase erfolgreich abgeschlossen ist, kann das Angebot für Wanderer erweitert und um die oben genannten Produkte für weitere Zielgruppen ergänzt werden. Zudem ist eine kontinuierliche Weiterentwicklung und Generierung von Ideen von Bedeutung, damit das Gesamtprodukt ständig an die Bedürfnisse der Kunden angepasst werden kann und damit Wettbewerbsvorteile erzielt werden.

5 Fazit und Ausblick

Damit die deutschen Mittelgebirge einen Wiederaufschwung erleben und von einer steigenden touristischen Wertschöpfung profitieren, müssen unbedingt neue Produkte entwickelt und etabliert werden, die das Image nachhaltig verbessern. Dazu kann ein strukturierter Prozess, wie oben an einem Praxisbeispiel beschrieben, beitragen. Allerdings hat auch der Innovationsprozess seine Hürden und Grenzen, so dass für Destinationen bestimmte Maßnahmen von Vorteil sind, damit der Entwicklungsprozess von Produkten reibungsloser abläuft.

Auf Grund der Beteiligung vieler Akteure in einer Destination sollten sich diese Beteiligten regelmäßig zusammenfinden, damit Probleme identifiziert und Ideen generiert werden. Regelmäßig stattfindende Konferenzen sind dazu gut geeignet, weil dort nicht nur Probleme und Problemlösungen aufgedeckt und gefunden, sondern auch Widerstände gegen Produktideen erkannt werden können. Dies ist Grundlage für einen Interessensausgleich zwischen konträren Parteien. Des Weiteren sollte ein dauerhaftes oder temporär arbeitendes Fachgremium für die Bewertung der Ideen und Produktentwicklung zusammengestellt werden. Dabei ist es durchaus von Vorteil, die Kreativität von Externen zu nutzen und

Best Practice-Beispiele als Vorbilder zu sehen, von denen man lernen kann. Um den Entwicklungsprozess in geordneten Bahnen ablaufen zu lassen, müssen zudem bestimmte Rahmenbedingungen wie Ziele, Strategien oder Richtlinien vorhanden sein, damit v. a. die Arbeit mit vielen Beteiligten strukturiert verläuft. Ähnliches gilt für die Erfolgskontrolle. Auch hier ist ein standardisiertes System von Vorteil, damit bei allen Akteuren Klarheit darüber herrscht, welche Kennzahlen zur Bewertung des Erfolgs herangezogen und erhoben werden müssen. Darüber hinaus sollten zudem während des gesamten Entwicklungsprozesses stets der Kunde, seine Wünsche und sein Vorteil im Mittelpunkt stehen, damit das Risiko, ein für den Kunden unattraktives Produkt zu erstellen, verringert wird.

Mit Hilfe dieser Hinweise können deutsche Mittelgebirge kreativer und effektiver Produkte entwickeln, um im globalen Kampf um den Touristen erfolgreicher zu agieren. Zeitgemäße, innovative Produkte helfen den deutschen Mittelgebirgsregionen das Image aufzupolieren und sich im Wettbewerb neu zu positionieren, so dass das touristische Potenzial der deutschen Mittelgebirge besser genutzt werden kann.

Literaturverzeichnis

Antz, C. & M. T. Schreiber (2004): Kinder-, Jugend- und Familientourismus in Sachsen-Anhalt. Magdeburg

Aregger, K. (1976): Innovation in sozialen Systemen – Einführung in die Innovationstheorie der Organisation. Bern

Baiersbronn Touristik (2008): Der Seenstieg. 5 Etappen, 1 Erlebnis, unzählige Eindrücke. Baiersbronn

Barnett, H. G. (1953): Innovation: The basis of cultural change. Michigan

BfN (= Bundesamt für Naturschutz) (2009): Definition ökologischer Tourismus, Naturtourismus. URL: http://www.bfn.de/0323 iyeoeko.html, 23.10.2009

Bremer, M. (2007): Befragung zum Wandern und Reisen 2006. Niederkassel

Butler, R. W. (2006): The Tourism Area Life Cycle. Vol. 1. Toronto

DAV (= *Deutscher Alpenverein*) (2009): Hütten des Alpenvereins. http://www.alpenverein.de/template_loader.php?tplpage_id=68, 23.10.2009

Dean, B. V. & J. D. Goldhar (1980): Management of research and innovation. Michigan.

Dreyer, A. (1995): Der Markt für Sporttourismus. In: *Dreyer, A. & A. Krüger* (Hrsg.): Sporttourismus. München. S. 9-51

DTV (= Deutscher Tourismusverband e. V.) (2002): Die Entwicklung des Tourismus in Deutschland 1902-2002. Bonn.

Freyer, W. (2009a): Tourismus. Einfühung in die Fremdenverkehrsökonomie. 9. Aufl. München

Freyer, W. (2009b): Tourismus-Marketing. 6. Aufl. München

F.U.R. (= *Forschungsgemeinschaft Urlaub und Reisen*) (2010): Die Urlaubsreisen der Deutschen. Kurzfassung der Reiseanalyse 2009. Kiel

Hauschildt, J. (2004): Innovationsmanagement. 3. Aufl. München.

Hipp, C. (2000): Innovationsprozesse im Dienstleistungssektor. Eine theoretisch und empirisch basierte Innovationstypologie. Heidelberg

Kirstges, T. (2000): Marktanalyse Incentive-Reisen in Deutschland: Umfang, Motive und Organisationsformen. Wilhelmshaven

Krüger, A. (2010): Historie des Wanderns. In: *Dreyer, A., A. Menzel & M. Endreß* (Hrsg.): Wandertourismus. Kundengruppen, Destinationsmarketing, Gesundheitsaspekte. Wien/München. S. 15-21

Menzel, A., M. Endreß & A. Dreyer (2008): Wandertourismus in deutschen Mittelgebirgen. Produkte – Destinationsmarketing – Gesundheit. Hamburg

Nationalpark Eifel (2009): Der Wildnis-Trail in 4 Tagen durch den Nationalpark Eifel, Schleiden-Gemünd

Neumann, C. (2005): Deutschland-Tourismus und seine Entwicklung. Trier.

NZTRI (= *New Zealand Tourism Research Institute*) (2009): Hiking/Trekking Tourism in New Zealand and Australia. Auckland

Opaschowski, H. (2008): Deutschland 2030. Wie wir in Zukunft leben. München

Ostdeutscher Sparkassenverband (Hrsg.) (2009): Tourismusbarometer Jahresbericht 2009. Berlin

o. V. (2009): Wanderhütten an der Rennsteigbaude; http://www.wanderhuetten-am-rennsteig.de/15443.html?*session*id*key*=*session*id*val*, 23.10.2009

PEG (= Permanente Gästebefragung Sachsen-Anhalt) (2007): Permanente Gästebefragung Sachsen-Anhalt 2006/07. Köln

Pleschak, F. & H. Sabisch (1996): Innovationsmanagement. Stuttgart.

Rickards, T. (1985): Stimulating innovation: a system approach. Basingstoke

Roberts, E. B. (1987): Generating technological innovations. Oxford

Rogers, E. M. (1983): Diffusion of innovations. New York.

Schmookler, J. (1966): Invention and economic growth. Michigan

Statistisches Bundesamt (2009): Onlinerecherche Gemeindeverzeichnis, http://www.destatis.de/gv/suche_gv2000.htm, 06.10.2009

Tourist Information Feldberg (2009): Hosentaschen-Ranger. http://www.feldberg-steig.de/fst/hosentaschen_ranger, 23.10.2009

Trendscope (2009): Radreisen der Deutschen 2008. Köln

Tushman, M. L. & W. L. Moore (1982): Readings in the Management of innovations. Madison

Uhlmann, L. (1978): Der Innovationsprozeß in westeuropäischen Industrieländern. Berlin

Vahs, D. & R. Burmester (2005): Innovationsmanagement. Von der Produktidee zur erfolgreichen Vermarktung. 3. Aufl. Stuttgart

Vedin, B.-A. (1980): Innovation organization: from practice to theory and back. Lund

Walder, B. (2007): Tourismus. Management von Innovationen. Marburg

Woratschek, H., S. Roth & S. Pastowski (2004): Markttests innovativer Dienstleistungen aus der Perspektive unterschiedlicher Geschäftsmodelle. In: *Bruhn, M. & B. Strauss* (Hrsg.): Dienstleistungsinnovationen. Wiesbaden. S. 381-411

Zaltman, G., R. Duncan & J. Holbek (1973): Innovations and organizations. Michigan

Andreas Kagermeier & Joachim Willms (eds.): Tourism Development in Low Mountain Ranges.
Mannheim 2010, p. 135 - 152 (= Studien zur Freizeit- und Tourismusforschung, Vol. 3)

Winter tourism in the Sauerland
– Will it soon be history?

Julia Raulf (Bochum)

1 Introduction

Today climate change is a theme that is always being discussed. The consequences of climate change affect different sectors, also including tourism. However not all kinds of tourism are affected by climate change and its consequences to the same extent. Especially beach tourism and ski or rather winter tourism are being influenced by climate change, because of their strong dependence on climatic conditions. Besides, destinations that have a strong dependence on tourism, are considered to be especially vulnerable (cf. *Elsasser/Bürki* 2007, p. 866 et sqq.). The Sauerland as a region of wintersports belongs to it, too. Its future against the background of climate change shall be analysed.

The Sauerland is situated in the west of Germany and is located quite near to the conurbation of the Ruhr (see fig. 1). It mainly covers the province of North Rhine-Westphalia and partially Hesse. The Sauerland ranks among the German low mountain ranges and is part of the Rhenish Slate Mountains. It is run through by the Rothaargebirge and its highest peaks are the Langenberg and the Hegekopf near Willingen with 843 m and the Kahler Asten near Winterberg with 841 m (cf. *Kracht* 2005, p. 15; *Liedtke* 2002, p. 114).

The economy of the Sauerland is determined by the producing business, but it mainly consists of small and medium-sized companies. Because of the mountainous relief there have never been any settlements of industries. However, the Sauerland as a region of tourism has reached high name recognition, with respect to summer as well as winter tourism (cf. *Roth et al.* p. A-7 et sqq.).

2 Tourism at the Sauerland

Today the Sauerland has many offers of winter and summer tourism. At the homepage of the Sauerland *(www.sauerland.com)* it is advertising many activities that can be carried out in leisure time. Winter offers are for example Nordic skiing, Alpin skiing or tobogganing, whereas in summer hiking and biking are in the foreground (cf. *Sauerland-Tourismus e. V. 2009*, n. pag.).

History

The Sauerland has been influenced by tourism for more than 100 years. The beginnings of tourism go back to the second half of the 19th century. In 1862 the Lenne-Sieg-Bahn and later the Ruhrtal-bahn (1872) were built. Connecting the Ruhr and the city of Kassel, they largely improved the accessibility of the Sauerland. At that time the first guests of the Rhenish-Westphalian industrial area travelled as summer visitors to the Sauerland to recover from every day life of their work. In the course of the 20th century an expansion of tourism, which in the beginning had only been limited to the prosperous part of the population, to all social classes took place. Besides, the accessibility of the Sauerland has been further improved by the construction of different railway routes (cf. *Harrer* 1996, p. 18; *HB Verlag* 1992, p. 51; *Michels* 1989, p. 39).

Fig. 1: Position of the Sauerland within Germany

Source: Microsoft Corporation 2004, n. pag.

Simultaneously, a winter season was established in mountain regions like the Sauerland. This was caused by the improved local public infrastructure or rather accessibility of such regions and also by the "discovery" of the scenic beauty of mountain regions. In 1907 the first ski club, the "Sauerländer Skiclub", was founded in the Sauerland. From now on winter tourism became more and more popular and many towns, like for example Winterberg, saw it as a second source of income in addition to the summer season (see fig. 2) (cf. *Harrer* 1996, p. 18; *WDR Köln* 2008, n. pag.).

In the 1950ies tourism in the Sauerland experienced a boom, as a result of the economic miracle, the rise in the number of automobiles and the expansion of leisure time. Thus, until the 1970ies winter tourism in the Sauerland flourished. But in the middle of the 1980ies demand started to decline and winter tourism in the Sauerland lost its importance (cf. *Ermlich* 2002, n. pag.; *HB Verlag* 1992, p. 52; *Schürmann* 1977, p. 61).

Fig. 2: First groups of skiers at Winterberg

Source: Michels 1989, p. 42

Economic importance

Today, winter tourism in the Sauerland is still an important factor for the economy of winter sport resorts or even single districts. Within the scope of the "Masterplan "Wintersport im Sauerland und Siegerland-Wittgenstein" (2001) the economic importance of winter/snow tourism in the Sauerland has been analised. But the results cannot be published in here, because they are not meant for the public at the moment.

Winter sports resorts

Today Winterberg, Willingen and Schmallenberg are the biggest resorts of winter sports in the Sauerland. Besides many other skiing areas exist, which spread out over different villages or single districts of the Sauerland. The skiing areas of the Wintersport-Arena Sauerland have altitudes between 500 m and 843 m above sea level and are equipped with altogether 148 ski lifts (cf. *Wintersport-Arena Sauerland e.V.* 2007, p. 5).

Because Winterberg (450 m to 843 m above sea level) is a traditional resort of winter sports, it shall be further introduced, exemplary and acting for the Sauerland. Winterberg has with the "Skiliftkarussel Winterberg" the biggest skiing area of the Wintersport-Arena Sauerland. Beside it there are many other skiing areas in Winterberg and also a fun-park for snowboarders, skiers and tobogganists (cf. *Wintersport-Arena Sauerland e.V.* 2007, p. 30 et sqq., 48 et sqq.).

Apert from the skiing areas, Winterberg has a bob run too, that is beeing used for international competitions. Moreover the St. Georg ski jump is situated in the "Skiliftkarussel Winterberg". It is used for competitions and offers 20.000 seats (see fig. 3). In Winterberg many meetings with national and international character, that draw many visitors, take place, for example the toboggan or bob world championships, the Wok world championship or the snowball fight championship (cf. *Stadt Winterberg* 2008a, *Stadt Winterberg* 2008b, *Stadt Winterberg* 2008d).

Fig. 3: Skiing area with the St. Georg ski jump

Source: own photo 2008

Winterberg is to a high degree influenced by tourism, especially winter tourism. The biggest group of tourists apart from the Germans are the Dutch. These represent for the whole area of the Sauerland an important group of tourists, what becomes clear in Winterberg above all. Almost all signs that are relevant for tourists are written in German and Dutch or only in Dutch. Examples are a sign to the tourist information (VVV) or a sign to a ski school (see fig. 4).

Besides, hints on shops that can be rented or bought are written in Dutch. This shows that the Dutch are not only spending their leisure time in Winterberg, but they also work there or are economically active. The hotel "Der Brabander", which has a Dutch management and is aimed at Dutch guests, is a good example for that.

Fig. 4: Sign to a ski school

Source: own photo 2008

3 Climate change at the Sauerland

Winter tourism at the Sauerland is highly affected by the consequences of climate change. In the 1980ies and the 1990ies the effects of climate change, in the form of snow-deficient winters, were already noticeable. The consequences, which can emanate from temporary snow-deficiency, are seen as a threat to the touristic structures, especially in traditional regions of winter sports like the Sauerland.

Snow-deficient winters: Consequences and strategies – Excursus Switzerland

Snow-deficient winters affect the supply side as well as the demand side, as can be made clear with the example of winter tourism in Switzerland. Around the end of the 1980ies there were already snow-deficient winters. These led to considerable losses of sales in different areas like cable-way companies, hotels, the market for articles of winter sports etc., which again caused a highly reduced supply of part-time jobs or even the dismisssal of employees (cf. *Abegg/Elsasser* 1996a, p. 117 et seq.).

A survey among skiers that was conducted in different skiing areas of the cantons Obwalden and Nidwalden gave knowledge of the change of the demand side as a result of snow-deficient winters. It indicated that the majority of the skiers would move to snow-reliable areas or ski more rarely. This would lead to a considerable loss of guests in the inspected skiing areas, which again would have negative effects on the economy (cf. *Bürki* 1998, p. 156 et seq.).

In Switzerland the increase of snow-deficient winters led to a discussion about the consequences for Swiss tourism, because this is to a high degree aimed at ski sport. Therefore different strategies, which shall contribute to the preservation of tourism in the Swiss mountain area, have been developed. These strategies can be subdivided into adaptation and avoiding strategies that are transferable to other regions of winter sports (see fig. 5) (cf. *Abegg/Elsasser* 1996b, p. 737 & 740).

Measures that belong to the adaptation strategies are for example ones that preserve the ski sport, such as the construction of artificial snow-making facilities or the development of higher terrains for ski sport. Besides completions of supply in winter tourism, in form of alternatives at temporary snow-deficiency as well as general alternatives to ski tourism, belong to it. Avoiding strategies aim at the reduction of the emission of gases that are relevant to climate (especially CO_2). These are for example measures that optimise the efficiency of energy at tourist companies and reduce traffic that is caused by tourism (cf. *Abegg & Elsasser* 1996b, p. 740 ff; *Elsasser et al.* 2000, p. 39).

Studies and forecasts

The effects of climate change on climate and options for winter sports at the Sauerland have been investigated rarely up to now. Apart from a thesis by *Harrer* (1996), in which the economic-geographical effects of a changed ecological situation and the resulting consequences for winter tourism in Germany have been investigated, there is a more recent study by the Sporthochschule Köln from 2006. In this

Fig. 5: Adaptation and avoiding strategies

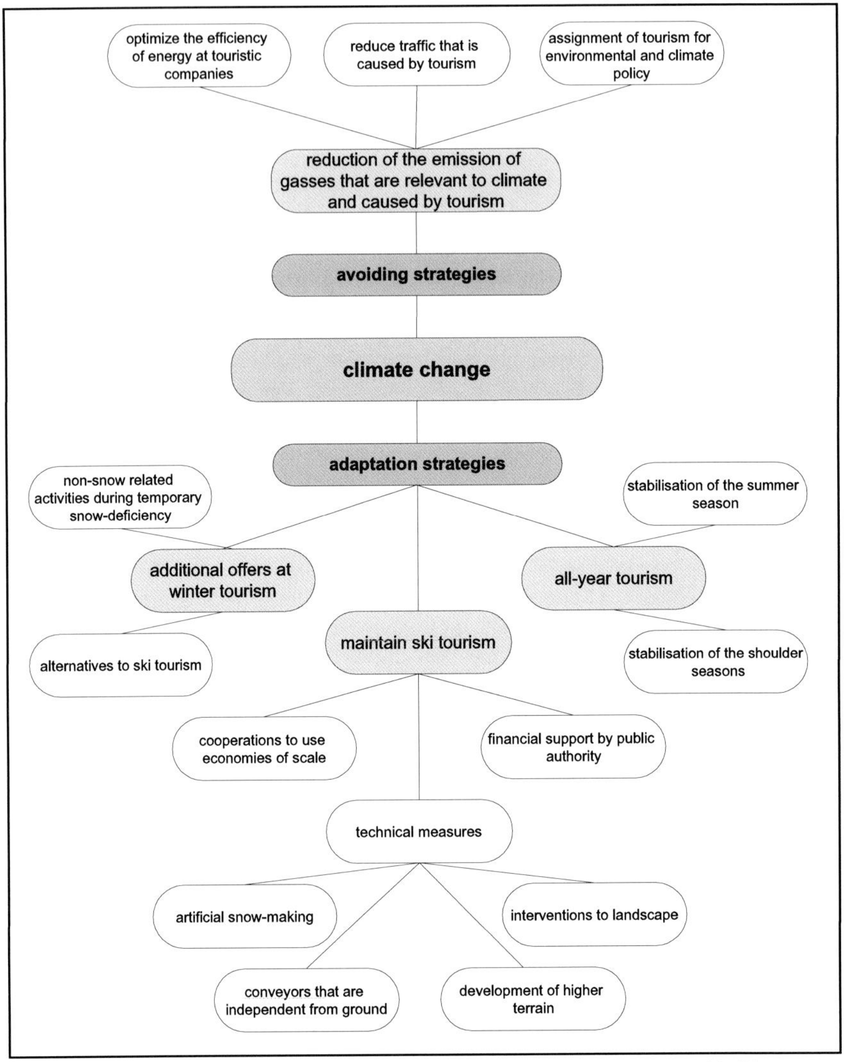

Source: own changed graph according to Abegg/Elsasser 1996 b, p.741; Elsasser et al. 2000, p.39

study the snow-reliability and the options for the production of artificial snow at the German low mountain ranges or rather at the Sauerland have been analysed climatologically. This shall be represented in more detail in the following paragraph.

First of all some definitions that form the basis of the study shall be given:

The season of snow sports lasts from the 15th of December until the 31st of March. For the description of the current status the mean values of the dates from the period from 1980 to 2002 have been used. This created a more reliable basis of the data and thus the bad situation of snow cover at the end of the 1990ies has not been overrated (cf. *Schneider* 2006, p. 7 et seq.).

For the determination of days with snow cover the definition is that days with a height of snow cover of 9 cm or more count as a ***snow day***. But here it has to be critically remarked that for downhill run a snow depth of at least 20 cm and for cross-country skiing a snow depth of at least 10 cm are necessary (cf. *Roth et al.* 2001, p. A-99, A-115; *Schneider* 2006, p. 12). Therefore in the study it was assumed, in the favour of the Sauerland, that the snow days have a sufficient snow cover for the respective ski sport. Because of this the results of the studies have to be regarded critically from a scientific point of view. Beyond that, they cannot be taken as concrete results, but they can be used as a dim clue for the further possible development of the Sauerland with regard to winter sports.

For the determination of the ***potential options for the production of artificial snow*** as threshold value, from which on artificial snow making (without additions that support crystallization) is acceptable under financial and temporary points of view, a dew-point temperature of -4°C has been chosen. For it an air temperature that at most only just exceeds the dew-point temperature is necessary (cf. *Schneider* 2006, p. 13).

The study contains three different scenarios with a varying number of days with snow and days, at which artificial snowmaking is possible. The years 2012 and 2025 have been chosen as time-cuts. Up to these years calculations about the middle increase of the air temperature have been made. On the basis of the calculated dependence of the durability of the snow cover and the potential options for the production of artificial snow on the air temperature it has been determined, about how many days the durability of the snow cover and the potential options for the production of artificial snow go down, at the respective increase of the air temperature. These determined values represent the middle scenario. For the minimum scenario and the maximum scenario the minimal and maximal increase of the air temperature, which have to be expected, have been determined on the basis of the modified model runs of the IPCC (Intergovernmental Panel on Climate Change) for central Europe and the winter season (cf. *Schneider* 2006, p. 21).

In the following table the forecast for the number of days with potential options for the production of artificial snow and the snow days at middle, minimum and maximum increase of the air temperature is being shown. The values of the year 2000 represent the current status (cf. tab. 1).

For downhill run at the Sauerland an average number of at least 80 days of operation has been fixed, so that an economical running of a skiing area or a ski lift company can be ensured (cf. *Roth* et al. 2001, p. A-76). Based on this background the following conclusions can be made:

In 2012 at each of the calculated scenarios as many as 80 days (snow days and days with potential options for the production of artificial snow) with a snow cover of at least 9 cm can be reached. But with consideration of the spatial distribution, which is also shown in the study, it has to be established, that these 80 days can only be reached in the Hochsauerland, for example in the area around Willingen and Winterberg. In the remaining area of the Sauerland the number of days with a snow cover in places drops under 20 days, while the number of days with potential options for the production of artificial snow does not drop under 21 days.

Tab. 1: Forecast for the number of days with potential options for the production of artificial snow and the snow days at the Sauerland/Rothaargebirge

middle scenario		
days with potential options for the production of artificial snow		
2000: 28-35	*2012:* 21-28	*2025:* 14-28
snow days		
2000: 30-60	*2012:* <20-50	*2025:* <20-40
minimum scenario		
days with potential options for the production of artificial snow		
2000: 28-35	*2012:* 21-35	*2025:* 21-28
snow days		
2000: 30-60	*2012:* <20-60	*2025:* <20-50
maximum scenario		
days with potential options for the production of artificial snow		
2000: 28-35	*2012:* 21-28	*2025:* 14-21
snow days		
2000: 30-60	*2012:* <20-50	*2025:* <20-30

Source: own graph according to Schneider 2006, p.81 et seq.

In the year 2025 the situation will be different, like the forecasts promise. Only if the minimum scenario becomes true, still around 80 days with a snow cover of at least 9 cm can be reached. However this area would be very restricted and would only be a small part of the Sauerland. In the remaining area of the Sauerland at most 68 days with a snow depth of 9 cm could be reached. The middle and maximum scenario clearly show smaller values. Especially the maximum scenario only shows selective areas with as many as 30 snow days. The days with potential options for the production of artificial snow are distributed over a small area and do not count more than 21 days. Therefore only at a few areas of the Sauerland 51 days with a snow depth of at least 9 cm could be reached. But it has to be taken into account that this number in the large part of the Sauerland is most 34 days.

Therefore a number of 80 days of operation, which is necessary for Alpine skiing, can in 2012 only be reached in the Hochsauerland and in 2025 just in parts of the Hochsauerland, if the minimum scenario becomes true. For 2025 the forecasts for the Sauerland as a region for Alpine skiing are rather bad. With regard to Nordic skiing, for which a number of at least 50 days of operation is necessary, it can be noticed that the Sauerland can be graded at least in parts as suitable, according to the study, even if the maximum scenario becomes true (cf. *Roth et al.* 2001, p. A-99).

However, it has to be pointed out once again, that the study is based on the assumption that ski sport is already possible from a snow depth of 9 cm, even if normally minimum snow depths of 10 cm (Nordic skiing) or rather 20 cm (Alpine skiing) are provided. It comes along that every day with a minimum snow depth of 9 cm is counted as snow day in the study. But nevertheless it has not been taken into account whether the snow depth would be sufficient for Alpine skiing. Here a differentiation between snow days with a snow depth of 10 cm up to 20 cm and at least 20 cm should have taken place. So more reliable forecasts for the future of the Sauerland as a region of winter sports could have been given and more reliable statements could have been made.

Apart from the study of the Sporthochschule Köln (2006), there is the project "Climate change in North Rhine-Westphalia – Regional estimation of the proneness of selected sectors", which has been assigned by the Ministry of Environment and Conservation, Agriculture and Consumer Protection of North Rhine-Westphalia. The scientific investigations have been carried out by the Potsdam Institute for Climate Impact Research (PIK). Within the scope of the project, the proneness of winter tourism in the Sauerland to climate change has been analysed among other things. The results have been published in a final report in April 2009 and shall be explained in greater detail in the following part.

The regional model of climate CCLM has been used for the analysis of the development of the natural snow days (cf. fig. 6). Therefore a decline in the snowfall (in mm) of about 40 % to 60 % in the period of 2036-2065 compared with the period of 1960-1990 is expected (cf. *Kropp et al.* 2009, p. 207). Because a minimum snow depth of 20 cm is necessary for Alpine skiing, it has also been analysed, in which way the average annual days with a snow depth of more than 20 cm of fresh-fallen snow will change in the period of 2036-2065 compared to the period of 1961-1990 (see fig. 6; cf. *Kropp et al.* 2009, p. 207). Therefore an extensive decline of more than 87,5 % is expected (cf. *Kropp et al.* 2009, p. 208).

Besides the options for the production of artificial snow (number of days at which artificial snow-making is possible on the basis of the climatic circumstances) has been analysed. This has been analysed on the basis of days with a wet-bulb temperature of -2°C and -4°C, because these are decisive for the use of artificial snow-making facilities. For the investigation of the options for the production of artificial snow, the climate models STAR (statistical model of regionalization) and CCLM have been applied. In table 2 the expected changes of the annual days with the potential options for the production of artificial snow (in %) in the Sauerland in the period of 2016-2025, 2031-2060 and 2071-2100 compared with the period of 1961-1990 are shown. For limits the wet-bulb temperatures (wet-bulb temp.) of -2°C and -4°C have been served (cf. *Kropp et al.* 2009, p. 208, 213).

Fig. 6: Change of the annual number of days with a snow depth of 20 cm in the period of 2036-2065 compared with the period of 1961-1990 in %

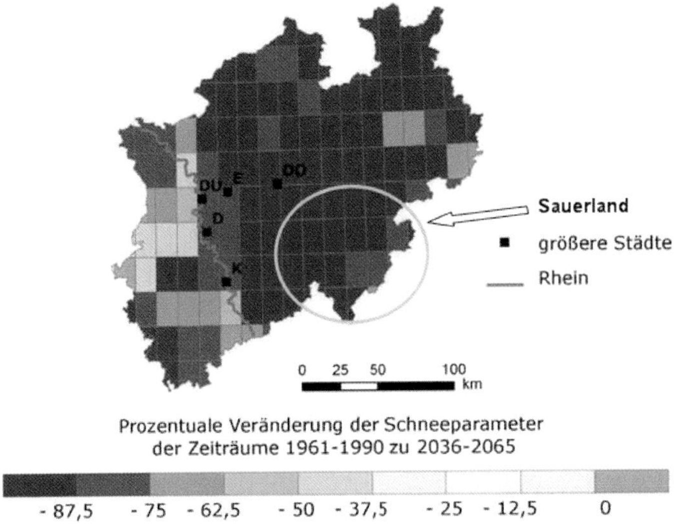

Source: changed graph according to Kropp et al. 2009, p.208

Tab. 2: Change of the options for the production of artificial snow

	wet-bulb temp. < -4°C		**wet-bulb temp. < -2°C**	
period	STAR	CCLM	STAR	CCLM
2016-2025	-21% - -41%	-11%	-15% - -35%	-17%
2031-2060	-39% - -59%	-49%	-31% - -47%	-38%
2071-2100	-	-77%	-	-69%

Source: own graph according to Kropp et al. 2009, p.213

The results show that the next years will be marked by further declining options for the production of artificial snow (cf. *Kropp et al. 2009*, p. 213). Therefore the decline of natural snowfall cannot be cushioned by the use of artificial snow-making facilities in the future. In addition, the number of natural snow days will strongly decline.

Altogether the PIK comes to the result that winter tourism can be seen as very vulnerable facing climate change, because a high decline of snow-reliability is expected. It recommends the development of alternative forms of tourism to compensate for economical losses in winter tourism (cf. *Kropp* et al. 2009, p. 214).

However it has to be pointed out, that the climate models in general have certain uncertainties and the results are therefore not 100 per cent reliable. Nevertheless they can deliver first important clues concerning the further development of winter tourism (cf. *Kropp et al.* 2009, p. 207).

Measures and strategies

The unsatisfactory situation of tourism or rather winter tourism in the Sauerland, which for example has been shown by the decline of the days of operation of ski lifts since the season of 1988/89, has already been discussed at a meeting of substitutes of the Ministry of Economics of North Rhine-Westphalia, the tourism association of North Rhine-Westphalia and the Hochsauerlandkreis, as well as other concerned bodies in 1998. Consequently a masterplan for the Sauerland has been prepared in the following years, which was completed in 2001. In November 2002 it was supplemented by the "Masterplan Sauerland/Siegerland-Wittgenstein Stufe II". There the foundation of a central institution, which coordinates and controls the development of the infrastructure in the central zone of winter sports (Winterberg and environs) and which also looks after the regional marketing concept, has been recommended. Consequently in 2002 the "Wintersport-Arena Sauerland/Siegerland-Wittgenstein e.V.", in which 57 skiing areas of the Sauerland were united, was founded. Investment activities could be coordinated and adjusted to one another by it and by the common design, and marketing of the region of winter sports synergetic effects could be used (cf. *Ift* 2008, p. 6; *Roth et al.* 2001, p. 103).

The strategies that are employed at the Wintersport-Arena are dominated by the use of artificial snow-making facilities, which is the mean factor of the strategies (see fig. 7). The development of the supply shows that, too. From 1999 to 2007 the number of snow cannons increased from 22 to 173, which corresponds to an improvement of 686 % (cf. *Ift* 2008, p. 11).

Fig. 7: Snow cannon at a skiing area of Winterberg

Source: own photo 2008

Besides, snow-farming and the development of higher terrain for ski sports take place. Apart from these measures, which are all lined up on the maintenance of ski sport, other measures with the aim of becoming more independent from ski sport, like the creation of non-snow related activities in winter, are being taken.

All-year tourism represents another strategy. In Winterberg and Willingen the slopes and ski lifts are partly used in summer too: new kinds of sports like mountainboarding come to the fore. Besides, a bikepark with slopes of an overall length of 9 km - the first German Mountainboardpark - opened in summer 2008 at the Poppenberg in Winterberg. The sport mountainboarding has already experienced a boom in the USA and England and can be best described by snowboarding in summer or skateboarding in the countryside (see fig. 8). The return transport up to the mountain is carried out by lifts, like at the bikepark (cf. *Wintersport-Arena Sauerland e. V.* 2008, n. pag.; *Bikepark Winterberg* n. d., *Stadt Winterberg* 2008c).

Fig. 8: Mountainboarder at Winterberg

Source: SevenOne Intermedia GmbH 2008

There are also slopes that in summer can be ridden down with bullracers (outsized tricycles) or hillracers (tobogganing like in snow), that are not motorised (see fig. 9 & 10). Besides, summertubing is being offered. There, the participants slide down the courses with big, air-filled tyres. The president of the Wintersport-Arena, Michael Beckmann, who is also the chief executive of tourism in Winterberg, emphasises that such projects enrich the offers during the seasons without snow and moreover represent an aditional source of income for the people who are running the ski lifts (cf. *Stadt Winterberg* 2008c).

The Wintersport-Arena Sauerland generally focuses on sport tourism, especially Nordic sports and fun sports. The Nordic sports are Nordic walking, Nordic trekking and Nordic blading. In the area of the Wintersport-Arena Sauerland many Nordicaktiv-centres and routes that have been conceived by the German skiing association are located. There is further the Bike-Arena Sauerland, the region of bikes at the Sauerland, which has a net of cycle tracks with altogether 1.700 km of length. Besides many companies have adjusted to cycling tourists (cf. *Standpunkt-Verlag GmbH* 2008, p. 7; *Wintersport-Arena Sauerland* 2008, p. 15). There is also an all-year offer of hiking activities in the Sauerland. Apart from many footpaths, like the Rothaarsteig for example, there are also marked footpaths in and around Winterberg that are cleared from snow in winter (cf. *Kracht* 2005, p. 18; *Standpunkt-Verlag GmbH* 2008, p. 48).

In addition to these offers there are many events that can also be assigned to the strategy of fun sports and sports. Examples are the "Wok-WM" (wok world championship) or the "ISOSTEEL Schneeball-Schlacht Weltmeisterschaft" (Snowball

Fig. 9: Bullracer

Source: Siegerlandkurier; Sauerlandkurier 2007

Fig. 10: Hillracer

Source: Focus Online n. d.

fight world championship) in Winterberg or the "FIS Weltcup Skispringen" (ski jumping worldcup) in Willingen (cf. *Tourist Information Winterberg* 2008, n. pag.; *Wintersport-Arena Sauerland/Siegerland-Wittgenstein* e. V. et al. 2008, p. 19).

In the last years the offers of the Wintersport-Arena have been complemented by offers that do not depend on the weather conditions. For example an indoor-playground in Winterberg and a kart- and bowlingcentre in Willingen have been created. With such offers a temporary phase of bad weather conditions can at least be partly bridged (cf. *Ift* 2008, p. 17).

Fig. 11: Snowball fight world championship

Source: Stadtmarketing Winterberg mit seinen Dörfern 2009, p.37

Apart from these adaptation strategies there is also planned an avoiding strategy or rather a project that contributes to the reduction of the emission of gases that are relevant to climate and caused by tourism at the Wintersport-Arena: The creation of a region of winter sports that is neutral to climate. But this project is still in the phase of planning (cf. *Ift* 2008, p. 43 et sqq.).

Previous implementation and effects of the measures

In the update of the masterplan of 2008 the previous implementation and effects of the measures of the masterplan have been analysed by the ift Freizeit- und Tourismusberatung GmbH (Köln). The centre of the analysed area was formed by the communities Winterberg, Willingen and Schmallenberg, because 95,8 % of the investments have been transacted there (cf. *Ift* 2008, p. 26).

The offer at the Wintersport-Arena has been clearly developed further in the period from 1999 to 2007. The number of ski lifts only increased to a minor degree (from 148 to 156), whereas the capacity of visitors increased about 135 % (from 1.012.739 to 2.378.016). This shows that above all investments have been put into the modernisation of ski lifts. The number of snow cannons, as already said, increased by 686 %. This again illustrates the importance that the use of artificial snow-making facilities has in the struggle against snow-deficient winters (cf. *Ift* 2008, p. 11).

The following figure shows the development of the snow-covered areas and the days of operation at the Wintersport-Arena during the seasons from 1988/89 to 2006/07.

Fig. 12: Development of the snow-covered areas and the days of operation at the Wintersport- Arena 1988/89 - 2006/07

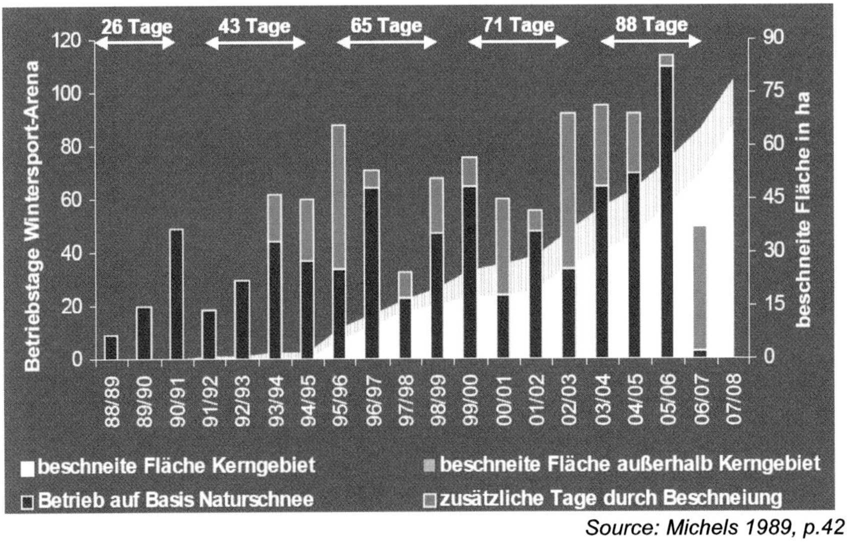

Source: Michels 1989, p.42

It is shown that the natural snow cover is subjected to considerable variations. The regarded period shows both snow-deficient and snowy winters. The winters of 1988/89 and 2006/07 were especially snow-deficient. In the season of 1988/89 the number of days of operation in the area of the Wintersport-Arena was under 10 days, however in 2006/07 it was despite a snow-deficiency about 50 days of operation. This shows that with the help of artificial snow-making facilities the natural snow-deficiency – without artificial snow-making facilities at best three days of operation would have been possible – can be compensated to a certain degree. At the same time it is being shown that the size of the area that has been covered by snow cannons with artificial snow, especially at the centre zone, has increased continuously since the middle of the 1990ies (cf. *Ift* 2008, p. 12).

Fig. 13: Areas at which investments have taken place

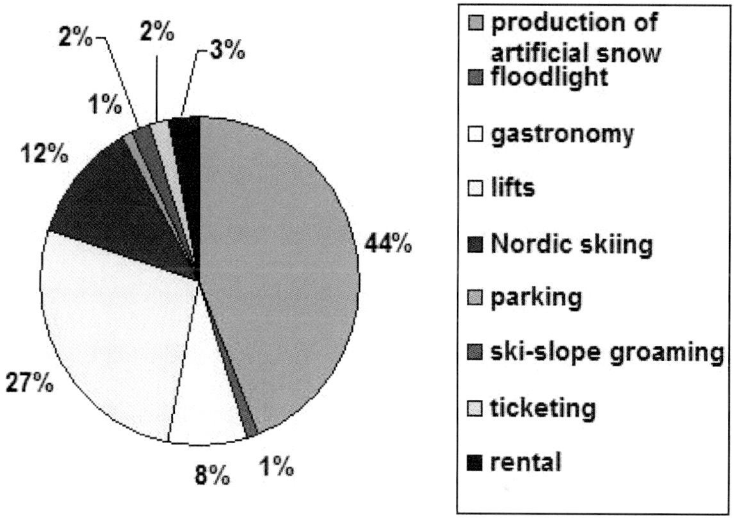

Source: own changed graph according to Ift 2008, p.15

An interview among the operators provided information on the areas in which the investments into the infrastructure of winter sports in the Wintersport-Arena has been raised (cf. *Ift* 2008, p. 15).

It is being shown that it has been invested mostly into artificial snow-making facilities (44 %) and ski lifts (27 %). This again makes clear that the use of artificial snow-making facilities is regarded as necessary and that these already form part of the basic infrastructure of the skiing areas. It has been invested into the offers of the summer, too. The Mountain-Bike-Park Kappe or the Bullracing at the Ruhrquelle are examples for that (cf. *Ift* 2008, p. 17).

The whole investments into the infrastructure of the Wintersport-Arena amounted to around 60 mio. € in the period from 1999 to 2007 (cf. *Ift* 2008, p. 18).

4 Future prospects and recommendations

Besides tourism there is only the producing business as a big area of the economy, because of the circumstances of the relief. Investigations in Switzerland have shown that snow-deficient winters lead to losses in the tourism economy and also have a negative effect on other areas of the economy. The consequences of sporadic snow-deficient winters can mostly be compensated. But the question arises as to how long successive snow-deficient winters can be compensated before bigger economical "damages" arise. To avoid such scenarios, at the Wintersport-Arena, snow cannons are being used for the improvement of snow-reliability and big hopes are being put in it. This is connected with high costs and besides it is to note that artificial snow and the use of artificial snow-making facilities have negative effects on nature and environment, too. Apart from that, other measures, like the provision of subsidies or cooperations between single skiing areas, to maintain ski tourism, take place at the Wintersport-Arena too. Above all it is being worked on the expansion of the all-year tourism, what has been shown by the comments on the strategies of the Wintersport-Arena.

The forecasts for climate change in Sauerland however show bad future prospects for winter tourism at the Sauerland. In the future the exercise of winter sports will be more and more spatially limited and only be possible sporadically in the Sauerland. The economic efficiency that is being ensured from 80 days of operation (Alpine skiing) or rather 50 days of operation (Nordic skiing), will not be reached in the large part of the skiing areas any more. Against this background a break with the too strong focus on snow cannons as a remedy for snow-deficiency should take place and instead the development of offers that are not dependent on climate and weather conditions, for example in the sector culture, should be supported.

By establishing types of tourism that are independent from seasons and by developing summer tourism, the dependence on winter tourism can be reduced. Here the Wintersport-Arena is on the right track. Hiking tourism with the Rothaarsteig or sport tourism with the new trend sports have to be mentioned. But the last-mentioned should be more competed for supraregionally.

However, the measures and strategies focus too strongly on the area around Winterberg and Willingen. Alternatives for winter tourism in the remaining areas of the Sauerland, where only sporadic offers of winter sports do exist, should be developed as well. Especially these areas will be affected by the consequences of climate change in comparison with the higher located area Winterberg/Willingen and it will not be able to offer winter sports any more. There, a stronger focus on hiking and cycling tourism, as well as sports such as Nordic sports would be meaningful. In the long term, in the Sauerland a general re-orientation in tourism and a focus on summer tourism or types of tourism that are independent from snow, has to take place.

With regard to the forecasts about climate change that promise anything but good prospects for winter tourism in the Sauerland, this will even be soon history at the Sauerland.

Bibliography

Abegg, Bruno & Hans Elsasser (1996a): Klimarisiken aus touristischer Sicht. In: *Abegg, Bruno* (ed.): Klimarisiken – Herausforderung für die Schweizer Wirtschaft: Thesen zu Klimaänderungen und Naturkatastrophen. Zürich. p. 115-125

Abegg, Bruno & Hans Elsasser (1996b): Klima, Wetter und Tourismus in den Schweizer Alpen. In: Geographische Rundschau 48/12, p. 737-742

Bikepark Winterberg (n. d.): Bikepark Winterberg. Winterberg

Bürki, Rolf (1998): Klimaänderung und Skitourismus – Wie wirkt sich eine Klimaänderung auf die skitouristische Nachfrage aus? In: Geographica Helvetica, 1998/4, p. 155-161

Elsasser, Hans, Rolf Bürki, & Bruno Abegg (2000): Klimawandel und Schneesicherheit. In: Petermanns Geographische Mitteilungen 144/4, p. 34-41

Elsasser, Hans & Rolf Bürki (2007): Auswirkungen von Umweltveränderungen auf den Tourismus - dargestellt am Beispiel der Klimaänderung im Alpenraum. In: *Becker, Christoph, Hans Hopfinger & Albrecht Steinecke* (eds.): Geographie der Freizeit und des Tourismus – Bilanz und Ausblick. München. 3rd edition. p. 865-875

Ermlich, Günter (2002): Lasst die Kanonen sprechen. URL: http://hermes.zeit.de/pdf/archiv/2002/48/Sauerland.pdf, call date: 29.10.2008

Focus Online (ed.) (n. d.): ISPO – Vom Sommerrodel zum Airbag-Rucksack. URL: http://www.focus.de/finanzen/news/ispo_did_18240.html?slide=1, call date: 05.02.2009

Harrer, Bernhard (1996): Wirtschaftsgeographische Auswirkungen einer veränderten ökologischen Situation – Konsequenzen für den Wintertourismus in Deutschland. München (= Schriftenreihe des Deutschen Wirtschaftswissenschaftlichen Instituts für Fremdenverkehr an der Universität München, 47)

HB Verlag (= HB Verlags- und Vertriebsgesellschaft mbH) (ed.) (1992): Sauerland. Hamburg (= Bildatlas, 110)

Ift (= Ift Freizeit- und Tourismusberatung GmbH) (ed.) (2008): Masterplan Wintersport-Arena Sauerland/Siegerland-Wittgenstein – Fortschreibung des Masterplans mit Handlungsstrategien und Impulsprojekten. Köln

Kracht, Peter (2005): Sauerland, Siegerland und Wittgensteiner Land. Münster. 2nd edition (= Regionen in Nordrhein-Westfalen, 1)

Kropp, J. et al. (2009): "Klimawandel in Nordrhein-Westfalen – Regionale Abschätzung der Anfälligkeit ausgewählter Sektoren". Potsdam (= Abschlussbericht des Potsdam-Instituts für Klimafolgenforschung (PIK) für das Ministerium für Umwelt und Naturschutz, Landwirtschaft und Verbraucherschutz Nordrhein-Westfalen)

Liedtke, Herbert (2002): Namen und Abgrenzungen von Landschaften in der Bundesrepublik Deutschland. Flensburg. 3rd edition (= Forschungen zur deutschen Landeskunde, 239)

Michels, Bärbel (ed.) (1989): Wintersport im Sauerland in früherer Zeit. Brilon

Roth, Ralf et al. (2001): Masterplan im Sauerland und Siegerland-Wittgenstein. Köln

Sauerland-Tourismus e.V. (2009): Aktivitäten. URL: http://www.sauerland.com/sauerland/aktivitaeten__1, call date: 15.09.2009

Schürmann, Frank (1977): Vom Eisen zur weißen Industrie. In: Merian 30, p. 60-65

Schneider, Christoph (2006): Klimatologische Analyse der Schneesicherheit und Beschneibarkeit von Wintersportgebieten in deutschen Mittelgebirgen. Köln (= Schriftenreihe Natursport und Ökologie, 19)

Sevenone Intermedia GmbH (2008): Mountainboarding: Mit Riesen-Skateboard bergab. URL: http://www.n24.de/news/newsitem_1157922.html, call date: 17.01.2009

Siegerlandkurier & Sauerlandkurier (2007): Bullracer: Ultimativer Downhill-Spaß. URL: http://www.sauerlandkurier.de/bullracer-ultimativer-downhill-spass-sauerlandkurier_kat131_id24697.html#, call date: 05.01.2009

Stadtmarketing Winterberg mit seinen Dörfern e. V. (ed.) (2009): Ferienwelt Winterberg – Schneeinfo (= information brochure). Winterberg

Stadt Winterberg (ed.) (2008a): Bobbahn. URL: http://www.winterberg.de/tourismus/de/sehen-und-erleben/bobbahn/der-eiskanal/index.php?navanchor=1010181, call date: 12.12.2008

Stadt Winterberg (ed.) (2008b): Eventkalender. URL: http://www.winterberg.de/tourismus/de/sehen-und-erleben/events/eventkalender/index.php?navanchor=1010031, call date: 12.12.2008

Stadt Winterberg (ed.) (2008c): Funsport. URL: http://www.winterberg.de/tourismus/de/aktiv-und-entspannen/funsport/index.php? navanchor=1010038, call date: 12.01.2009

Stadt Winterberg (ed.) (2008d): St. Georg Schanze. URL: http://www.winterberg.de/tourismus/de/aktiv-und-entspannen/winter/st-georgschanze/index.php?navanchor=1010179, call date: 12.12.2008

Standpunkt-Verlag GmbH (ed.) (2008): Ferienwelt Winterberg – Gästeführer (= information brochure). Rietberg-Mastholte

Tourist Information Winterberg (ed.) (2008): Ferienwelt Winterberg - Veranstaltungskalender Januar-März 2009 (= information brochure). Winterberg

Westdeutscher Rundfunk Köln (WDR Köln) (ed.) (2008): Wie der Wintersport ins Sauerland kam. URL: http://www.wdr.de/tv/wdrdok_af/sendungsbeitraege/2008/1212/index.jsp, call date: 22.12.2008

Wintersport-Arena Sauerland e. V. (ed.) (2007): Wintersport-Arena Sauerland – ... das größte Schneevergnügen nördlich der Alpen (= information brochure). Winterberg

Wintersport-Arena Sauerland e. V. (ed.) (2008): Mit Bikes und Boards, Hillracern und Bullracern grüne Skihänge hinab. URL: http://www.wintersport-arena.de/de/presse/artikel/2008_08_01.pdf, call date: 05.12.2008

Wintersport-Arena Sauerland (ed.) (2008): Wintersport-Arena Express (= information brochure). Winterberg

Wintersport-Arena Sauerland/Siegerland-Wittgenstein e. V.; Karstadt Sports & Karstadt Warenhaus GmbH (eds.) (2008): Wintersport-Arena Sauerland – ... das größte Schneevergnügen nördlich der Alpen! (= information brochure). Dortmund

Veröffentlichungen im Verlag MetaGIS Fachbuch

Berichte des Zentrums für Regionalforschung
Würzburg

Herausgegeben von U. Ante, Ch. Daxelmüller, H. Flachenecker, J. Kopf, J. Rauh

ISSN 1869-473X

Band 1: *Rauh, Jürgen (Hrsg.):*
Facetten und Perspektiven der Regionalforschung in Unterfranken.
2009, 184 Seiten mit zahlreichen Abbildungen, Fotos und Tabellen
24,00 €, ISBN: 978-3-936438-28-4

Band 2: *Holste, Sybille:*
Die Vernetzung der Region Mainfranken mit den benachbarten Metropolregionen.
2010, 220 Seiten mit zahlreichen Abbildungen und Tabellen
24,00 €, ISBN: 978-3-936438-32-1

Studien zur Freizeit- und Tourismusforschung
Trier

Herausgegeben von Hans Hopfinger, Andreas Kagermeier und Monika Rullo

ISSN 1869-7909

Band 2: *Soboll, Anja (Hrsg.):*
Deutschland als Incoming-Destination.
2009, 152 Seiten mit 61 Abbildungen und 8 Tabellen
24,00 €, ISBN: 978-3-936438-31-4

Band 3: *Andreas Kagermeier & Joachim Willms (Hrsg.):*
Tourism Development in Low Mountain Ranges.
2010, 152 Seiten mit zahlreichen Abbildungen und Tabellen
24,00 €, ISBN: 978-3-936438-34-5

Studies on Mobility and Transport Research

Herausgegeben von W. Gronau und A. Kagermeier

ISSN 1868-5811

Vol. 1: *Gronau, Werner (Ed.):*
Passenger Intermodality
Current Frameworks, Trends and Perspectives.
2008, 158 Seiten, 31 Abbildungen und 24 Tabellen
25,00 €, ISBN: 978-3-936438-23-9

Vol. 2: *Gronau, Werner (Ed.):*
Transport Planing and Challengers in Eastern Mediterranean countries (AT)
Barriers and Potential Solutions.
In Druckvorbereitung - erscheint Sommer 2010
ISBN: 978-3-936438-26-0

Vol. 3: *In Druckvorbereitung - erscheint Herbst 2010*

Studien zur Mobilitäts- und Verkehrsforschung

Herausgegeben von M. Gather, A. Kagermeier und M. Lanzendorf

ISSN 1868-5803

Band 1: *Gather, Matthias & Andreas Kagermeier (Hrsg.):* **Freizeitverkehr – Hintergründe, Probleme, Perspektiven** 2002, 140 Seiten, 47 Abbildungen und 17 Tabellen 15,50 €, ISBN: 978-3-936438-00-0

Band 2: *Kagermeier, Andreas, Thomas J. Mager & Thomas W. Zängler (Hrsg.):* **Mobilitätskonzepte in Ballungsräumen**
2002, 306 Seiten, 121 Abbildungen, 30 Tabellen und 12 Fotos
25,00 €, ISBN 978-3-936438-01-7

Band 3: *Fliegner, Steffen:*
Car Sharing als Alternative?
Mobilitätsstilbasierte Potenziale zur Autoabschaffung
2002, 290 Seiten, 33 Abbildungen und 44 Tabellen
23,50 €, ISBN 978-3-936438-02-4

Band 4: *Hautzinger, Heinz (Hrsg.):*
Freizeitmobilitätsforschung – Theoretische und methodische Ansätze.
2003, 120 Seiten, 34 Abbildungen und 21 Tabellen
15,00 €, ISBN 978-3-936438-04-8

Band 5: *Dalkmann, Holger, Martin Lanzendorf & Joachim Scheiner (Hrsg.):*
Verkehrsgenese - Entstehung von Verkehr sowie Potenziale und Grenzen der Gestaltung einer nachhaltigen Mobilität
2004, 282 Seiten, 43 Abbildungen und 25 Tabellen
ISBN 978-3-936438-05-5 - ***vergriffen***

Band 6: *Feldkötter, Michael:*
Das Fahrrad als städtisches Verkehrsmittel. Untersuchungen zur Fahrradnutzung in Düsseldorf und Bonn.
2003, 216 Seiten, 37 Abbildungen, 37 Tabellen und 4 Karten
25,50 €, ISBN 978-3-936438-06-2

Band 7: *Schiefelbusch, Martin (Hrsg.):*
Erfolgreiche Eventverkehre: Analysen und Fallstudien.
2004, 262 Seiten, 66 Abbildungen, 24 Tabellen und 18 Fotos
30,00 €, ISBN 978-3-936438-07-9

Band 8: *Monheim, Heiner (Hrsg.):*
Fahrradförderung mit System. Elemente einer angebotsorientierten Radverkehrspolitik.
2005, 326 Seiten, 56 Abbildungen, 33 Tabellen und 16 Fotos
38,00 €, ISBN 978-3-936438-08-6

Band 9: *Gronau, Werner:*
Freizeitmobilität und Freizeitstile. Ein praxisorientierter Ansatz zur Modellierung des Verkehrsmittelwahlverhaltens an Freizeitgroßeinrichtungen
2005, 166 Seiten, 58 Abbildungen und 18 Tabellen
28,00 €, ISBN 978-3-936438-09-3

Band 10: *Kagermeier, Andreas (Hrsg.):*
Verkehrssystem- und Mobilitätsmanagement im ländl. Raum.
2004, 422 Seiten, 134 Abbildungen, 42 Tabellen und 17 Fotos
ISBN 978-3-936438-10-9 - ***vergriffen***

Band 11: *Neiberger, Cordula & Heike Bertram (Hrsg.):*
Waren um die Welt bewegen.
Strategien und Standorte im Management globaler Warenketten.
2005, 128 Seiten, 32 Abbildungen und 5 Tabellen
22,00 €, ISBN 978-3-936438-11-6

Band 12: *Poppinga, Enno:*

Auf Nebenstrecken zum Kunden. Verkehrliche und wirtschaftliche Impulse für den ländlichen Raum in Deutschland durch Markenführung im regionalen Schienenverkehr.
2005, 200 Seiten, 12 Abbildungen 9 Tabellen und 2 Karten
32,00 €, ISBN 978-3-936438-12-3

Band 13: *Freitag, Elke:*

Bedeutung und Chancen von Freizeitverkehrsangeboten des ÖPNV – dargestellt am Beispiel von Fahrradbuslinien in Deutschland.
2005, 254 Seiten, 96 Abbildungen und 20 Tabellen
34,00 €, ISBN 978-3-936438-13-0

Band 14: *Lenz, Barbara & Claudia Nobis (Hrsg.):*

Wirtschaftsverkehr: Alles in Bewegung?
2007, 262 Seiten, 52 Abbildungen und 20 Tabellen
ISBN 978-3-936438-14-7 - ***vergriffen***

Band 15: *Glogger, Andrea Felicitas*

Telearbeit und Mobilitätsverhalten.
2006, 146 Seiten, 33 Abbildungen und 38 Tabellen
24,00 €, ISBN 978-3-936438-15-4

Band 16: *Martin, Niklas:*

Einkaufen in der Stadt der kurzen Wege? Einkaufsmobilität unter dem Einfluss von Lebensstilen, Lebenslagen, Konsummotiven und Raumstrukturen.
2006, 282 Seiten, 54 Abbildungen, 29 Tabellen und 14 Karten
38,00 €, ISBN 978-3-936438-18-5

Band 17: *Schmöe, Hinrich:*

Öffentlicher Personennahverkehr in kleinen und mittelgroßen Kommunen. Untersucht anhand ausgewählter Fallbeispiele in Ostwestfalen-Lippe und Südniedersachsen.
2007, 366 Seiten, 68 Abbildungen und 57 Tabellen
44,00 €, ISBN 978-3-936438-19-2

Band 18: *Schneider, Martin:*

Multimodales Marketing nachhaltiger Mobilität als Teil integrierten Mobilitätsmanagements.
2007, 180 Seiten, 58 Abbildungen und 17 Tabellen
ISBN 978-3-936438-20-8 - ***vergriffen***

Band 19: *Achen, Mathias, Mathias Gather & Peter Pez (Hrsg.):*

Konsum und Handel, Mobilität und Verkehr.
2008, 189 Seiten, 58 Abbildungen und 17 Tabellen
28,00 €, ISBN 978-3-936438-21-5

Band 20: *Niedzballa, Uwe:*
Mobilität im Grossaum Algier. Vor dem Hintergrund der siedlungsstrukturellen Dispersion und der Liberalisierung im Verkehrsmarkt.
2007, 180 Seiten, 58 Abbildungen und 17 Tabellen
28,00 €, ISBN 978-3-936438-22-2

Band 21: *Grischkat, Sylvie:*
Umweltbilanzierung von individuellem Mobilitätsverhalten. Methodische und gestaltungsrelevante Ansätze.
2008, 278 Seiten, 41 Abbildungen und 50 Tabellen
38,00 €, ISBN 978-3-936438-25-3

Band 22: *Buba, Hanspeter; Grötzbach, Jochen und Monheim, Rolf (Hrsg.):*
Nachhaltige Mobilitätskultur.
2010, 234 Seiten, zahlreiche Abbildungen und Tabellen
24,00 €, ISBN 978-3-936438-29-1

Einzelpublikationen

Pfarrgemeinde St. Laurentius Mannheim-Käfertal (Hrsg.):
175 Jahre St. Laurentius. Canite laudem excelsam exsultante voce - Singet ein hohes Lob mit jubelnder Stimme.
2010, 186 Seiten, zahlreiche Abbildungen und Tabellen und 1 CD im Anhang mit weiterem Bild und Tonmaterial
15,00 €, ISBN 978-3-936438-30-7

Ledl, Jürgen:
Kernberuflichkeit in der Luftfahrt - Verschiedene Ausbildungswege mit einem Ziel. Diss. 2009, Bremen.
2010, 272 Seiten, zahlreiche Abbildungen und Tabellen
19,50 €, ISBN 978-3-936438-33-8

Die Bände dieser Reihen und die Einzelpublikationen sind zu beziehen über:
MetaGIS – Systems - Enzianstr.62 – D-68309 MANNHEIM
E-Mail: info@metagis.de
Tel.: +49 621 72739120 - Fax.: +49 621 72739122
Bestellformular: http://www.metagis.de/verlag/liste.htm

Und über jede gut sortierte Buchhandlung